英語の組み立て方＋話す

AREA式で英語2分間スピーキング

森 秀夫 著

Gakken

はじめに

現代のグローバル社会では、単なる日常英会話だけでなく、社会問題について英語で論理的に考え、議論し、説得する力が求められています。英語で議論する能力の重要性はますます高まっています。

現在、英検、TOEIC、TOEFL などのテストでは、スピーキングテストを受けることが一般的になってきています。これらのテストでは、「論理的に明確に主張を伝える力」や「社会的な問題について即興で 2 分間のスピーチをする能力」が求められています。

本書は 2 つのパートに分かれています。スピーチパートでは、30 のトピックについて、200 ～ 300 語の賛成・反対の意見を収録しており、合計 60 のスピーチが学べます。ダイアローグパートでは、20 のトピックに関して 2 人の登場人物が 300 語前後で意見を交換しています。

また、英検 1 級の二次試験でよく出題されるトピックのように「科学・テクノロジー」、「ビジネス・経済」、「社会・政治・法律・制度」、「自然・環境」、「教育」、「医学・健康」、「メディア・文化」、「ライフスタイル・趣味」の 8 つのジャンルに分類しています。

本書の特徴

① AREA 式スピーチ　すべてのスピーチは AREA 式（→ p.7）で書かれています。論理的な思考力を養い、建設的な意見を述べる習慣が身につきます。

② コンセプトマップ　各トピックにはキーワードを使ったスピーチのリテリングや即興スピーチの練習ができるコンセプトマップが付いています（→ p.10）。

③ 語彙(こい)力強化　各トピックで必要な約 1,700 語の英単語やフレーズがチェック形式で整理されており、発音を音声で確認し、練習できます。

④ 背景知識　スピーチ＋ダイアローグ計 50 のトピックに関する背景知識が身につきます。

⑤ フレーズ集　賛成・反対の意見を述べる際に必要な強調、理由、追加などを示すフレーズが、492 の例文とともに整理されています。

⑥ 試験対策　英検、TOEIC、TOEFL、IELTS などのスピーキングテストへの対策ができます。

本書の制作にあたり、株式会社 Gakken の安達正氏と編集担当の恩田明香氏には多大なご支援をいただきました。また、英文校正においては、友人の Sharon Rodrigues 氏から貴重なアドバイスをいただきました。おかげさまで、新しいタイプの一冊を完成させることができました。心より感謝申し上げます。

著者　森　秀夫

本書は 2018 年に（株）ディーエイチシーより刊行された『図式で攻略！　英語スピーキング』を最新の情報にアップデートし、音声とイラストを再収録してリニューアルしたものです。

CONTENTS

AREA 式で英語スピーキングを攻略しよう

「AREA 式」とは？

「AREA」とは、Assertion、Reason、Example、Assertion の頭文字です。

具体的には、始めに Assertion ＝主張を示し、次に Reason ＝理由を述べ、その根拠となる Example ＝例を示し、最後にもう一度、Assertion ＝主張を繰り返します。最後の Assertion が Conclusion ＝結論となります。なお、Example を Evidence と置き換える考え方もあります。例を証拠として示すので、根拠が強まります。

Assertion 主張 → Reason 理由 → Example 例 → Assertion 主張

この「AREA」という考え方は、元来、ディベートの限られた時間内で、自分の意見の論理性を示すために用いられてきました。AREA 式に従って話すことで、スピーチの意見に説得力が増します。主張のあとに理由と例を示すことで、話を論理的に展開することができるからです。AREA 式を身につけることにより、日常で発する意見にも説得力が増し、より建設的な意見が言えるようになります。また、論理的に伝えることで、相手の記憶にも強く残ります。

なお、AREA を、OREO や PREP と置き換える考え方もあります。OREO は「Opinion → Reason → Example → Opinion」で、PREP は「Point → Reason → Example → Point」を表します。

ここで、AREA 式のメリットを整理しておきましょう。

❶「主張→理由→例→主張」という論理的な構成により、説得力ある話し方が身につきます。
❷ 社会問題に対して、深く考える習慣が身につきます。
❸ 理由と例を分けて考えることで、自分の主張の根拠の中身を精査する力が身につきます。
❹ 相手の記憶に残る話し方が身につきます。

グローバル社会では、英語で論理的に議論する力が求められています。ここで、「議論する」"argue" の定義を確認してみます。（下線は筆者）

◆ *Longman Dictionary of Contemporary English*, 1995
argue: "To state, giving clear reasons, that something is true, should be done etc."

◆ *Collins Cobuild English Dictionary*, 1995
argue: "If you argue for or against an idea or policy, you state the reasons why you support or oppose it, in order to persuade people that it is right or that it is wrong." "If you argue, you support your opinions with evidence in an ordered or logical way."

下線部だけを訳すと、「意見を述べる」、「明確な理由を述べる」、「賛成、反対の理由を述べる」、「人を説得するため」、「証拠で意見を支持する」、「整理して」、「論理的に」となり、argue の定義は AREA の内容と一致していることがわかります。このことからも、AREA 式は、英語で議論する上で最適な方法の 1 つと言えます。

グローバル社会で生き残るためには、使える英語を身につけ、自分の主張と理由に基づき、意見を述べることが求められます。使える英語とは、実際のディベート、交渉、裁判などの場面で、まず主張を、次に明確な理由を述べて相手を説得できる英語のことです。物事の是非や白黒をはっきりさせるため、意見を筋道立てて述べたり、反論したり、相手を説得したりできる英語のスピーキング力は、極めて重要です。

次に、AREA 式の基本型を 2 分間のスピーチに当てはめて考えてみます。ここでは、スピーキングで役に立つキーフレーズと目安の時間配分だけを示します。

AREA 基本型	スピーキングで役に立つキーフレーズ	時間配分
Assertion（主張）	I agree / disagree ～. I have two points to make.	15 秒
Reason 1（理由）	First, ～.	10 秒
Example 1（例）／Evidence 1（証拠）	For example, ～. Furthermore, ～. Therefore, ～.	35 秒
Reason 2（理由）	Second, ～.	10 秒
Example 2（例）／Evidence 2（証拠）	For example, ～. In addition, ～. As a result, ～.	35 秒
Assertion（主張）／Conclusion（結論）	In conclusion, ～. Once again, I agree / disagree ～.	15 秒

本書では、60のスピーチ中の約7割をこの基本型のキーフレーズを用いて作成しました。また、表現のバリエーションを増やせるように、約3割のスピーチで他の表現を使っています。例えば、Assertionの中で、「2つの理由があります」を示すキーフレーズ I have two points to make. のバリエーションとしては、次のような表現が挙げられます。

I have two reasons why I think so.
I have two reasons to support my opinion.
I have two reasons to give.
I have two reasons for my opinion.
I have two reasons for my agreement.
I have two reasons for my disagreement.

今後は、高校入試や大学入試でスピーキングテストがますます導入されることが予想されます。これにより、英語の学び方を大きく変えていかなければ、対応が難しくなるでしょう。しかし、これは悪い変化ではありません。今までは試験に合格するための「英語の学び方」でしたが、これからは、学校や社会でも役立つ「英語の学び方」へと変えていく必要があるのです。

テスト対策としてAREA式を習得し、スピーキングテストに臨むことで、スピーキングの論理力と説得力を高めることができます。特に、本書に収載した60のスピーチは、すべてAREA式で構成されているため、基本型を徹底的にトレーニングできます。本書のAREA式スピーチで学習し、是非、考える習慣、論理的思考力、批判力、分析力や問題解決力を身につけてください。

AREA 式コンセプトマップを活用しよう

「コンセプトマップ」とは、概念と概念を線で結び、概念間の関係を視覚化するもので、本来はプレゼンテーションなどの際に用いられます。本書では、AREA 式で行うスピーチの内容整理のために、コンセプトマップを用いていますので、AREA 式コンセプトマップと言えます。その使い方について説明しましょう。

❶ 右ページのコンセプトマップのひな型をコピーして使う場合 難易度 ★★★

スピーチのタイトルだけを見て、自分の立場を決め、コンセプトマップに自分の考えを書き込む（1 分間）

▼

即興スピーチを行う（2 分間）

ポイント 本書のサンプルスピーチを読む前に、「どれだけトピックに対する知識があるか」、「どれだけトピックに関する英単語力があるか」などを確認できる。

❷ 本書のキーワード付きのコンセプトマップを使う場合 難易度 ★★☆

各スピーチに掲載されているコンセプトマップを確認

・「賛成」「反対」いずれかの立場が設定されている

・サンプルスピーチから選んだキーワードが記載されている

▼

スピーチのタイトルとキーワードを頼りに、即興スピーチを行う（2 分間）

ポイント キーワードは少なめに精選してあるので、自分の能力に応じて内容を追加できる。

❸ その他の使い方

(1) サンプルスピーチを読む前に、自分の持っている英語力のみでコンセプトマップを使う → 自分の現在の英語力を試すことができる

(2) サンプルスピーチを読んだあとにコンセプトマップを使い、定着度を確認するために内容をリテリングする → スピーキングが特に苦手な方におすすめ

いずれの場合でも、キーワードだけを書くことが重要です。几帳面に英文をすべて書き込む人がいますが、英文を書くと、どうしても文字を追って読み上げたくなります。書かれた英文を読むだけでは、スピーキングのトレーニングにはなりません。キーワードだけを頼りに、実際にスピーキングで文として使ってみることが大切です。

また、試験対策としてよく挙げられる、「スピーチの丸暗記」も 1 つの方法ですが、長続きしません。丸暗記しても、同じ問題が出る保証はありません。暗記による英語の定着は大切ですが、英語の発信力を磨くことが何より大切です。定着のためのトレーニングと発信のためのトレーニングの両方を意識して行うことが重要なのです。キーワードだけを頼りに、30 秒でも中身のある英語を話せるようになることが、大きな進歩になります。

コンセプトマップ

Assertion

Reason 1

Reason 2

Example 1

Example 2

Assertion (Conclusion)

英語スピーキングへの苦手意識を克服しよう

一般的に、英語のスピーキングが苦手な人の特徴は、7つあります。

❶ トピックについて考える習慣がなく、明確な自分の意見をもっていない

本書では、賛否両論の立場から合計80のスピーチとダイアローグを扱っています。学習する前には、トピックのタイトルを見て、自分の立場、つまりテーマについて賛成の立場なのか反対の立場なのかを決めてから、ページを開いてください。自分の立場を決めて学習することで、英語のスピーキング力、英単語力に加えて、トピックについて考える力も向上するのです。英語で考える力は、英語を学習する上では、非常に大切な力の1つです。

❷ 英語の間違いを恐れる

文法的な間違いを気にする人がいますが、スピーキングでは、不完全な英語を使ってもコミュニケーションは成立しています。スピーキングもライティングも、間違いながらも実際に英語を使うことでしか力は身につきません。

❸ 問題集に時間と労力をかけ、TOEIC 等で高得点を取って満足してしまう

英単語や英語に関する知識は増えますが、スピーキングでは使えない英語を覚えているにすぎません。発信するための英語は、使うことでしか身につきません。実際に英単語やフレーズなどを自分の発話として使いながら覚えると、飛躍的に定着しやすくなります。英語をインプットすることだけで満足するのではなく、発信するためのトレーニングを行うことが必要です。

❹ アクティブボキャブラリーとパッシブボキャブラリーを意識していない

アクティブボキャブラリーとは、理解もできるし、使うこともできるレベルの英単語を指します。パッシブボキャブラリーとは、リーディングやリスニングでは理解できるけれども、スピーキングやライティングでは使いこなせない英単語を指します。本書では、アクティブボキャブラリーを増やすために、コンセプトマップやフレーズ形式で自発的に英語を使えるように、工夫しています。

❺ 発言が苦手だからと、小さな声で自信なさそうに話す

発音や英語が苦手以前に、英語が通じない原因の多くは、相手に声が届いていないことです。知っている英単語を使って、アクセントに注意して大きな声で話すだけでも、意思疎通ができます。自信をもって大きな声で話すことが大切です。

❻ 社会問題やニュースなどへの関心が低く、知識がない

英語で話しかけても、トピックについて知識がなくて、会話が続かないことがあります。トピックについて関心がなく知らなければ、日本語でも英語でも話が続きません。

❼ スピーキングの基本型や有効なトレーニング方法を知らないので、意見を整理して伝えられない

本書では、AREA 式とコンセプトマップを活用して、視覚的に型を理解し、英語を発信するためのトレーニングができます。

この１冊にじっくり取り組めば、これらの弱点はすべて克服できますし、各種資格試験のスピーキングテストの対策も万全です。AREA 式とコンセプトマップを十分に活用して、さまざまなトピックについて考える訓練を積めば、本書で取り上げていないテーマが出題された際にも十分対応できるはずです。

例えば、「安楽死は認められるべきか」、「救急車利用に課金すべきか」、「在宅勤務を推進すべきか」、「核兵器は廃絶されるべきか」、「日本はもっと移民を受け入れるべきか」など、ニュースになっているトピックは、スピーキングテストの課題として使われる可能性があります。こういった新聞やテレビのニュースには、日ごろから常に関心を持ち、英文記事を集めて、トピックに関するキーワードとなる英単語を集めておきましょう。そしてコンセプトマップにキーワードだけをメモして、徹底的にトレーニングすればよいのです。本書が、英語のスピーキングが苦手な人にとって、大きな効果を発揮するものと確信しています。

本書の構成と段階的実践トレーニング

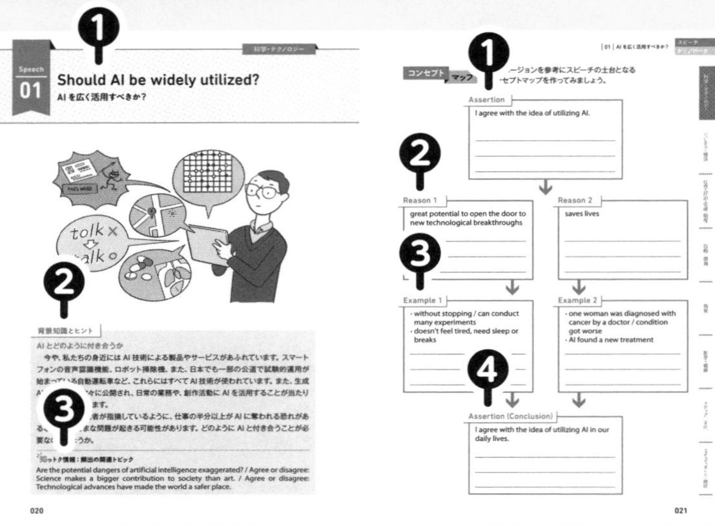

トピック

❶ テーマ

自分が賛成の立場をとるか、反対の立場をとるかを決めて考えをまとめましょう。

❷ 背景知識とヒント

トピックの背景を理解し、自分の主張をまとめる参考にしてください。

❸ 知っトク情報

実際に英検等で過去に出題された関連するトピックの問題のリストです。

コンセプトマップ

❶ Assertion

主張したい一文を書き込みます。

❷ Reason

理由を 2 つ、キーワードで書き込みます。

❸ Example

理由を支える例を、キーワードで書き込みます。

❹ Assertion (Conclusion)

❶～❸を踏まえ、最も主張したい一文でスピーチを締めます。

段階的実践トレーニング

STEP 1 ▸ 背景知識の学習

テーマとイラストを見て、まずは自分の立場を考えます。馴染みのないテーマの場合は、「背景知識とヒント」を読んで参考にしてください。

STEP 2 ▸ コンセプトマップの活用

空欄に、自分の考えに関するキーワードをメモします。キーワードだけを頼りに、まずは試しに即興で 2 分間のスピーチをしてみましょう。（→ p.10 ～ p.11）

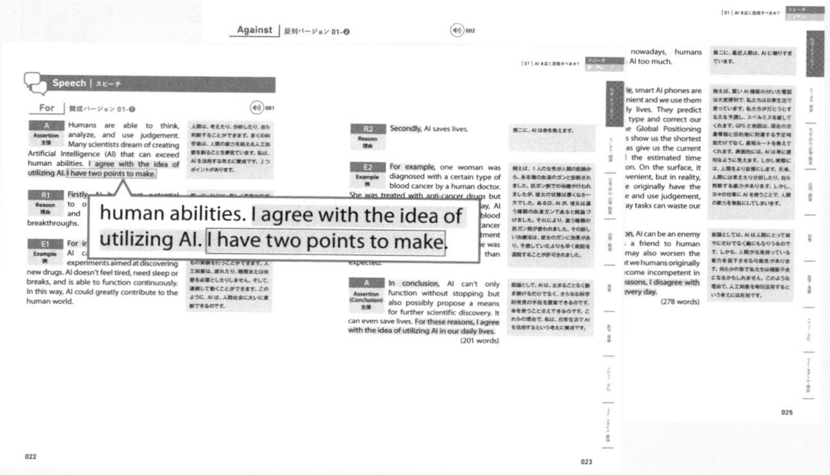

human abilities. I agree with the idea of
utilizing AI. I have two points to make.

スピーチ（For 賛成バージョン・Against 反対バージョン）

線で囲まれた表現は、「論理的に展開するためのキーフレーズ」です。続くページにある「Words and Phrases」や「Tips」でバリエーションを紹介しています。マーカーが引かれているのは、AREA 式の指標となる重要な表現です。このマーカーに注目して、AREA 式の各パートを読んでいきましょう。

段階的実践トレーニング

STEP 3 ▸ リスニング

サンプルスピーチの音声を、まずは通して全体を聞いて、理解します。聞き取れない単語があったら、チェックしておきましょう。

STEP 4 ▸ リーディング

本文を読んで、内容を理解します。本文に出てくる英単語やフレーズ、訳例を確認しましょう。

STEP 5 ▸ 音読練習

再度音声を聞き、音読します。マーカーの表現を意識しつつ、アクセントやイントネーションに気をつけて取り組みましょう。

STEP 6 ▸ オーバーラップリーディング

英文を見ながら、音声の英語に合わせて同時に音読します。

STEP 7 ▸ ディクテーション

音声を聞きながら、英文を書き写します。慣れてきたら、テキストを見ないで書き起こせるようにしましょう。

STEP 8 ▸ シャドウイング

テキストは見ないで、音声に合わせて英文を口に出します。非常に難易度の高い勉強法ですが、スピーキング能力を高めるためには最適の方法です。

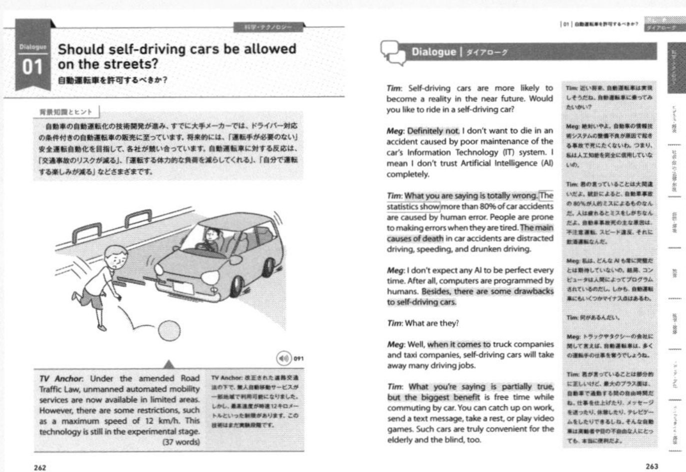

科学・テクノロジー

Dialogue 01

Should self-driving cars be allowed on the streets?

自動運転車を許可するべきか？

背景知識とヒント

自動車の自動運転化の技術開発が進み、すでに大手メーカーでは、ドライバー対応の条件付きの自動運転車の販売に至っています。将来的には、「運転手が必要のない」安全運転自動化を目指して、各社が競い合っています。自動運転車に対する反応は、「交通事故のリスクが減る」、「運転する体力的な負荷を減らしてくれる」、「自分で運転する楽しみが減る」などさまざまです。

091

TV Anchor: Under the amended Road Traffic Law, unmanned automated mobility services are now available in limited areas. However, there are some restrictions, such as a maximum speed of 12 km/h. This technology is still in the experimental stage. (37 words)

TV Anchor: 改正された道路交通法の下で、無人自動移動サービスが一部地域で利用可能になりました。しかし、最高速度が時速12キロメートルといった制限があります。この技術はまだ実験段階です。

262

| 01 | 自動運転車を許可するべきか？ ダイアローグ

Dialogue | ダイアローグ

Tim: Self-driving cars are more likely to become a reality in the near future. Would you like to ride in a self-driving car?

Meg: Definitely not. I don't want to die in an accident caused by poor maintenance of the car's Information Technology (IT) system. I mean I don't trust Artificial Intelligence (AI) completely.

Tim: What you are saying is totally wrong. The statistics show more than 80% of car accidents are caused by human error. People are prone to making errors when they are tired. The main causes of death in car accidents are distracted driving, speeding, and drunken driving.

Meg: I don't expect any AI to be perfect every time. After all, computers are programmed by humans. Besides, there are some drawbacks to self-driving cars.

Tim: What are they?

Meg: Well, when it comes to truck companies and taxi companies, self-driving cars will take away many driving jobs.

Tim: What you're saying is partially true, but the biggest benefit is free time while commuting by car. You can catch up on work, send a text message, take a rest, or play video games. Such cars are truly convenient for the elderly and the blind, too.

Tim: 近い将来、自動運転車は実現しそうだね。自動運転車に乗ってみたいかい？

Meg: 絶対いやよ。自動車の情報技術システムの整備不良が原因で起きる事故で死にたくないわ。つまり、私は人工知能を完全に信用していないの。

Tim: 君の言っていることは大間違いだよ。統計によると、自動車事故の80%が人的ミスによるものなんだ。人は疲れるとミスをしがちなんだよ。自動車事故死の主な原因は、不注意運転、スピード違反、それに飲酒運転なんだ。

Meg: 私は、どんなAIも常に完璧だとは期待していないの。結局、コンピュータは人間によってプログラムされているのだし。しかも、自動運転車にもいくつかマイナス点はあるわ。

Tim: 何があるんだい。

Meg: トラックやタクシーの会社に関して言えば、自動運転車は、多くの運転手の仕事を奪うでしょうね。

Tim: 君が言っていることは部分的に正しいけど、最大のプラス面は、自動車で通勤する間の自由時間だね。仕事を仕上げたり、メッセージを送ったり、休憩したり、テレビゲームをしたりできるしね。そんな自動車は高齢者や目の不自由な人にとっても、本当に便利だよ。

263

Part2 ダイアローグ

報道ニュースを聞いた2人が、そのニュースについてディスカッションをします。自分の考えをコンセプトマップで整理し、スピーチを構成してみましょう。

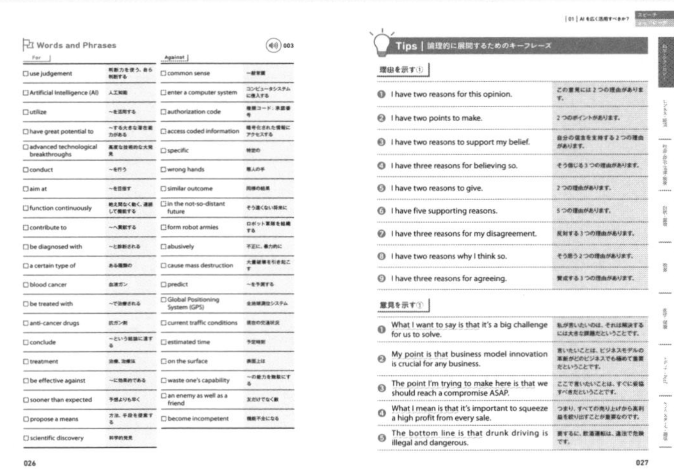

Words and Phrases 003

For		Against	
□use judgement	判断力を使う、自ら判断する	□common sense	一般常識
□Artificial Intelligence (AI)	人工知能	□enter a computer system	コンピュータシステムに侵入する
□utilize	～を活用する	□authorization code	権限コード；承認番号
□have great potential to	～する大きな潜在能力がある	□access coded information	暗号化された情報にアクセスする
□advanced technological breakthroughs	高度な技術的な大発見	□specific	特定の
□conduct	～を行う	□wrong hands	悪人の手
□aim at	～を目指す	□similar outcome	同様の結果
□function continuously	絶え間なく動く、連続して機能する	□in the not-so-distant future	そう遠くない将来に
□contribute to	～へ貢献する	□form robot armies	ロボット軍隊を組織する
□be diagnosed with	～と診断される	□abusively	不正に、暴力的に
□a certain type of	ある種類の	□cause mass destruction	大量破壊を引き起こす
□blood cancer	血液ガン	□predict	～を予測する
□be treated with	～で治療される	□Global Positioning System (GPS)	全地球測位システム
□anti-cancer drugs	抗ガン剤	□current traffic conditions	現在の交通状況
□conclude	～という結論に達する	□estimated time	予定時刻
□treatment	治療、治療法	□on the surface	表面上は
□be effective against	～に効果的である	□waste one's capability	～の能力を無駄にする
□sooner than expected	予想よりも早く	□an enemy as well as a friend	友だけでなく敵
□propose a means	方法、手段を提案する	□become incompetent	機能不全になる
□scientific discovery	科学的発見		

026

| 01 | AIを広く活用すべきか？ スピーチ

Tips | 論理的に展開するためのキーフレーズ

理由を示す①

❶ I have two reasons for this opinion.	この意見には2つの理由があります。
❷ I have two points to make.	2つのポイントがあります。
❸ I have two reasons to support my belief.	自分の信念を支持する2つの理由があります。
❹ I have three reasons for believing so.	そう信じる3つの理由があります。
❺ I have two reasons to give.	2つの理由があります。
❻ I have five supporting reasons.	5つの理由があります。
❼ I have three reasons for my disagreement.	反対する3つの理由があります。
❽ I have two reasons why I think so.	そう思う2つの理由があります。
❾ I have three reasons for agreeing.	賛成する3つの理由があります。

意見を示す①

❶ What I want to say is that it's a big challenge for us to solve.	私が言いたいのは、それは解決するには大きな課題だということです。
❷ My point is that business model innovation is crucial for any business.	言いたいことは、ビジネスモデルの革新がどのビジネスでも極めて重要だということです。
❸ The point I'm trying to make here is that we should reach a compromise ASAP.	ここで言いたいことは、すぐに妥協すべきだということです。
❹ What I mean is that it's important to squeeze a high profit from every sale.	つまり、すべての売り上げから高利益を絞り出すことが重要なのです。
❺ The bottom line is that drunk driving is illegal and dangerous.	要するに、飲酒運転は、違法で危険です。

027

Words and Phrases

トピックで必要な英単語やフレーズです。巻末には日本語から引ける「逆引き索引」をまとめています（p.354 ～）。

Tips 論理的に展開するためのキーフレーズ

賛成・反対の意見を述べる際に必要なテクニックとなる、強調、理由、追加等を示すフレーズです。機能別にまとめた一覧（p.343 ～）もあります。

段階的実践トレーニング

STEP 9 ▸ コンセプトマップでリテリング (→ p.10)

一通りサンプルスピーチを学び終えたら、コンセプトマップのひな型を使ってリテリング（スピーチの再構築）を行い、定着度を確認しましょう。

STEP 10 ▸ 実践トレーニングの継続

本書の内容をマスターしたら、コンセプトマップのひな型を活用し、スピーキングの練習を、できれば毎日継続してください。体力の向上を図るには毎日のトレーニングが不可欠なことと同じです。

実践トレーニングを効果的に行うための小道具

❶ タイマー

資格試験では、必ず時間制限があります。英検 1 級の二次試験であれば、タイトルを選んでから、1 分間の考慮時間があり、それから 2 分間でスピーチをします。2 分を過ぎると、話の途中であっても中止させられます。その後 4 分間、スピーチの内容やトピックに関連した質問が出題されます。このように試験対策として、実際の試験に応じて時間を設定して、練習することが大切です。

❷ ボイスレコーダー

練習の際には、なんとなく練習をするのではなく、必ず 1 週間に 1 度は、自分のスピーチを録音します。2 分間のスピーチには、約 200 語以上が必要になります。内容あるスピーチが 2 分間、適切な時間配分でできているかを確認するのです。

❸ スマートフォン

スマートフォンに自分のスピーキングを録画して、自分で分析します。

❹ ノート

コンセプトマップのコピーを貼り、メモを書き込みます。また、実践トレーニングの時間を記録します。学習した記録時間が増えるごとに、自信が増していきます。

いかがでしょうか？

スピーキングに苦手意識を持っている日本人は非常に多いのですが、AREA 式を理解して身につければ、誰でも飛躍的に英語スピーキング力を向上させることができます。加えてダイアローグから、使える表現を実践的に覚えて強化すれば、資格試験対策も完璧です。

それでは、一緒にスピーキング学習の第一歩を踏み出してみましょう。

音声のご利用方法

方法 1

音声再生アプリで再生する

右の QR コードをスマホなどで読み取るか、下の URL にアクセスしてアプリをダウンロードしてください。ダウンロード後、アプリを起動して『AREA 式で英語 2 分間スピーキング』を選択すると、端末に音声がダウンロードできます。

https://gakken-ep.jp/extra/myotomo/

方法 2

MP3 形式の音声で再生する

上記の方法 1 の URL、もしくは QR コードでページにアクセスし、ページ下方の【語学・検定】から『AREA 式で英語 2 分間スピーキング』を選択すると、音声ファイルがダウンロードされます。

ご利用上の注意

お客様のネット環境およびスマホやタブレット端末の環境により、音声の再生やアプリの利用ができない場合、当社は責任を負いかねます。また、スマホやタブレット端末へのアプリのインストール方法など、技術的なお問い合わせにはご対応できません。ご理解いただきますようお願いいたします。

Part 1

Speech

スピーチ

60

賛成 30 ＋ 反対 30

Speech 01

Should AI be widely utilized?

AIを広く活用すべきか？

背景知識とヒント

AIとどのように付き合うか

今や、私たちの身近にはAI技術による製品やサービスがあふれています。スマートフォンの音声認識機能、ロボット掃除機、また、日本でも一部の公道で試験的運用が始まっている自動運転車など、これらにはすべてAI技術が使われています。また、生成AIサービスが次々に公開され、日常の業務や、創作活動にAIを活用することが当たり前になりつつあります。

一方、一部の識者が指摘しているように、仕事の半分以上がAIに奪われる恐れがあるなど、さまざまな問題が起きる可能性があります。どのようにAIと付き合うことが必要なのでしょうか。

知っトク情報：頻出の関連トピック

Are the potential dangers of artificial intelligence exaggerated? / Agree or disagree: Science makes a bigger contribution to society than art. / Agree or disagree: Technological advances have made the world a safer place.

コンセプトマップ

賛成バージョンを参考にスピーチの土台となるコンセプトマップを作ってみましょう。

Assertion

I agree with the idea of utilizing AI.

Reason 1

great potential to open the door to new technological breakthroughs

Reason 2

saves lives

Example 1

- without stopping / can conduct many experiments
- doesn't feel tired, need sleep or breaks

Example 2

- one woman was diagnosed with cancer by a doctor / condition got worse
- AI found a new treatment

Assertion (Conclusion)

I agree with the idea of utilizing AI in our daily lives.

Speech | スピーチ

For | 賛成バージョン 01-❶

001

A
Assertion
主張

Humans are able to think, analyze, and use judgement. Many scientists dream of creating Artificial Intelligence (AI) that can exceed human abilities. I agree with the idea of utilizing AI. I have two points to make.

人間は、考えたり、分析したり、自ら判断することができます。多くの科学者は、人間の能力を超える人工知能を創ることを夢見ています。私は、AI を活用する考えに賛成です。2 つポイントがあります。

R1
Reason
理由

Firstly, AI has great potential to open the door to new and advanced technological breakthroughs.

第一に、AI には、新しく高度な技術的大発見へのドアを開く、大きな潜在能力があります。

E1
Example
例

For instance, without stopping, AI can conduct millions of experiments aimed at discovering new drugs. AI doesn't feel tired, need sleep or breaks, and is able to function continuously. In this way, AI could greatly contribute to the human world.

例えば AI は、止まることなく、新薬を発見することを目指して何百万回もの実験を行うことができます。人工知能は、疲れたり、睡眠または休憩を必要としたりしません。そして、連続して動くことができます。このように、AI は、人間社会に大いに貢献できるのです。

R2
Reason
理由

Secondly, AI saves lives.

第二に、AIは命を救えます。

E2
Example
例

For example, one woman was diagnosed with a certain type of blood cancer by a human doctor. She was treated with anti-cancer drugs but her condition only got worse. One day, AI concluded she had a different type of blood cancer. So, different kinds of anti-cancer drugs were then used. The new treatment was effective against her cancer and she was allowed to leave the hospital sooner than expected.

例えば、１人の女性が人間の医師から、ある種の血液のガンと診断されました。抗ガン剤での治療が行われましたが、彼女の状態は悪くなる一方でした。ある日、AIが、彼女は違う種類の血液ガンであると結論づけました。それにより、違う種類の抗ガン剤が使われました。その新しい治療法は、彼女のガンに効果があり、予想していたよりも早く病院を退院することが許可されました。

A
Assertion (Conclusion)
主張

In conclusion, AI can't only function without stopping but also possibly propose a means for further scientific discovery. It can even save lives. For these reasons, I agree with the idea of utilizing AI in our daily lives.

(201 words)

結論として、AIは、止まることなく動き続けるだけでなく、さらなる科学的発見の手段を提案できるのです。命を救うことさえできるのです。これらの理由で、私は、日常生活でAIを活用するという考えに賛成です。

Against | 反対バージョン 01-❷

 002

A
Assertion
主張

AI means Artificial Intelligence. It neither thinks freely nor feels as humans do. It doesn't even have common sense. How can we trust such a thing? I disagree with the idea of utilizing AI. I have two points to make.

AIとは、人工知能を意味します。AIは、人間のように自由に考えたり、感じたりしません。一般常識も持っていません。そのようなものを、どのように信頼できるのでしょうか。私は、AIを活用するという考えに反対です。2つのポイントがあります。

R1
Reason
理由

Firstly, there is a possibility that AI can be dangerous.

第一に、AIは危険である可能性があります。

E1
Example
例

For example, a virus created by AI has already entered some computer systems and stolen user IDs in order to control authorization codes and access coded information. If the control of a specific AI gets into the wrong hands, it may lead to a similar outcome. What I mean is that in the not-so-distant future, AI may form robot armies and could use them abusively somehow. It may even cause mass destruction.

例えば、AIによって作られたウイルスは、すべての権限コードを管理し、暗号化された情報にアクセスするために、すでにコンピュータに侵入し、利用者のIDを盗み出しているのです。ある特定の人工知能が、悪人の手に落ちれば、同じ結果に至るかもしれません。私が言いたいことは、それほど遠くない将来に、AIがロボット軍隊を組織して、悪用するかもしれないということです。大量破壊を引き起こすかもしれません。

R2
Reason
理由

Secondly, nowadays, humans depend on AI too much.

第二に、最近人間は、AIに頼りすぎています。

E2
Example
例

For example, smart AI phones are very convenient and we use them in our daily lives. They predict what we are going to type and correct our errors in spelling. The Global Positioning System (GPS) and maps show us the shortest routes to take as well as give us the current traffic conditions and the estimated time to reach our destination. On the surface, it seems AI is simply convenient, but in reality, it makes us lazier. We originally have the ability to think, analyze and use judgement, but using AI for everyday tasks can waste our capabilities.

例えば、賢いAI機能の付いた電話は大変便利で、私たちは日常生活で使っています。私たちが打とうとする文を予測し、スペルミスを直してくれます。GPSと地図は、現在の交通情報と目的地に到達する予定時刻だけでなく、最短ルートを教えてくれます。表面的には、AIは単に便利なように見えます。しかし実際には、人間をより怠惰にします。元来、人間には考えたり分析したり、自ら判断する能力があります。しかし、日々の仕事にAIを使うことで、人間の能力を無駄にしてしまいます。

A
Assertion (Conclusion)
主張

In conclusion, AI can be an enemy as well as a friend to human beings. It may also worsen the abilities that we humans originally have. We may even become incompetent in some way. For these reasons, I disagree with the idea of utilizing AI every day.

(278 words)

結論としては、AIは人間にとって味方にだけでなく敵にもなりうるのです。しかも、人間が元来持っている能力を低下させる可能性があります。何らかの形で私たちは機能不全になるかもしれません。このような理由で、人工知能を毎日活用するという考えには反対です。

Words and Phrases

For

□ use judgement	判断力を使う、自ら判断する
□ Artificial Intelligence (AI)	人工知能
□ utilize	～を活用する
□ have great potential to	～する大きな潜在能力がある
□ advanced technological breakthroughs	高度な技術的な大発見
□ conduct	～を行う
□ aim at	～を目指す
□ function continuously	絶え間なく動く、連続して機能する
□ contribute to	～へ貢献する
□ be diagnosed with	～と診断される
□ a certain type of	ある種類の
□ blood cancer	血液ガン
□ be treated with	～で治療される
□ anti-cancer drugs	抗ガン剤
□ conclude	～という結論に達する
□ treatment	治療、治療法
□ be effective against	～に効果的である
□ sooner than expected	予想よりも早く
□ propose a means	方法、手段を提案する
□ scientific discovery	科学的発見

Against

□ common sense	一般常識
□ enter a computer system	コンピュータシステムに侵入する
□ authorization code	権限コード；承認番号
□ access coded information	暗号化された情報にアクセスする
□ specific	特定の
□ wrong hands	悪人の手
□ similar outcome	同様の結果
□ in the not-so-distant future	そう遠くない将来に
□ form robot armies	ロボット軍隊を組織する
□ abusively	不正に、暴力的に
□ cause mass destruction	大量破壊を引き起こす
□ predict	～を予測する
□ Global Positioning System (GPS)	全地球測位システム
□ current traffic conditions	現在の交通状況
□ estimated time	予定時刻
□ on the surface	表面上は
□ waste one's capability	～の能力を無駄にする
□ an enemy as well as a friend	友だけでなく敵
□ become incompetent	機能不全になる

Tips | 論理的に展開するためのキーフレーズ

理由を示す①

❶ I have two reasons for this opinion.	この意見には2つの理由があります。
❷ I have two points to make.	2つのポイントがあります。
❸ I have two reasons to support my belief.	自分の信念を支持する2つの理由があります。
❹ I have three reasons for believing so.	そう信じる3つの理由があります。
❺ I have two reasons to give.	2つの理由があります。
❻ I have five supporting reasons.	5つの理由があります。
❼ I have three reasons for my disagreement.	反対する3つの理由があります。
❽ I have two reasons why I think so.	そう思う2つの理由があります。
❾ I have three reasons for agreeing.	賛成する3つの理由があります。

意見を示す①

❶ What I want to say is that it's a big challenge for us to solve.	私が言いたいのは、それは解決するには大きな課題だということです。
❷ My point is that business model innovation is crucial for any business.	言いたいことは、ビジネスモデルの革新がどのビジネスでも極めて重要だということです。
❸ The point I'm trying to make here is that we should reach a compromise ASAP.	ここで言いたいことは、すぐに妥協すべきだということです。
❹ What I mean is that it's important to squeeze a high profit from every sale.	つまり、すべての売り上げから高利益を絞り出すことが重要なのです。
❺ The bottom line is that drunk driving is illegal and dangerous.	要するに、飲酒運転は、違法で危険です。

Should human cloning be undertaken?

クローン人間の是非

背景知識とヒント

クローン人間をめぐる議論

クローン技術を使って、1996年にイギリスで、世界で初めてのクローン羊が誕生しました。その後も、クローン技術に関する研究は進み、特に再生医療分野などへの貢献が期待されています。

クローン人間の作製については、各国でタブー視されており、日本でも罰則を科してこれを禁じています。しかし、クローン羊が誕生して以来、クローン人間に対するさまざまな議論が活発になされ、賛否両論の意見があります。

知っトク情報：頻出の関連トピック

Are you for or against human cloning? / Do the benefits of cloning outweigh the dangers? / Is the human race in danger of making itself extinct? / Will the human race one day destroy itself?

コンセプトマップ

反対バージョンを参考にスピーチの土台となるコンセプトマップを作ってみましょう。

Assertion

I disagree with the idea of cloning humans.

Reason 1

human cloning is abused

Reason 2

confusing to have one's exact clone

Example 1

- clones will be used as human bombs
- replace an elite member

Example 2

- distinguish the original person from his clones
- legally and scientifically prove

Assertion (Conclusion)

I disagree with the idea of cloning humans.

Speech | スピーチ

For | 賛成バージョン 02-❶

 004

A
Assertion
主張

Cloning humans is an amazing achievement in biology and it has had a profound effect on society. I strongly believe human cloning has the potential to offer great benefits to people. I agree with the idea of cloning humans. I have two points to make.

ヒトクローンは生物学における素晴らしい成果で、それは社会に大きな影響を及ぼしました。私は、ヒトクローンは、人間に大きなメリットをもたらす可能性があると強く信じます。ヒトクローンの考えに賛成です。2つのポイントがあります。

R1
Reason
理由

Firstly, cloning humans will make us happy.

第一に、ヒトクローンは人間を幸せにします。

E1
Example
例

For example, infertile couples will have the chance to have children using their DNA. Though they may desire to have children, some couples have difficulty reproducing naturally. And others may have lost their children through accidents or illness. Emotional pain may be alleviated by cloning oneself or one who has passed away; relatives will feel much joy. In addition, doctors can clone organs from a sick person's tissues or the tissues of a relative. This enables them to help patients, especially those who are waiting their turn on a long donor receiver list.

例えば、不妊症のカップルは自分のDNAを使って子どもを授かるチャンスがあります。子どもを授かりたいと切望しながら、自然に子どもを授かるのが難しいカップルがいます。また、事故や病気で子どもを失った人もいるかもしれません。精神的な苦痛は、自分自身や他界した人のクローンを作ることで和らげることができるかもしれません。親族も喜びを感じるでしょう。さらに、医師は病人の組織や親族の組織から臓器のクローンを作ることができます。このことによって患者、特に長いドナー受取人リストで自分の順番を待っている人を、助けることができます。

R2
Reason
理由

Secondly, cloning humans will make our lives more convenient. Some great minds have passed away. If we bring them back using cloning technology, their cloned copy could discover even more theories and invent even more gadgets.

第二に、ヒトクローンは生活をもっと便利にします。他界した偉人がいます。もし彼らをクローン技術により生き返らせられれば、彼らのクローンはより多くの理論を発見し、もっと多くの装置を発明するかもしれません。

E2
Example
例

For example, there's Steve Jobs, Thomas Edison, and the like; the list goes on and on. There could be more and more of these cloned geniuses revitalizing our world. Why, possibly dozens of Thomas Edisons could work hard on multiple inventions! I would be thrilled to use all these new gadgets that would make my life more convenient.

例えば、スティーブ・ジョブズ、トーマス・エジソンなど、例を挙げればきりがありません。クローンで生み出されたこれらの天才たちは、世界を活気づけることでしょう。もちろん、おそらく多数のトーマス・エジソンたちは、多数の発明に熱心に取り組むことでしょう！　生活を便利にしてくれる、これらすべての新しい装置を使うことに、きっと私はワクワクすることでしょう。

A
Assertion (Conclusion)
主張

In conclusion, I think it would be nice to see many familiar faces. Besides, there is also the possibility that cloning technology can be used to cure diseases as well as replace body parts. To reiterate , I agree with the idea of cloning humans.

(283 words)

結論として、たくさんのなじみの顔に会うことは素晴らしいと思います。さらに、クローン技術は、体の一部分を取り換えるだけでなく、病気を治すことに使われる可能性があります。繰り返し言いますが、ヒトクローンの考えに賛成です。

Against | 反対バージョン 02-❷

005

A
Assertion
主張

Cloning humans is against the will of God. God is the Creator and we should not play God. Moreover, human cloning raises even more ethical issues. Do the original human and his clones have the same rights? How can we tell them apart? I disagree with the idea of cloning humans. I have two points to make.

ヒトクローンは神の意思に反します。神は創造者で、私たちは神のようにふるまうべきではありません。さらに、ヒトクローンは、さらなる倫理的問題をもたらします。元の人間とそのクローンは、同じ権利を持つのでしょうか。どのようにして彼らを識別できるのでしょうか。ヒトクローンの考えに反対します。2つのポイントがあります。

R1
Reason
理由

Firstly, in almost all science fiction stories, human cloning is abused. Once cloning humans becomes possible, it will pose a danger to society.

第一に、ほとんどすべての SF 小説の中で、ヒトクローンは、悪用されています。いったんヒトクローンが可能になれば、社会に危険を及ぼすでしょう。

E1
Example
例

For example, it's possible that thousands of super clones will be used as human bombs in acts of terrorism. Why, a clone could even replace an elite member of a religion or government! Furthermore, even if we destroy current clones, newborn clones will eventually appear somewhere. Once again, who will take responsibility for endangering the daily lives of people all over the planet?

例えば、何千というスーパークローンがテロ行為の中で人間爆弾として使われるでしょう。もちろん、あるクローンが、宗教や政府のエリートの一員に取って代わることもありえます。さらに、たとえ現在のクローンを処分しても、最終的には、新生のクローンがどこかで出現するでしょう。繰り返しますが、世界中の人々の日々の生活を脅かすものに対し、誰が責任を取るのでしょうか。

R2
Reason
理由

Secondly, it would be strange and confusing to have one's exact clone somewhere on the earth. How should we treat cloned human beings? Do they have the same rights as the original humans from which they were cloned? Cloning means two genetically identical and potentially similar people exist at the exact same time.

第二に、地球上のどこかにいる人の完全なクローンがいることは、不思議で紛らわしいことです。クローンをどのように扱うべきなのでしょう。クローンと、クローンの元の人間とは、同じ権利を持つのでしょうか。クローンの意味するところは、遺伝学的に同じです。潜在的に似た人間が、同じ時間に存在していることなのです。

E2
Example
例

For example, clones of the same origin all look alike. Which is which? Furthermore, how can we distinguish the original person from his clones? Last but not least, how can we legally and scientifically prove which is the original human being?

例えば、元が同じ人間のクローンは、すべて同じに見えます。どちらがどちらなのでしょうか。さらに、オリジナルとクローンとをどのように区別するのでしょうか。最後になりますが、法的にも科学的にもどちらがオリジナルの人間なのか、どのように証明できるのでしょうか。

A
Assertion (Conclusion)
主張

In conclusion, one big drawback to cloning humans is that it's against religious and governmental ethics. In other words, human clones are not acceptable from an ethical point of view. As such, cloning humans should not be allowed. To reiterate, I disagree with the idea of cloning humans.

(285 words)

結論として、ヒトクローンを作製することの大きな欠点は、宗教倫理や政治倫理に反することです。言い換えると、倫理的な観点からすると、ヒトクローンは、受け入れられません。同様に、ヒトクローンは、許されるべきではありません。繰り返しますが、ヒトクローンの考えに反対です。

Words and Phrases

006

For

□ cloning humans	ヒトクローン
□ have a profound effect on	～に大きな影響を及ぼす
□ offer great benefits to	～に大きなメリットをもたらす
□ infertile couple	不妊症のカップル
□ DNA (deoxyribonucleic acid)	デオキシリボ核酸
□ reproduce	生殖させる
□ emotional pain	精神的な苦痛
□ alleviate	～を軽減する、和らげる
□ clone organs	臓器のクローンを作る
□ tissue	（細胞の）組織
□ wait one's turn on a long donor receiver list	長いドナー受取人リストで順番を待つ
□ great minds	偉人
□ invent a gadget	装置を発明する
□ and the like	（具体例に続けて）など
□ The list goes on and on.	例を挙げればきりがない。
□ revitalize	～を活性化させる
□ be thrilled to	～することにワクワクする
□ cure diseases	病気を治す
□ replace body parts	体の一部分を取り換える
□ to reiterate	繰り返しになるが

Against

□ against the will of God	神の意思に反する
□ the Creator	創造者、神
□ play God	神のようにふるまう、全能であろうとする
□ raise ethical issues	倫理的問題をもたらす
□ tell ~ apart ...	～と…を識別する
□ science fiction story	SF小説
□ abuse	～を悪用する
□ pose a danger to society	社会に危険を及ぼす
□ human bombs in acts of terrorism	テロ行為での人間爆弾
□ newborn clones	新生クローン
□ take responsibility for	～の責任をとる
□ have one's exact clone	正確なクローンがいる
□ genetically identical	遺伝学的に同じである
□ last but not least	最後になりますが
□ legally and scientifically prove	法的にも科学的にも証明する
□ drawback	欠点
□ acceptable	容認できる
□ from an ethical point of view	倫理的な観点からすると

Tips | 論理的に展開するためのキーフレーズ

繰り返しを示す①

❶	As I have described previously, it's risky to enter into a new business market.	前にも述べたように、新しいビジネス市場へ参入するのはリスクがあります。
❷	As I stated before, our company will be taken over by an investment company.	先に触れたように、わが社は、投資会社に吸収合併されるでしょう。
❸	As I explained earlier, a particular gesture can cause misunderstandings in communication.	先に説明したように、ある特定のジェスチャーは、コミュニケーションに誤解を生むことがあります。
❹	As I explained earlier, I cannot agree to price revisions.	先に説明したように、価格の見直しには賛成できません。
❺	As I repeated before, I am not in favor of a consumption tax rise.	先に繰り返したように、消費税の引き上げには賛成しません。
❻	As I mentioned earlier, new customer development is the priority.	先に述べたように、新規顧客開拓が最優先です。

強調を示す①

❶	Without a doubt, it's one of the most effective ways to assess the quality of the data.	間違いなく、それはデータの質を評価する最も効果的な方法の１つです。
❷	There is no doubt that the top priority is to offer quality goods.	最優先の課題が、質の高い製品を提供することであるのは間違いありません。
❸	There is no question that we should protect confidential documents.	機密文書を保護すべきだということは、間違いありません。
❹	Undoubtedly, this situation has to be changed.	間違いなく、この状況は変えられるべきです。
❺	What I'd like to stress is the importance of publicizing new products.	強調したいことは、新製品を宣伝することの重要性です。

Should people be replaced by robots?

人はロボットにとってかわられるのか？

背景知識とヒント

職場へのロボット導入が進む日本

国と産業界は、職場へのロボット導入により、安全で効率の高い職場環境を実現してきました。近年では介護施設などで、身体機能補助ロボットやコミュニケーション型の介護ロボットの導入が進められています。

しかし、「人間の仕事が奪われる」、「コミュニケーションは人間同士でなければ意味がない」など、否定的な意見もあります。人間の仕事を奪わずに、ロボットの導入はスムーズに進むでしょうか。

知っトク情報：頻出の関連トピック

Will the increasing reliance on robots and computers pose a threat to society? / The future role of robots in daily life. / Will Japan's predicted labor shortage cause a major crisis?

反対バージョンを参考にスピーチの土台となるコンセプトマップを作ってみましょう。

Assertion

I disagree with the idea of robots replacing people.

Reason 1

have a negative impact

Reason 2

work at dangerous places like battlefields

Example 1

- people are losing their jobs
- unemployment rate

Example 2

- robot soldiers
- don't get tired or feel sadness
- continue fighting

Assertion (Conclusion)

I disagree with the idea of robots replacing people.

Speech | スピーチ

For | 賛成バージョン 03-❶

007

A
Assertion
主張

Robots have become common in recent years. Cleaning robots and talking robots are good examples. I agree with the idea of robots replacing people. I have two points to make.

最近、ロボットが普及しています。掃除ロボットや対話型ロボットが良い例です。ロボットを人の代わりに使うという考えに賛成です。2つのポイントがあります。

R1
Reason
理由

Firstly, robots are more productive than humans.

第一に、ロボットは人間よりはるかに生産性が高いです。

E1
Example
例

For instance, robots don't get tired or feel bored. They don't need any sleep, vacation, or salary. Once robots are programmed to perform certain tasks, they will do them accurately and consistently 24/7. All they need is regular maintenance and enough energy to perform.

例えば、ロボットは疲れたり飽きたりしません。睡眠、休暇、給料を必要としません。ロボットは、いったん特定のタスクを実行するようにプログラムされると、毎日24時間、正確に着実に実行します。必要なことは、定期的なメンテナンスと動くための十分なエネルギーです。

R2
Reason
理由

Secondly, robots can perform tasks even in harsh environments.

第二に、ロボットは厳しい環境でもタスクを実行できます。

E2
Example
例

For instance, they can go to faraway planets and explore space without needing air. They can also work in nuclear power plants. They can even fight in a war. Furthermore, robots can be manipulated remotely by humans who are watching the robots' movements on monitors. Humans don't have to risk their lives in dangerous environments. Robots can contribute a lot to reduce the number of human lives lost in such situations.

例えば、遠く離れた惑星に行って、空気を必要とせずに宇宙を探査することができます。ロボットは原子力発電所でも働けます。戦争で戦うことさえできます。さらに、モニターで動きを見ている人間が、ロボットを遠隔操作することもできます。人間は、危険な環境で命をかける必要がありません。ロボットは、そのような状況で失われる人命の数を減らすことに大きく貢献できます。

A
Assertion (Conclusion)
主張

In conclusion, as I mentioned before, robots have so many advantages. They are always ready to perform their tasks with incredible precision, productivity, and efficiency. Therefore, I agree with the idea of robots replacing people.

(196 words)

結論として、すでに述べたように、ロボットには非常に多くのメリットがあります。ロボットは信じられないほどの正確さ、生産性と効率性で、タスクをいつでも実行できます。そのため、ロボットを人間の代わりに使うという考えに賛成です。

Against | 反対バージョン 03-❷

 008

A
Assertion
主張

Since robots can perform tasks such as cleaning and talking, it seems that they would make people's lives much easier and more convenient. Far from it. I disagree with the idea of robots replacing people. I have two points to make.

ロボットは掃除や対話といったタスクを実行できるので、人間の生活をより簡単で便利にするだろうと思われます。いいえ、そんなことはありません。ロボットを人間の代わりに使うという考えに反対です。2つのポイントがあります。

R1
Reason
理由

Firstly, robots have a negative impact on people.

第一に、ロボットは人間に悪影響を及ぼします。

E1
Example
例

For example, due to robots and automation, people are losing their jobs. In other words, the unemployment rate will increase. In turn, many people find it hard to make ends meet because they don't have an adequate income. As a result, the less people use money, the worse the economy will become. Robots could cause a vicious cycle of unemployment, poverty, low spending, and a continuously declining economy.

例えば、ロボットと自動化により、人は仕事を失っています。言い換えると、失業率が上がるだろうということです。そうして、多くの人が十分な収入を得られず、家計のやりくりが難しくなるのです。その結果、人がだんだんお金を使わなくなり、経済はますます悪化するでしょう。ロボットは、失業、貧困、低迷する消費、継続的に低迷する経済という悪循環を招くでしょう。

R2
Reason
理由

Secondly, robots can replace the human workforce in dangerous places, such as battlefields. My biggest concern is using robot soldiers and unmanned drones on battlefields.

第二に、ロボットは、戦場のような危険な場所で、人間の労働力の代わりになります。一番の心配は、ロボット兵や、操縦士の必要のないドローンが戦場で使われることです。

E2
Example
例

For example, robot soldiers don't get tired or feel sadness, and they can continue fighting once they are programmed to do so. Since humans don't have to worry about losing their companions as casualties in battle, it may mean a greater potential for having large-scale wars. Once a war with these soldiers starts, who is responsible for it?

例えば、ロボット兵は疲れることもなく、悲しみも感じません。いったんロボットが戦うようにプログラムされたら、戦い続けます。人間は、戦闘の犠牲者として仲間を失う心配をする必要がないので、大規模な戦争になる大きな可能性があります。いったんロボット兵が戦争を始めたら、誰が責任をとるのでしょうか。

A
Assertion (Conclusion)
主張

In conclusion, it's true that robots are taking over some human jobs in various fields little by little, but we can't be too careful about overusing robots. Moreover, robots may be able to do hard work instead of people. But once these robots are in trouble, many of them are too complex for the average person to fix. What benefit does an irreparable robot offer? Therefore, I disagree with the idea of robots replacing people.

(275 words)

結論として、さまざまな分野で、ロボットが徐々に人間の仕事を引き継いできているのは事実です。しかし、ロボットの使いすぎには用心が必要です。さらに、ロボットは人間の代わりにきつい仕事ができるかもしれません。しかし、いったんこれらのロボットが故障したら、ロボットの多くは、普通の人には複雑すぎて修理できません。修理不可能なロボットがどんな利益をもたらすというのでしょう。そのため、ロボットを人間の代わりに使うという考えに反対です。

Words and Phrases

For

□ become common	普及する、一般的になる
□ productive	生産性の高い
□ get tired	疲れる
□ be programmed to perform certain tasks	特定のタスクが実行できるようにプログラムされている
□ accurately and consistently 24/7	毎日24時間正確に、着実に
□ all they need is	必要なことは～である
□ regular maintenance	定期的なメンテナンス
□ in harsh environments	厳しい環境で
□ faraway planets	遠く離れた惑星
□ explore space	宇宙を探査する
□ furthermore	さらに
□ be manipulated remotely by	～によって遠隔操作される
□ watch movements on monitors	モニターで動きを見る
□ contribute	貢献する
□ reduce	～を減らす
□ as I mentioned before	すでに述べたように
□ have so many advantages	非常に多くのメリットがある
□ with incredible precision, productivity and efficiency	信じられないほどの正確さ、生産性と効率性で

Against

□ Far from it.	それどころではない。
□ due to robots and automation	ロボットと自動化により
□ unemployment rate	失業率
□ make ends meet	家計をやりくりする
□ adequate income	十分な収入
□ the less ~, the worse …	～が少なくなるほど、…は悪化する
□ cause a vicious cycle of	～の悪循環を招く
□ declining economy	低迷する経済
□ workforce	労働力
□ my biggest concern is	一番の心配は～である
□ lose companions	仲間を失う
□ casualties in battle	戦場での犠牲者
□ large-scale war	大規模な戦争
□ little by little	徐々に
□ can't be too careful about	～に用心するにこしたことはない
□ overuse	使いすぎる
□ be in trouble	故障している
□ fix	～を修理する
□ irreparable	修理不可能な

Tips | 論理的に展開するためのキーフレーズ

繰り返しを示す②

1	To reiterate, this research is outdated.	繰り返しますが、この研究は時代遅れです。
2	To reiterate, voting in elections is not compulsory in Japan.	繰り返しますが、選挙での投票は日本では強制ではありません。
3	I want to reiterate that it's critical to cut down on advertising costs.	広告費を削減することが大切だと、繰り返し言いたいです。
4	Once again, what we really need is to boost our company's profits.	もう一度言いますが、本当に必要なことは、会社の利益を上げることです。
5	I just don't want to repeat what I have said.	言ったことを繰り返したくないです。

言い換えを示す①

1	Your performance in the speech didn't reach the required level. In other words, you failed.	スピーチの能力は必要な水準まで達しませんでした。言い換えると、あなたは不合格です。
2	We minimized the size of the company. In other words, 30% of workers were fired.	会社の規模を縮小しました。言い換えると、従業員の30%を解雇しました。
3	The tax system revision affects people with an annual income exceeding 10 million yen; in other words, the rich.	税制改正は年収1,000万円を超える人に影響を与えます。言い換えると、金持ち、ということです。
4	Smoking makes your blood thick and sticky. To put it another way, you should stop smoking.	タバコを吸うと、血液が濃くドロドロになります。言い換えると、タバコを吸うことを止めるべきです。
5	This book is very difficult. To put it differently, it's too early for you to read this.	この本は、非常に難しいです。言い換えると、あなたが読むには早すぎます。

Is it worthwhile to change careers several times during our life?

人生で、何度も転職する方が良い？

背景知識とヒント

転職の価値とは？

転職やヘッドハンティングには、何か人を引きつける響きがあります。確かに、職場が変われば新しい気持ちで働くことができ、新たな環境で自身の可能性を切り開くことができるかもしれません。

しかし、「転職＝仕事のやりがい」、「ヘッドハンティング＝年収アップ」とは限りません。転職を検討する前に、メリットとデメリットの両方を検討することが必要です。

知っトク情報：頻出の関連トピック

Should job promotions be based on performance or on seniority? / Should everyone be guaranteed a job?

コンセプトマップ

賛成バージョンを参考にスピーチの土台となるコンセプトマップを作ってみましょう。

Assertion

I agree with the idea of changing careers.

....

....

....

Reason 1

accepting employment in the same field quick career growth

....

....

....

Reason 2

new jobs mean new possibilities

....

....

....

Example 1

- promotions
- are accustomed to the basics of the job

....

....

....

Example 2

- attractive high salary
- new place stimulating work

....

....

....

Assertion (Conclusion)

I agree with the idea of changing careers.

....

....

....

Speech | スピーチ

010

For | 賛成バージョン 04-❶

A
Assertion
主張

We expect many things from our jobs. We want to meet our needs, achieve self-satisfaction, and gain new skills. It's worthwhile and challenging to switch from one job to another. Therefore, I agree with the idea of changing careers several times during our life. I have two points to make.

私たちは仕事に多くのことを期待します。自分の欲求を満たしたり、自己満足を得たり、新しいスキルを身につけたりしたいのです。転職することは、価値があってやりがいがあります。そのため、一生の間に、何度か転職するという考え方に賛成です。２つのポイントがあります。

R1
Reason
理由

First, accepting employment in the same field elsewhere leads to quick career growth.

第一に、他の場所で同じ分野の仕事に就くことは、迅速なキャリアアップにつながります。

E1
Example
例

For example, if we change jobs but remain in our area of expertise, it will lead to promotions. This is because we are accustomed to the basics of the job, the job environment, and the job-related problems of our field. However, if we change jobs and move into a different field, it will be difficult to start a career from scratch.

例えば、転職したとしても、同じ専門分野に留まれば、昇進につながります。これは、仕事の基本や職場環境、専門分野の職務上の問題に慣れているからです。しかし、転職して違う分野に進出するなら、仕事をゼロから始めるのは難しいでしょう。

R2
Reason
理由

Second, new jobs mean new possibilities.

第二に、新しい仕事は新しい可能性を意味します。

E2
Example
例

For example, we may have new opportunities, such as a very high salary at our new place of employment. On average, we are supposed to work for about 40 to 50 years. Working at the same company for such a long time will make us bored and impatient because the work routine is the same day after day. New job possibilities could offer us a much more satisfying and stimulating work environment.

例えば、私たちは新しい勤務先での高賃金といった、新しいチャンスをつかむかもしれません。平均して、私たちは40年から50年働くことになります。長期間同じ会社に勤めると、仕事の手順が毎日同じなので、退屈でイライラすることになります。新しい仕事の可能性は、より満足できて刺激的な職場環境を提供してくれるはずです。

A
Assertion (Conclusion)
主張

Overall, there are numerous benefits to changing companies, such as new job opportunities and possibilities, salary increases, and different learning experiences. Moreover, working for the same company for a long time makes us fed up because the work routine stays the same. Therefore, I agree with the idea of changing careers several times during our life.

(258 words)

全体的に、会社を変えることには多数のプラス面があります。例えば、新しい仕事のチャンスと可能性、昇給、異なる学びの体験などです。さらに、同じ会社に長く勤務すれば、仕事の手順が同じなので、飽き飽きしてしまいます。そのため、一生の間に数回転職するという考えに賛成です。

Against | 反対バージョン 04-❷

011

A
Assertion
主張

These days, seeking new job opportunities is becoming more common. People want to earn more and more money by changing their careers. However, there are both pros and cons to changing one's career. The cons outweigh the pros. I disagree with the idea of changing careers several times during our life. I have two points to make.

最近、転職の機会を探すことが、より一般的になってきています。人は転職することにより、より多くのお金を稼ぎたいのです。しかし転職にはプラス面とマイナス面があります。マイナス面がプラス面よりも勝っています。一生の間に、数回転職するという考えには反対です。2つのポイントがあります。

R1
Reason
理由

First, changing careers causes a lot of problems.

第一に、転職することで多くの問題を引き起こします。

E1
Example
例

For example, it may take a long time to adapt to our new working conditions. We would have to start a new type of job from scratch. This may cause discomfort, stress, and depression. To make matters worse, the older we get, the more difficult it becomes for us to adapt to changes.

例えば、新しい職場環境に適応するのに長い時間がかかるかもしれません。新しいタイプの仕事をゼロから始めなければならないでしょう。これが不快感、ストレス、うつ状態を引き起こすかもしれません。さらに悪いことには、年を重ねれば重ねるほど、変化に適応することが難しくなっていきます。

R2
Reason
理由

Second, there is always some risk in changing careers.

第二に、転職には、いつもいくつかのリスクが伴います。

E2
Example
例

For example, it may be difficult to achieve outstanding job performance in our new field because of the new job's various work conditions, such as different colleagues, a different budget, different experiences, or a lack of experience, and so on. As a result, we may be unsuccessful, lose our new position and end up unemployed.

例えば、新しい仕事のさまざまな職場環境のため、新しい分野で優れた仕事の業績を達成することは難しいかもしれません。例を挙げると、違う同僚や違う予算、違う経験、もしくは経験不足などです。結果として、失敗し、新しい地位を失い、失業するかもしれません。

A
Assertion (Conclusion)
主張

Overall, companies want us to be loyal to their company and work for them for many decades. Working at the same company has lots of advantages, such as stability and the comfort of familiarity. Therefore, I disagree with the idea of changing careers several times during our life.

(230 words)

全体的に、企業は、私たちがその会社に忠実であり、何十年も勤務してほしいと思っています。同じ会社に勤務することには多くの利点があります。例えば、安定性やなじみのある居心地の良さです。そのため、私は一生の間に、数回転職するという考えに反対です。

Words and Phrases

For

□ meet one's needs	自分の欲求を満たす
□ achieve self-satisfaction	自己満足を得る
□ gain new skills	新しいスキルを身につける
□ it's worthwhile and challenging to	～することは価値とやりがいがある
□ switch from one job to another	転職する
□ accept employment	仕事に就く
□ lead to quick career growth	早い出世につながる
□ area of expertise	専門分野
□ lead to promotions	昇進につながる
□ job-related	仕事に関連する、業務上の
□ be accustomed to	～することに慣れている
□ start a career from scratch	仕事をゼロから始める
□ place of employment	勤務先
□ on average	平均して、概して
□ be supposed to	～することになっている
□ impatient	イライラして
□ work routine	仕事の手順
□ satisfying and stimulating work environment	満足できて、刺激的な職場環境
□ there are numerous benefits to ～ing	～には多数のメリットがある
□ be fed up	飽き飽きしている

Against

□ seek a new job opportunity	新しい仕事の機会を探す
□ there are both pros and cons to ～ing	～には良い点と悪い点がある
□ The cons outweigh the pros.	マイナス面がプラス面よりも勝る。
□ change one's career	転職する
□ cause a lot of problems	多くの問題を引き起こす、迷惑をかける
□ adapt to	～に適応する
□ working conditions	職場環境、労働条件
□ cause discomfort, stress and depression	不快、ストレス、うつ状態を引き起こす
□ to make matters worse	さらに悪いことには
□ achieve outstanding job performance	優れた仕事上の業績を達成する
□ budget	予算
□ a lack of	～の不足
□ end up unemployed	結局失業する
□ be loyal to	～に忠実である
□ for many decades	何十年もの間
□ have lots of advantages	たくさんの利点がある
□ stability	安定性、信頼性
□ comfort	居心地の良さ
□ familiarity	よく知っていること；親しさ

Tips | 論理的に展開するためのキーフレーズ

因果関係を示す①

1	Overworking can lead to stress and more serious health problems.	働きすぎは、ストレスやより深刻な健康問題につながります。
2	Drinking sugary beverages too much can lead to obesity.	糖分の多いものを飲みすぎると肥満につながります。
3	Overworking can lead to high blood pressure and insomnia.	働きすぎは高血圧や不眠症につながります。
4	Drinking alcohol could trigger high blood pressure or worsen diabetes.	飲酒は高血圧を引き起こしたり、糖尿病を悪化させたりします。
5	Installing security cameras might bring about a decrease in the overall crime rate.	監視カメラを設置することで、全体的な犯罪率の減少につながるかもしれません。
6	Taking action on small problems can bring about larger outcomes.	小さな問題について行動を起こすことで、より大きな成果をもたらすことになります。
7	What factors could bring about a change in climate?	どんな要因が気候の変化をもたらすのでしょうか。

意見を示す②

1	There are both pros and cons to being vegetarian.	ベジタリアンになるのには良い点と悪い点があります。
2	There are both merits and demerits to promoting a smoking ban.	禁煙条例を推進することには、メリットとデメリットの両方があります。
3	Your proposals have both advantages and disadvantages.	あなたの提案には、メリットとデメリットの両方があります。
4	Your strength can compensate for my weakness and vice versa.	あなたの長所は、僕の弱点を補います。また逆に、僕の長所は、あなたの弱点を補います。
5	There are arguments for and against online dating.	オンラインデートには賛否両論があります。

Is being a freelancer a worthwhile alternative to being an employee?

フリーランサーは、会社員に代わる選択肢になりうるか？

背景知識とヒント

働き方の選択

会社に就職すれば、組織の一員として、社会のルールやマナーを学ぶことができます。また、一定の給料や福利手当等が保証され、生活も安定します。

一方、フリーランサーになると、収入も安定しないで、仕事量が増えます。誰も仕事を教えてはくれず、責任も自分一人でとらなければならなくなります。しかし、仕事の自由度は高く、努力次第で高収入も期待できます。

知っトク情報：頻出の関連トピック

Should people always put their families before their work? / Do you think work is less important to people today than in the past? / Telecommuting—the pros and cons of working from home.

コンセプトマップ

賛成バージョンを参考にスピーチの土台となるコンセプトマップを作ってみましょう。

Assertion

I agree with the idea of becoming a freelancer.

Reason 1

becoming a freelancer is the flexibility

Reason 2

potentially more income

Example 1

- choose business hours
- take the afternoon off / take a nap
- cafe / library / park / living room

Example 2

- the more active you are, the more business offers
- no middleman taking his cut

Assertion (Conclusion)

I agree with the idea of becoming a freelancer.

Speech | スピーチ

For | 賛成バージョン 05-❶

013

A
Assertion
主張

Becoming a freelancer can be a life-changing decision. It seems that the rewards outweigh the risks. It's worth a try. Therefore, I agree with the idea of becoming a freelancer. I have two points to make.

フリーランサーになることは、人生を変える決断になります。利益がリスクに勝るように思われます。やってみる価値はあります。そのため、フリーランサーになるという考えに賛成です。２つのポイントがあります。

R1
Reason
理由

The first benefit of becoming a freelancer is the flexibility.

フリーランサーになる第一の利点は、融通性です。

E1
Example
例

For example, you can choose your business hours. If you want to take the afternoon off, you can do that. If you want to take a nap in the daytime, go for it. When it comes to your work environment, you can choose to work wherever you want, for example, at a cafe, at the library, in a park, or in your living room. You can choose times and workplaces that suit your lifestyle. On-the-job flexibility is the biggest benefit for many freelancers.

例えば、勤務時間を選ぶことができます。もし午後に休みたければ、そうすることもできます。もし日中に仮眠をとりたければ、どうぞしてください。働く環境に関して言えば、働きたい場所で働けます。例えば、カフェ、図書館、公園、または自宅のリビングルームです。自分のライフスタイルに合わせて勤務時間と仕事場を選べます。勤務中の柔軟性は、多くのフリーランサーにとって最も大きな利点です。

R2
Reason
理由

The second benefit is potentially more income.

第二の利点は、収入が増える可能性があることです。

E2
Example
例

For example, once you are established as a freelancer, the more active you are, the more business offers you'll receive. As a freelancer, you'll also be able to profitably charge clients fees worthy of the customized work. As a result, with no middleman taking his cut, you can pocket more after all your expenses are paid. In this respect, you have more potential income.

例えば、いったんフリーランサーとして世間に認められれば、積極的に活動すればするほど、より多くの仕事のオファーを受けられるでしょう。フリーランサーとして、特別注文の仕事に見合った報酬を顧客に請求できます。結果として、中間業者の取り分がないので、必要経費を払ったあとは、大きな利益を手に入れることができます。この点で、より多くの収入を得る可能性があります。

A
Assertion (Conclusion)
主張

To conclude, the success of your freelance business depends on your commitment and the effort you make on the job. However, freelancing has several advantages, such as flexibility regarding times and workplaces, more business opportunities and potential income, and so on. With no middleman, you can reap 100% of the profits. Therefore, I agree with the idea of becoming a freelancer.

(261 words)

結論として、フリーランサーとして成功するかどうかは、仕事への献身と努力次第です。それでもフリーランスで働くことには、いくつかの利点があります。例えば、時間や仕事場の融通性、多くのビジネスチャンスと収入の見込みなどです。中間業者がいないので、利益の100%を得ることができます。そのため、フリーランサーになる考えに賛成です。

Against | 反対バージョン 05-❷

A
Assertion
主張

Nowadays, many people want to become a freelancer to balance their work and private lives. In my book, it will make your life more stressful. Therefore, I'm opposed to the idea of becoming a freelancer. I have two points to make.

最近、仕事と私生活のバランスをとるために、多くの人はフリーランサーになりたがります。私の考えでは、生活にストレスが多くなります。そのため、フリーランサーになるという考えに反対です。２つのポイントがあります。

R1
Reason
理由

The first drawback of becoming a freelancer is that you have to wear many hats.

第一のマイナス面は、いろいろな役割を担わなければならないことです。

E1
Example
例

For example, you have to do all the administrative work, such as paying invoices, billing and dealing with other accounting matters. You also have to do your own sales, advertising and marketing. In a nutshell, you are responsible for every aspect of your new business and thus every task related to it. All of this could be very stressful.

例えば、請求書に対する支払い、請求書の作成、他の経理に関する案件の処理など、すべての管理業務をこなさなくてはいけません。営業、広告やマーケティングもしなければいけません。一言で言えば、新しい仕事のあらゆる面とそれに関するすべての仕事に責任があります。これらすべてが大きなストレスになります。

R2
Reason
理由

The second drawback is instability.

第二のマイナス面は、不安定さです。

E2
Example
例

Take the money issue, for example. It's a fact that you are at risk of not getting paid. In that respect, every now and then, you may be required to work as a debt collector. Freelancing affects your financial security a lot. Your income and workload are unstable and inconsistent. This, in turn, will make it difficult to plan for the future.

お金の件を例にとってみましょう。報酬が支払われないリスクがあることは事実です。その点では、債権回収者として働くことを求められることがあるかもしれません。フリーランスで働くことは経済的安定に影響を及ぼします。収入や仕事量は、不安定で一貫性がありません。そうして、将来について計画を立てることが難しくなるのです。

A
Assertion (Conclusion)
主張

To conclude, freelancing has more negative aspects than positive aspects, such as mountains of administrative work and job instability. You may suffer stress daily from the possibility of missing business opportunities and thereby losing work. This is the biggest difference between employed workers and self-employed workers. Therefore, I'm opposed to the idea of becoming a freelancer considering these two points.

(242 words)

結論として、フリーランスはプラス面よりもマイナス面が多いのです。例えば、山のような管理業務や仕事の不安定さです。ビジネスチャンスを失う可能性や、それにより失業する可能性で毎日ストレスを感じるかもしれません。これは、会社員と自営業者との最も大きな違いです。そのため、これらの２つの点を考慮して、フリーランサーになるという考えに反対です。

Words and Phrases

For

□ life-changing decision	人生を変える決断
□ the rewards outweigh the risks	利益の方がリスクより勝る
□ business hours	業務時間
□ take ~ off	~を休みにする
□ take a nap in the daytime	昼間に仮眠をとる
□ when it comes to	~に関して言えば
□ suit one's lifestyle	ライフスタイルに合わせる
□ be established as ~	~として世間に認められた
□ receive business offer	仕事を受ける
□ profitably charge clients fees	利益になるように顧客に料金を請求する
□ worthy of ~	~に値する
□ customized work	特別注文の仕事
□ middleman	中間業者
□ take one's cut	~の分け前をとる
□ pocket	~を手に入れる
□ expense	経費
□ in this respect	この点で
□ commitment	尽力、貢献
□ reap 100% of the profits	利益の 100%を得る

Against

□ in my book	私の考えでは
□ the first drawback of	~の最初の欠点
□ wear many hats	いろいろな役割を担う
□ do all the administrative work	すべての管理業務をやる
□ pay invoices	請求書に対する支払いをする
□ billing	請求書の作成
□ accounting matters	経理に関する案件
□ advertising and marketing	広告とマーケティング
□ in a nutshell	一言で言えば
□ be responsible for	~に責任がある
□ instability	不安定さ
□ Take the money issue, for example.	例えばお金の問題を例にとってみる。
□ it's a fact that	~なのは事実である
□ be at risk of	~するリスクがある
□ every now and then	時々
□ debt collector	債権回収者
□ workload	仕事量
□ unstable and inconsistent	不安定で一貫性のない
□ suffer stress daily from	~から日々ストレスを受ける
□ employed workers and self-employed workers	会社員と自営業者

Tips | 論理的に展開するためのキーフレーズ

可能・能力を示す

❶	Politicians should be capable of making decisions and implementing policies to overcome crises.	政治家は、危機を克服するために、決断をして、政策を実施できなければならないのです。
❷	You are able to tackle and handle various problems.	あなたは、さまざまな問題に対処できます。
❸	This conflict can be solved only by negotiations not by military force.	この対立は、軍事力にではなく、交渉によってのみ解決されます。
❹	I believe it is possible to prove their guilt with this evidence.	この証拠で彼らの罪を証明することができると信じます。
❺	He is competent enough to cope with various troubles.	彼は、さまざまな問題に対処できる十分な能力があります。

反論を示す①

❶	You are mistaken about that.	それについては間違っています。
❷	You are terribly mistaken.	あなたはとんでもない間違いをしています。
❸	What you said is not true.	あなたが言ったことは、事実ではありません。
❹	I'm opposed to the death penalty.	死刑に反対です。
❺	I'm totally against living together before marriage.	結婚前の同棲には大反対です。
❻	That's not the way I see it.	私はそう思いません。

Speech 06 Should bicycle use for commuting be promoted?

自転車通勤を推進すべきか？

背景知識とヒント

自転車通勤の魅力と欠点とは？

自転車通勤には、鉄道やバスの移動では得られない魅力があります。まず、新鮮な空気でリフレッシュできることです。同時に体力の向上やダイエット効果もあります。また、環境にやさしく、渋滞や満員電車を避けることができます。しかし、事故が起きた際に生じる加害者や、被害者としての被害の大きさなど、見過ごせないデメリットも多くあります。自転車通勤は、奨励されるべきなのでしょうか。

知っトク情報：頻出の関連トピック

Pros and cons of public transportation. / The advantages and disadvantages of living in the city. / How safe is public transportation?

コンセプトマップ

賛成バージョンを参考にスピーチの土台となるコンセプトマップを作ってみましょう。

Assertion

I agree with promoting bicycle use for commuting.

Reason 1

good for your health

Reason 2

environment-friendly

Example 1

- by car, don't move your body
- by bicycle, ride your bike

Example 2

- bicycles don't emit air pollutants
- cost-saving and energy-saving

Assertion (Conclusion)

I agree with the idea of promoting bicycle use for commuting.

Speech | スピーチ

For | 賛成バージョン 06-❶

016

A
Assertion
主張

Cycling is a more convenient way to get around, especially in crowded cities. Bicycles also take up less space than cars, and there are other benefits as well. Therefore, I agree with promoting bicycle use for commuting. I have two points to make.

特に混雑した都市部では、サイクリングは、あちこち移動するのにより便利な方法です。自転車は車ほど場所も取りません。おまけに、他の利点もあります。そのため、私は自転車通勤を推進する考えに賛成です。2つのポイントがあります。

R1
Reason
理由

First, riding a bicycle is good for your health.

第一に、自転車に乗ることは健康に良いです。

E1
Example
例

For example, as a car driver, you are not required to greatly move your body when commuting to your workplace. However, as a bicycle rider, you are required to ride your bike from home to work. According to a study, the added physical activity you get by switching from car to bike for your commute may add as much as 14 months to your life. This shows how healthy commuting by bicycle is.

例えば、自動車ドライバーの場合、職場へ通勤するときに身体を動かすことはそれほど求められません。しかし、自転車に乗る人は、家から職場まで自転車をこいで移動するのです。ある研究によれば、通勤を自動車から自転車に切り替えることで運動量が増え、寿命が14か月も延びる可能性があるということです。これは、自転車通勤がいかに健康的であるかを示しています。

R2
Reason
理由

Second, needless to say, bicycles are environmentally friendly.

第二に、言うまでもなく、自転車は環境にやさしいのです。

E2
Example
例

For example, most big cities are getting overcrowded with more and more cars. These vehicles emit carbon dioxide and other air pollutants. On the other hand, bicycles and their riders don't. What's more, compared with cars, bicycles are both cost-saving and energy-saving.

例えば、ほとんどの大都市はますます多くの車で混雑しています。これらの車は、二酸化炭素や他の大気汚染物質を排出します。一方、自転車と自転車に乗る人は排出しません。さらに、自動車と比べると、自転車は経費削減にも省エネにもなります。

A
Assertion (Conclusion)
主張

In conclusion, it's obvious that commuting by bicycle has plenty of advantages. A bike doesn't take up as much space and costs less than a car. Cycling is good for our health and the environment. Therefore, I agree with the idea of promoting bicycle use for commuting.

(222 words)

結論として、自転車による通勤には多くのメリットがあることは明らかです。自転車はスペースをとらないし、車ほど経費もかかりません。サイクリングは健康と環境に良いのです。そのため、私は自転車通勤を推進する考えに賛成です。

Against | 反対バージョン 06-❷

A
Assertion
主張

Some say that bicycles are the best way to commute in big cities. However, other means of transportation such as cars, buses, and the subway system are more convenient. Therefore, I disagree with the idea of promoting bicycle use for commuting. I have two points to make.

大都市では、自転車が通勤に最も良い方法だと言う人がいます。しかし、車、バスそして地下鉄など他の交通手段のほうが便利です。そのため、私は自転車通勤を推進するという考えに反対します。２つのポイントがあります。

R1
Reason
理由

First, bicycles are a dangerous way to commute.

第一に、自転車は、通勤するのに危険な方法です。

E1
Example
例

For example, these days, the number of bicycle-related accidents are about seventy thousand per year these days. When you have a bicycle accident, it's possible to protect your head with a helmet, but nothing can protect your body. In other words, there is the potential to be critically or life-threateningly wounded.

例えば、自転車が関係する事故は、最近では１年に約７万件もあります。自転車事故を起こしたら、ヘルメットで頭を保護することは可能ですが、あなたの身体を保護してくれるものは何もありません。言い換えれば、重傷を負い、命を脅かすケガをする可能性があるのです。

R2
Reason
理由

Second, bicycles are not good for a long-distance commute.

第二に、自転車は長距離通勤には向きません。

E2
Example
例

For example, many business people live a long distance from their workplace. For everyday commuting, it's not possible to travel long distance by bicycle because cycling is hard work. In addition, they are also subject to weather conditions, such as heat, cold humidity, wind, and the like. Therefore, it's neither realistic nor reasonable to commute by bicycle.

例えば、多くのビジネスパーソンが職場から遠くに住んでいます。毎日の通勤において、サイクリングはハードワークなので、自転車で長距離を通勤することは不可能です。さらに、暑さ、寒さ、湿度や風などの天候状況にも左右されます。そのため、自転車で通勤することは、現実的でも合理的でもありません。

A
Assertion (Conclusion)
主張

In conclusion, considering all the disadvantages of commuting by bicycles, such as safety issues and weather problems, I disagree with promoting bicycle use for commuting.

(197 words)

結論として、安全上の問題や天候といった、自転車で通勤することに関するすべての欠点を考慮すると、自転車通勤を推進するという考えに反対です。

Words and Phrases

 018

For

□ get around	あちこち移動する
□ take up space	場所をとる
□ commute	通勤する
□ be good for	～にとってよい
□ be required to	～することを求められる
□ workplace	職場
□ according to a study	ある研究によれば
□ physical activity	身体活動
□ switch from car to bike	自動車から自転車に切り替える
□ needless to say	言うまでもなく
□ environmentally friendly	環境にやさしい
□ get overcrowded with	～でいっぱいになる、過密になる
□ air pollutants	大気汚染物質
□ what's more	さらに
□ cost-saving and energy-saving	経費削減で省エネの
□ have plenty of advantages	たくさんの利点がある

Against

□ a means of transportation	1つの交通手段
□ subway system	地下鉄網
□ bicycle-related accidents	自転車が関係する事故
□ per year	1年につき
□ these days	最近
□ protect	～を保護する
□ with a helmet	ヘルメットで
□ in other words	言い換えれば
□ there is the potential to	～になる可能性がある
□ be critically or life-threateningly wounded	重傷を負い、命を脅かすケガをしている
□ a long-distance commute	長距離通勤
□ live a long distance from	～から遠くに住む
□ be subject to	～に左右される
□ humidity	湿度
□ and the like	(具体例に続けて) など
□ neither ～ nor …	～と…のどちらでもない
□ realistic	現実的な
□ reasonable	合理的な
□ considering all the disadvantages	すべての利点を考慮すると

Tips | 論理的に展開するためのキーフレーズ

意見を示す③

1	Yoga is effective in alleviating sleep problems.	ヨガは、不眠症を緩和するのに効果があります。
2	Making university tuition free benefits the public.	大学の無償化は、国民の利益につながります。
3	Drug testing can be helpful in determining the cause of car accidents.	薬物検査は、自動車事故の原因を突き止めるのに役に立ちます。
4	Bicycles are not good for a long distance commute.	自転車は長距離通勤には向きません。
5	Early rising can be beneficial for you because it improves your performance.	早起きは能力を高めるので、メリットがあります。
6	Big data can be useful for deciding the next strategy.	ビッグデータは、次の戦略を決めるのに利用できます。

連結語①

1	Here is some drug abuse-related data.	ここに薬物乱用関連のデータがあります。
2	Car accident-related injuries happen a lot every day.	車の事故が関連する負傷は、毎日たくさん起きています。
3	How can we prevent alcohol-related accidents?	飲酒関連の事故をどのように防ぐことができるでしょうか。
4	A large number of people die from smoke-related diseases.	非常に多くの人が喫煙関連の疾患で死亡しています。
5	Can you think of any allergy-related chemicals?	何かアレルギーに関連している化学物質を思い出せますか。
6	I learned more about cancer-related pain.	ガンが関係する痛みについて多く学びました。
7	What is the most crucial diet-related issue?	最も重要な食に関する問題は何ですか。
8	We should not underestimate drug-related side effects.	麻薬による副作用を軽視すべきではありません。
9	Here are some computer-related business ideas.	ここにコンピュータ関連のビジネスのアイディアがいくつかあります。

Speech 07

Is restricting the use of credit cards for certain people necessary?

特定の人々に対するクレジットカードの使用制限は必要か？

背景知識とヒント

キャッシュレス化が進む社会

オンラインショッピングが盛んになり、クレジットカードや電子マネーが普及して、キャッシュレス社会化が進んでいます。クレジットカードの平均保有枚数は、今や 1 人あたり 3 枚になるといいます。

クレジットカードを使うメリットとしては、「現金を持つ必要がない」、「カードの履歴が家計簿代わりになる」、「ポイントがたまる」などです。一方、デメリットとしては、「お金を使いすぎてしまう」、「不正利用される危険性がある」、「お金の感覚が麻痺してしまう」などが挙げられます。クレジットカードを使う際には、メリットとデメリットをよく把握して、使いすぎに注意することが大切です。

知っトク情報：頻出の関連トピック

The increasing problem of credit card debt. / Should more controls be placed on the financial industry? / Should companies in financial trouble receive government support?

コンセプトマップ

賛成バージョンを参考にスピーチの土台となるコンセプトマップを作ってみましょう。

Assertion

I agree with restricting the use of credit cards for certain people.

Reason 1

the temptation to overspend

Reason 2

the security risks

Example 1

- impulse buying
- unnecessary purchases

Example 2

- steal credit card data
- become a victim of credit card fraud

Assertion (Conclusion)

I agree with restricting the use of credit cards for certain people.

Speech | スピーチ

019

For | 賛成バージョン 07-❶

A Assertion 主張

There are two types of credit card users: those who can use their credit cards responsibly and those who cannot. I agree with restricting the use of credit cards for certain people. It's important to remember that charging purchases to credit cards is a form of borrowing. We buy now and then pay later. Misusing credit cards will lead to debt and therefore a bad credit history. I have two reasons for my agreement.

クレジットカードの利用者には２つのタイプがあります。責任を持って使える人とそうでない人です。私は、特定の人々にクレジットカードの利用を制限することに賛成です。クレジットカードでの購入は借金の一形態であることを覚えておくことが重要です。今買って、後で支払うのです。クレジットカードの使い方を誤ると借金を招き、信用履歴が悪くなります。私が賛成する理由は２つあります。

R1 Reason 理由

The first drawback of credit cards is the temptation to overspend.

クレジットカードの第一の欠点は、浪費を誘発することです。

E1 Example 例

For example, once users start using credit cards, they tend to buy more than they can afford. Moreover, impulse buying and unnecessary purchases become common. As a result, it's sometimes difficult to keep track of how much we have spent and thus we become heavily indebted.

例えば、一度クレジットカードを使い始めると、利用者は自分の支払い能力を超えて買い物をする傾向があります。さらに、衝動買いや不必要な買い物も普通に行うようになります。その結果、自分がいくら使ったかを把握するのが難しくなり、多額の負債を抱えることになるのです。

R2
Reason
理由

The second drawback of credit cards is the security risk.

クレジットカードの二番目の欠点は、セキュリティーリスクです。

E2
Example
例

For example, many users often create one easily guessed password because they don't want to remember different passwords. This makes it easy for online thieves to steal credit card data. As such, everybody has the potential to become a victim of credit card fraud. Credit card fraud can happen in a variety of ways and so it's quite difficult to avoid.

例えば、多くの利用者は異なるパスワードを覚えることを望まず、簡単に推測できるパスワードを作成することがよくあります。これにより、オンライン上の窃盗犯はクレジットカード情報を簡単に盗めるようになります。そのため、誰もがクレジットカード詐欺の被害者になる可能性があります。クレジットカード詐欺はさまざまな方法で起こり、それを避けるのはかなり難しいです。

A
Assertion (Conclusion)
主張

In conclusion, restricting the use of credit cards for certain people is necessary to address the drawbacks I mentioned. Credit cards may be the starting point for multiple debts. Moreover, once a bad credit history has been created through debt, it can never be erased. In addition, avoiding credit card fraud is nearly impossible if our data is stolen due to easily guessed passwords. Therefore, I agree with restricting the use of credit cards for certain people.

(279 words)

結論として、私が述べた欠点に対処するためには、特定の人々にクレジットカードの利用を制限することが必要です。クレジットカードは複数の借金の始まりとなる可能性があります。さらに、借金を通じて悪い信用履歴が作成されてしまうと、それは決して消えることはありません。また、簡単に推測されるパスワードのせいでデータが盗まれた場合、クレジットカード詐欺を避けることはほぼ不可能です。したがって、私は特定の人々にクレジットカードの利用を制限することに賛成です。

Against | 反対バージョン 07-❷

020

A
Assertion
主張

While there is a concern that credit card use will increase debt, setting a reasonable monthly limit can reduce this risk. I disagree with restricting the use of credit cards for certain people. I have two reasons for my disagreement.

クレジットカードの使用が借金を増やすという懸念がある一方で、適切な月間限度額を設定することで、このリスクを軽減することができます。私は特定の人々にクレジットカードの利用を制限することには反対です。反対する理由は2つあります。

R1
Reason
理由

The first benefit of credit cards is their versatility in payment options.

クレジットカードの1つ目の利点は、支払いオプションの多様性です。

E1
Example
例

For example, whether it's making reservations for travel or purchasing goods online, credit cards provide a convenient and secure method of payment. In particular, credit cards are a must when we buy online. Moreover, they're safer to carry than a lot of cash, particularly when traveling abroad.

例えば、旅行の予約でも、オンラインでの商品の購入でも、クレジットカードは便利で安全な支払い方法を提供します。特に、オンラインでの購入時にはクレジットカードが必須です。また、特に海外旅行時には、多額の現金を持ち歩くよりも安全です。

R2
Reason
理由

The second benefit of credit cards is that credit cards are always insured.

クレジットカードの２つ目の利点は、常に保険がかかっていることです。

E2
Example
例

For example, in the unfortunate event of theft or unauthorized use, cardholders are not responsible for the expenses as long as they report the theft immediately. On the other hand, if money is taken by a robber, it's next to impossible to get the money back. In this sense, it's much safer to carry credit cards instead of cash.

例えば、盗難や不正利用の不幸な事件が発生した場合、即座に報告すれば、カード所有者に費用負担は課されません。一方、強盗によって金銭が奪われた場合、その金銭を取り戻すのはほぼ不可能です。この意味では、現金の代わりにクレジットカードを持ち歩く方が安全です。

A
Assertion (Conclusion)
主張

In conclusion, credit cards play a crucial role in modern-day transactions, such as for booking and shopping online and off, and also for traveling abroad. They also prevent thieves from successfully stealing our money. In addition, a good credit history should make it easier to get a financial loan in the future. Therefore, I disagree with restricting the use of credit cards for certain people.

(236 words)

結論として、クレジットカードは、オンライン・オフラインでの予約やショッピング、それに海外旅行といった現代の取引において重要な役割を果たしているのです。また、泥棒が私たちのお金を成功裏に盗むのを防ぎます。さらに、優良な信用履歴があれば、将来、金融ローンを組みやすくなるはずです。したがって、私は特定の人々にクレジットカードの利用を制限することには反対です。

Words and Phrases

For

□ use ～ responsibly	～を責任を持って使う
□ charge ～ to credit card	～をクレジットで買う、支払う
□ a form of borrowing	借金の一形態
□ drawback of	～の欠点、デメリット
□ temptation	誘惑
□ impulse buying	衝動買い
□ unnecessary purchases	不必要な買い物
□ keep track of	～の把握をする；～の記録をつける
□ become heavily indebted	大きな借金を抱える
□ security risk	セキュリティーリスク
□ create one easily guessed password	1つの推測されやすいパスワードを作る
□ as such	そのため；同様に
□ have the potential to	～する可能性がある
□ become a victim of credit card fraud	クレジットカード詐欺の被害に遭う
□ multiple debts	多重債務
□ erase	～を消す

Against

□ set a reasonable monthly limit	適切な月間上限額を設定する
□ versatility in payment options	支払いオプションの多様性
□ secure method of payment	安全な支払い方法
□ in particular	特に
□ must	必需品、なければならないもの
□ purchase online	インターネットで買い物をする
□ insure	～に保険をかける
□ be responsible for	～に対して責任がある、責任を負う
□ as long as	～しさえすれば、～である限りは
□ report a theft	盗難届を出す
□ robber	泥棒
□ it's next to impossible to	～するのは極めて困難である
□ get the money back	お金を取り戻す
□ instead of cash	現金の代わりに
□ shop online and off	インターネットでもリアルでも買い物をする
□ prevent ... from ～ing	…が～するのを妨げる
□ a good credit history	良いクレジット履歴
□ get a financial loan	ローンを組む

Tips | 論理的に展開するためのキーフレーズ

根拠を示す①

❶	The first upside of becoming a freelancer is flexibility on the job.	フリーランサーになる第一のメリットは、仕事の融通性です。
❷	The first advantage of commuting by bicycle is that it is good for your health.	自転車で通勤する第一のメリットは、健康に良いことです。
❸	On the positive side, people can remain anonymous on the Internet.	肯定的な面としては、インターネット上では、匿名でいられます。
❹	Is there any potential benefit to outsourcing IT operations?	IT 業務を外部委託することに潜在的メリットは何かありますか。
❺	What are the disadvantages of relocating the headquarters?	本部を移転することに何かデメリットはありますか。

必要性を示す

❶	It's necessary for us to know that there is a fair outcome for all customers.	すべての顧客に公正な成果があることを知ることは必要です。
❷	It's absolutely necessary to achieve our sales target.	販売目標を成し遂げることは絶対必要です。
❸	It's essential to protect our online reputation.	ネット上の評判を守ることは不可欠です。
❹	It's a must to maintain strict quality control to improve the bottom line.	最終利益を上げるために、厳しい品質管理を維持することは必須です。
❺	It's imperative to consider your opinion from different perspectives.	違う視点から自分の意見を検討することは必須です。
❻	It's indispensable to satisfy all customers through exceptional customer service.	素晴らしいカスタマーサービスで、すべての顧客を満足させることは必要不可欠です。

Should elderly drivers' licenses be revoked when they reach a certain age?

高齢者の運転免許を取り消すべきか?

背景知識とヒント

免許返納の是非

日本では 1998 年に運転免許証の自主返納制度ができましたが、当初はそれほど注目されませんでした。しかし、高齢者による不適切な運転操作が原因で起きる死亡事故などが増加し、運転免許証の自主返納が呼びかけられるようになりました。

一方で、公共交通機関が十分に発達していない地域では、運転免許証を返納してしまうと、買い物や病院への通院などで日常生活が不便になってしまいます。高齢者の運転免許証返納の是非については、慎重な議論が必要でしょう。

知っトク情報:頻出の関連トピック

Do local communities do enough to care for the elderly? / Do people get wiser as they get older? / Does society make full use of the talents of senior citizens?

コンセプトマップ

反対バージョンを参考にスピーチの土台となるコンセプトマップを作ってみましょう。

Assertion

I can't support revoking elderly drivers' licenses when they reach a certain age.

Reason 1

all people age differently

Reason 2

take away freedom in a rural area / inconvenient

Example 1

- my grandma is 80 years old / healthy and active
- elderly people are bedridden

Example 2

- not go shopping
- not meet friends
- not get medical care

Assertion (Conclusion)

I can't support revoking elderly drivers' licenses when they reach a certain age.

Speech | スピーチ

For | 賛成バージョン 08-❶

022

A
Assertion
主張

According to current news, the fatality rate for drivers over 80 is much higher than that of teenagers. I don't want senior citizens to be involved in fatal accidents. Therefore, I support revoking elderly drivers' licenses when they reach a certain age. I have two reasons for believing so.

最近のニュースによると、80 歳以上の運転手の死亡率が 10 代のそれよりもかなり高いということです。高齢者に死亡事故に関わってほしくありません。そのため、高齢者がある年齢に達したら、運転免許を取り消すことに賛成です。そう信じる 2 つの理由があります。

R1
Reason
理由

First, people's cognitive functions deteriorate with age. In other words, the older they get, the less they recall and the slower they process thoughts.

第一に、人の認知機能は年齢とともに低下します。言い換えると、年をとればとるほど、思い出すことが少なくなり、思考を処理するスピードが遅くなります。

E1
Example
例

For example, sometimes, they can't remember where they put the car keys. Other times, they even forget the rules of the road. Moreover, their responses become slower. Therefore, it's often difficult for elderly people to judge a turn against oncoming traffic correctly. Worst of all, some elderly people may actually suffer from dementia. Some drive the wrong way down the highway, cause an accident, and then don't even remember having caused it.

例えば、車のカギをどこに置いたか思い出せないことがあります。また、交通規則さえ忘れてしまうこともあります。さらに、反応も遅くなります。そのため高齢者にとっては、対向車に対して正しく曲がるタイミングを判断するのが難しいことがあります。最悪なことは、認知症を患っている高齢者がいることです。高速道路を逆走し、交通事故を起こし、事故を起こしたことさえ覚えていない人もいるのです。

R2
Reason
理由

Second, people lose physical strength with age.

第二に、体力が年齢とともに衰えます。

E2
Example
例

For example, as people get older, their arm and leg muscles become weaker and weaker. Therefore, they may tend to press the brake pedal more lightly than they think. Then, it may take longer for the car to stop. As a result, they may hit the car in front of them. Sometimes, they even lose control of the steering wheel. They'd have to be ready every time they drive for the worst-case scenario regarding traffic accidents; it would be so stressful.

例えば、年をとればとるほど、腕や足の筋力が弱くなります。そのため、ブレーキペダルを思ったよりも軽く踏んでしまうようになるかもしれません。そして、そのために車が停車するのが遅くなってしまうかもしれません。結果として、前の車に追突してしまうかもしれません。ハンドル操作を誤ることもあります。交通事故に関しては、運転するたびに、最悪のシナリオを想定しなければなりません。それは大きなストレスです。

A
Assertion (Conclusion)
主張

To conclude, the government should act responsibly and issue a regulation providing for the revocation of elderly drivers' licenses. This is necessary to avoid road tragedies harming not only senior citizens themselves but also innocent people. For these reasons, I support revoking elderly drivers' licenses when they reach a certain age.

(283 words)

結論として、政府は責任を持って対処し、高齢者の運転免許取り消しに備えて条例を公布すべきです。これは、高齢者自身だけでなく、罪なき人に危害を加える交通事故の悲劇を避けるために必要です。これらの理由で、高齢者がある年齢に達したら、運転免許を取り消すことに賛成です。

Against | 反対バージョン 08-❷

023

A
Assertion
主張

If we set a certain age for elderly people to have to give up their licenses, it would be a form of discrimination. It's a biased way of thinking. Obviously, not everyone ages in the same way. I can't support revoking elderly drivers' licenses when they reach a certain age. I have two reasons for saying so.

もし高齢者が運転免許証を諦めなければならない一定の年齢を設定したら、それは一種の差別になるでしょう。それは偏った考え方です。もちろん、誰もが同じように老いるわけではありません。高齢者がある一定の年齢に達したら、運転免許を取り消すことには賛成できません。2つの理由があります。

R1
Reason
理由

First, it's true that cognitive functions worsen with age, but all people age differently.

第一に、認知機能が年齢とともに低下するのは事実ですが、すべての人はそれぞれ違う形で老いるものです。

E1
Example
例

For instance, my grandma is 80 years old, and she is as healthy and active as a young person. I know some elderly people are bedridden and can't move freely. However , that does not mean we should treat all senior citizens similarly. Reflexes and senses, including eyesight and hearing, vary from person to person even among youths.

例えば、私の祖母は80歳です。そして若い人と同じくらい、健康的で活動的です。寝たきりで、自由に体を動かせないお年寄りがいることも知っています。しかし、それはすべての高齢者を同じように扱うべきだという意味ではありません。視力や聴力を含む反射神経や感覚は、若い人の間でさえ、人によって違います。

R2
Reason
理由

Second, revoking elderly drivers' licences is like taking away their freedom, especially if they reside in rural areas. Without a car, their life will be very inconvenient.

第二に、高齢者の運転免許証を取り上げることは、彼らの自由を取り上げることと同じです。もし地方に住んでいれば、特にそうです。車なしでは、生活は大変不便です。

E2
Example
例

For instance, they will not easily be able to go shopping, meet friends, dine out, get medical care and so on. This is because public transportation in rural areas is sometimes not available. If senior citizens want to be driven somewhere, they will have to find someone who can help them. Or they will have to take a taxi instead.

例えば、気軽に買い物に行ったり、友人に会ったり、外食をしたり、医療を受けたりすることなどはできないでしょう。これは、地方では公共交通機関が利用できないこともあるからです。もし高齢者がどこかへ車で送ってもらいたいときには、誰か助けてくれる人を見つけなくてはなりません。または、代わりにタクシーを使わなければなりません。

A
Assertion (Conclusion)
主張

To conclude, what is needed is to devise a driving test that checks their basic visual, mental, and reactive abilities. We can ask drivers of a certain age to take cognitive and strength tests to reveal any disabilities. Say, every year over 70 years old. For these reasons, I can't support revoking elderly drivers' licenses when they reach a certain age.

(276 words)

結論として、必要なことは、基本的な視力、知能、反応力を調べられる運転免許試験を工夫することです。ある一定の高齢者には、障害を調べるため認識力テストと体力テストを受けてもらうのです。例えば、70 歳以上の人が毎年対象です。これらの理由で、高齢者がある一定の年齢に達したら、運転免許を取り消すことには賛成できません。

Words and Phrases

024

For

□ revoke drivers' licenses	運転免許を取り消す、無効にする
□ according to current news	最近のニュースによると
□ fatality rate	死亡率
□ senior citizens	高齢者
□ be involved in fatal accidents	死亡事故に関わる
□ cognitive functions deteriorate with age	認知機能が年齢とともに低下する
□ recall	～を思い出す
□ process thoughts	思考を処理する
□ other times	一方、また
□ rules of the road	交通規則
□ judge a turn against oncoming traffic correctly	対向車に対して正しく曲がるタイミングを判断する
□ worst of all	最悪なことは
□ suffer from dementia	認知症を患う
□ cause an accident	事故を起こす
□ lose physical strength with age	年とともに体力が衰える
□ tend to press the brake pedal more lightly	ブレーキペダルを軽く踏む傾向がある
□ lose control of the steering wheel	ハンドル操作を誤る
□ for the worst-case scenario	最悪のシナリオを想定して
□ issue a regulation	条例を公布する
□ harm	～に危害を加える

Against

□ discrimination	差別
□ a biased way of thinking	偏見のある考え方
□ obviously	明らかに
□ not everyone ages in the same way	誰もが同じように老いるわけではない
□ as healthy and active as	～と同じく健康的で活動的な
□ be bedridden	寝たきりでいる
□ treat ～ similarly	～を同じように扱う
□ reflexes	反射神経
□ eyesight and hearing	視力と聴力
□ vary from person to person	人によって異なる
□ take away one's freedom	自由を奪う
□ reside in rural areas	地方に住む
□ inconvenient	不便な
□ dine out	外食する
□ get medical care	医療を受ける
□ public transportation	公共交通機関
□ what is needed is to devise	必要なことは～を工夫することである
□ check one's basic visual, mental, and reactive abilities	基本的な視力、知能、反応力を調べる
□ take cognitive and strength tests	認識力テストと体力テストを受ける
□ reveal disabilities	障害を調べる、明らかにする

Tips | 論理的に展開するためのキーフレーズ

同意を示す①

❶	I agree with the idea of meeting people through social media.	SNSを通して人と出会う考えに賛成します。
❷	I am strongly in favor of robots replacing people.	ロボットが人の代わりになることに強く賛成します。
❸	I support the idea of owning pets.	ペットを飼う考えに賛成です。
❹	I completely agree with the idea of abolishing nuclear power plants.	原子力発電所を廃炉にする考えに全面的に賛成です。
❺	I second the proposal for a compulsory voting system.	投票制度を義務化する提案に賛成です。

譲歩・逆接を示す①

❶	He is lazy, nonetheless, I love him.	彼は怠け者です。それにもかかわらず、彼を愛しています。
❷	Although some people agree with this plan, I personally disagree with it.	この計画に賛成する人はいますが、私は個人的にそれに反対です。
❸	Although it is important to set goals with your students, it is equally important to review their progress toward those goals regularly.	生徒と目標を設定することは重要ですが、目標に向けての進捗状況を定期的に点検することが同じく重要です。
❹	Three-star restaurants charge overly high prices, yet, customers keep visiting constantly.	三ツ星レストランはかなり高い値段を請求します。それでも、お客はいつも絶えません。
❺	About two-thirds of the residents voted in favor of the plan. However, the rest of them abstained from voting.	住民のおよそ3分の2がその計画に賛成票を投じました。しかし、残りは、投票することを棄権しました。

Speech 09

Should casinos be legalized in Japan?

日本でカジノを合法化すべきか？

背景知識とヒント

カジノの合法化は、日本に何をもたらす？

カジノは雇用創出の効果が大きく、経済の活性化が期待できると主張する人もいます。日本では、2018年にIR実施法が成立しました。IRとは統合型リゾート施設（Integrated Resort）の略で、ホテルやカジノ、劇場やショッピングモール、国際会議場などが集まった複合型施設のことです。この中にカジノが含まれています。カジノの合法化については、ギャンブル依存症の増加や治安の悪化などを心配する人もいます。経済成長と安心安全な社会と、どちらを優先すべきでしょうか。

知っトク情報：頻出の関連トピック

Agree or disagree: The advantages of legalized gambling outweigh the disadvantages. / Gambling: Harmless pastime or dangerous addiction? / Agree or disagree: Legalized gambling has a positive effect on a country's economy. / Are consumption taxes a good way to raise government revenue?

コンセプトマップ

反対バージョンを参考にスピーチの土台となるコンセプトマップを作ってみましょう。

Assertion

I am strongly against the idea of legalizing casinos in Japan.

Reason 1

gambling addiction is a serious problem

Reason 2

cause gambling-related social problems

Example 1

- 5% in Japan is addicted to gambling
- 1% in other countries impossible to control the urge to gamble

Example 2

- higher suicide rates
- debt burden
- family breakdowns
- gangsters

Assertion (Conclusion)

I am strongly against the idea of legalizing casinos in Japan.

Speech | スピーチ

025

For | 賛成バージョン 09-❶

A
Assertion
主張

Some people say we already have horse racing and Japanese pinball — pachinko — as forms of gambling, so we don't need to legalize casinos in Japan. But I don't agree. I believe casinos are an effective way to create new business opportunites and increase employment. I am strongly in favor of the idea of legalizing casinos in Japan. I have two reasons for believing so.

ギャンブルの形として、競馬や日本式ピンボール——パチンコ——がすでにあるので、日本でカジノを合法化する必要はないという人がいます。しかし、私は賛成しません。カジノは新しい事業のチャンスを創出し、雇用を増加させるのに効果的な方法だと信じているからです。日本でカジノを合法化することに強く賛成します。そう信じるのには、2つの理由があります。

R1
Reason
理由

Firstly, I'm sure casinos produce good economic effects like creating new businesses and more jobs.

第一に、カジノは新しい産業や多くの仕事を創出するなど、良い経済効果を生み出すと確信しています。

E1
Example
例

For example, more than 100 years ago, Las Vegas used to be a desert. After building casinos there, Las Vegas flourished into a profitable city thanks to its casino industry. Today, there are many places to work, such as hotels, amusement parks, and shopping malls. As a matter of fact, the Vegas casino industry has succeeded in creating thousands of jobs. Moreover, any government supporting casinos also profits through the collection of tax revenue.

例えば、100年以上前、ラスベガスは砂漠でした。そこにカジノを建設したあと、ラスベガスは、そのカジノ産業のおかげで利益を生む都市として繁栄しました。今日では、ホテルや遊園地、ショッピングモールなど、働くための多くの場所があります。実を言えば、ラスベガスのカジノ産業は、何千という仕事を創出することに成功しています。さらにカジノを支持するどの政府も、税収を集めることで利益を上げています。

R2
Reason
理由

Secondly, casinos are sure to attract lots of customers because, in casinos, there are lots of places for visitors to relax and enjoy themselves.

第二に、カジノは、必ず多くの客を引きつけます。というのも、カジノには、来場者が寛ぎ、楽しめる多くの場所があるからです。

E2
Example
例

For example, shopping malls and exciting forms of entertainment like magic shows, musicals, and concerts will all be available. Furthermore, casinos will attract a lot of tourists from all over the world. In addition, there are lots of elderly rich people in Japan, and they have become bored with their routine daily lives. I'm certain casinos will boost the Japanese tourist industry. As a result, they will also boost the Japanese economy.

例えば、ショッピングモールやマジックショー、ミュージカルやコンサートのようなエンターテインメントとして刺激的なものが、すべて利用できるのです。さらに、カジノは世界中から多くの観光客を引きつけます。また、日本にはたくさんの年配富裕層がいます。彼らは決まりきった毎日の生活に飽き飽きしているのです。カジノは、必ず日本の観光産業を活発にするでしょう。結果として、日本の景気を良くするでしょう。

A
Assertion (Conclusion)
主張

Overall, casinos provide customers with places to relax and enjoy themselves. As such, casinos are desirable places for them to spend their leisure time. In addition, they may live the dream of getting rich quick. Lastly, casinos create new businesses and increase employment and tax revenue. Therefore, I am strongly in favor of the idea of legalizing casinos in Japan.

(308 words)

全体的に、カジノはリラックスして楽しんでもらう場所を客に提供します。同様に、カジノは余暇を過ごすのに魅力ある場所です。さらに、一攫千金の夢に生きられるかもしれません。最後に、カジノは新しい産業を創出し雇用と税収を増やすでしょう。そのため、日本におけるカジノの合法化に強く賛成します。

Against | 反対バージョン 09-❷

026

A
Assertion
主張

Some customers get addicted to horse racing, and they continuously have to borrow money from consumer finance companies. Moreover, believing they can eventually win it all back, they keep on gambling even though they are deep in debt. As a result, they go bankrupt in the end. Naturally, they and their families will be miserable. I am strongly against the idea of legalizing casinos in Japan. I have two reasons to support my belief.

競馬にはまり、消費者金融からお金を借り続けなければならない客がいます。さらには、勝ってすべてを取り戻すことができると信じて、借金で身動きが取れないにもかかわらず、ギャンブルを続けるのです。結果として、彼らは最後に破産します。もちろん、彼らと家族は悲惨な状態になるでしょう。私は日本においてカジノを合法化するという考えに強く反対します。自分の信念を支持する2つの理由があります。

R1
Reason
理由

Firstly, gambling addiction is a serious problem.

第一に、ギャンブル依存は深刻な問題です。

E1
Example
例

Let me show you some statistical data. According to a survey, about 5% of the adult population in Japan is addicted to gambling. Compared with an approximately 1% rate in other countries, this figure is alarming. Besides, once one gets addicted to gambling, it's nearly impossible to control the urge to gamble again, and that's the main weakness of the addicted gambler.

いくつかの統計データを紹介しましょう。ある調査によれば、日本の成人人口の約5%がギャンブル依存だということです。他の国々のおよそ1%と比較すると、この数字は警戒すべきです。さらに、人がいったんギャンブル依存になると、もう一度ギャンブルしたいという衝動を抑えるのは、ほぼ不可能です。そして、それがギャンブル依存者の最大の弱点です。

R2
Reason
理由

Secondly, casinos may cause more gambling-related social problems.

第二に、カジノはギャンブルが関係する社会問題を引き起こすかもしれません。

E2
Example
例

For example, there are higher suicide rates, increased debt burden, family breakdowns, an increased number of gangsters, and so forth. Las Vegas is the gambling capital of the U.S.A. Gangsters once ruled the city. In fact, most of the above-mentioned problems were caused by them. Once gambling-related problems develop, it's very difficult to stop their progress and nearly impossible to reverse their effects.

例えば、高い自殺率、増えた借金、家庭崩壊、犯罪組織の構成員の増加などです。ラスベガスはアメリカでギャンブルの中心です。かつては、犯罪組織の面々が町を支配していました。実際、先に述べたほとんどの問題は、彼らによって引き起こされていました。いったんギャンブルが関係する問題が起こると、その進行を止めるのは不可能です。そしてその影響を改善することもほぼ不可能です。

A
Assertion (Conclusion)
主張

Overall, gambling is a serious problem, especially since it's not easy to diagnose gambling addiction. Furthermore, we have yet to find a proper cure for it. Finally, who is responsible for the resulting social problems mentioned earlier: the casinos, the adult customers themselves, the government, or all three? More statistical data is needed before we can make an informed decision. Therefore, I'm strongly against the idea of legalizing casinos in Japan.

(285 words)

全体的に、ギャンブルは深刻な問題です。特に、ギャンブル依存を診断するのは簡単ではないからです。さらに、その適切な治療がまだ見つかっていません。最後に、結果として生じる、先に述べたような社会問題に誰が責任をとるのでしょうか。カジノ、成人の客自身、政府、それとも三者全員でしょうか。情報に基づいて決定する前に、より多くの統計的データが必要です。そのため、日本においてカジノを法制化するという考えに強く反対します。

Words and Phrases

For		Against	
□ horse racing	競馬	□ get addicted to	～の中毒になる
□ pinball	ピンボール、パチンコ	□ continuously	絶えず
□ legalize casinos	カジノを合法化する	□ eventually	最終的に、結局は
□ be an effective way to	～する効果的な方法である	□ be deep in debt	借金で身動きがとれない
□ create new business opportunities	新しい事業のチャンスを創出する	□ go bankrupt	破産する
□ increase employment	雇用を増やす	□ statistical data	統計データ
□ I am strongly in favor of	～に強く賛成する	□ approximately 1% rate	およそ1%の割合
□ produce good economic effects	良い経済効果を生み出す	□ this figure is alarming	この数字は警戒するべきである
□ flourish	繁栄する	□ control the urge to	～する衝動を抑える
□ profitable	利益になる	□ addicted gambler	常習となったギャンブラー
□ as a matter of fact	実を言うと	□ gambling-related social problems	ギャンブルが関係する社会問題
□ profit through	～で収益を上げる	□ suicide rate	自殺率
□ collection of tax revenue	税収を集めること	□ debt burden	債務負担
□ available	入手できる、利用できる	□ family breakdown	家庭崩壊
□ become bored with	～で飽きる、退屈する	□ rule the city	その町を支配する
□ routine daily lives	決まり切った毎日の生活	□ reverse one's effects	影響を改善する
□ boost the Japanese tourist industry	日本の観光産業を活発にする	□ diagnose	～を診断する
□ overall	全体的に、概して	□ be responsible for	～に対して責任がある
□ desirable	好ましい、魅力がある	□ resulting	結果として生じる
□ leisure time	余暇	□ make an informed decision	情報に基づいて決定する

Tips | 論理的に展開するためのキーフレーズ

事実を示す

1	The fact is that one out of three business people are overweight.	実は、企業で働く人の３人に１人が肥満です。
2	The fact is that analyzing customer feedback is worthwhile.	顧客フィードバックを分析することは価値があるのは事実です。
3	The truth is that negotiating with any client is worth trying.	どんな顧客と交渉することも、試してみる価値があるのは事実です。
4	The truth is that such unreliable information is posted online anonymously.	そのような信頼できない情報が匿名でネット上に投稿されるのは本当です。
5	The reality is that it's important to meet customer demands.	現実には、顧客の声に応えることは大切です。
6	The reality is that we tend to ignore small problems until they have transformed into crises.	現実には、小さな問題が危機になるまで、それらを無視してしまう傾向にあります。

因果関係を示す②

1	Pollens can cause allergies.	花粉はアレルギーの原因となります。
2	I don't really know what could cause such a problem.	何がそのような問題を引き起こしたのか本当にわかりません。
3	Elderly drivers could cause a lot of fatal accidents.	高齢者の運転手は、多くの死亡事故を起こす恐れがあります。
4	Food poisoning is caused by bacteria.	食中毒は、細菌が原因で起きます。
5	Hundreds of car accidents are caused by drivers talking on smartphones.	スマートフォンで話し中の運転手が原因で、多くの自動車事故が起きています。
6	Several factors can give rise to a declining marriage rate.	いくつかの要因が、婚姻率の低下を生じさせています。

Speech 10

Should surveillance cameras be installed in all public places?

すべての公共の場に監視カメラをつけるべきか？

背景知識とヒント

監視カメラは防犯効果が高いが……

ひったくり、侵入窃盗、車上狙い、自転車窃盗などのニュースをよく耳にします。そのため、社会全体で防犯意識が高まってきており、公園や駅などの公共の場所はもちろん、自宅にも監視カメラを設置する人が増えています。監視カメラは、事件の抑止に効果があるだけでなく、事件が発生した際には、事件の証拠として使うことも可能です。

一般的に、その効果から監視カメラの設置には好意的な意見が多いのですが、プライバシーの侵害だと反対する人もいます。監視カメラを公共の場に設置することの、メリットとデメリットを考えてみましょう。

知っトク情報：頻出の関連トピック

Agree or disagree: Surveillance cameras should be installed in all public places. / Is the use of surveillance cameras in public places a good thing? / Privacy vs. security —the role of electronic surveillance in society. / The need to improve security in public places.

コンセプトマップ

賛成バージョンを参考にスピーチの土台となるコンセプトマップを作ってみましょう。

Assertion

I agree with installing surveillance cameras in all public places.

Reason 1

effective in monitoring public places

Reason 2

used as evidence in proving crimes

Example 1

- keep tabs on suspicious activities
- stop crimes

Example 2

- catch criminals
- evidence

Assertion (Conclusion)

I agree with installing surveillance cameras in all public places.

Speech | スピーチ

For | 賛成バージョン 10-❶

028

A
Assertion
主張

Governments are making efforts to install surveillance cameras in public places, such as shopping malls, parks, and streets. The reason is that these cameras will help ensure the safety of the society in question. I agree with installing surveillance cameras in all public places. I have two reasons for my opinion.

政府は、ショッピングモールや公園、道路などの公共の場所に監視カメラを設置する努力をしています。その理由は、これらのカメラは懸案の社会の安全を確保するのに役立つからです。すべての公共の場所に監視カメラを設置することに賛成します。2つの理由があります。

R1
Reason
理由

First, surveillance cameras are effective in monitoring public places for the safety of society in general.

第一に、監視カメラは、一般的に社会の安全のために公共の場所を監視するのに有効です。

E1
Example
例

For instance, such cameras enable us to keep tabs on suspicious activities and help stop crimes before they happen. In addition, most criminals try not to commit crimes while under surveillance. As a result, strategically placed cameras can be deterrents against criminal activity.

例えば、それらのカメラは、不審な行動を監視して、犯罪を未然に防止するのに役立ちます。さらに、ほとんどの犯罪者は監視下にいる間は、罪を犯そうとはしません。結果として、戦略的に配置されたカメラが犯罪活動に対して抑止力になりえます。

R2
Reason
理由

Second, camera images are effectively used as evidence in proving crimes.

第二に、カメラの画像は、犯罪を証明する証拠として効果的に用いられます。

E2
Example
例

For instance, camera images from crime scenes help to catch criminals and later can be used for their convictions. Small-time criminals, such as shoplifters, can also get caught via evidence from surveillance cameras. Wherever we go, surveillance cameras monitor and record our everyday behavior.

例えば、犯罪現場のカメラ画像は、犯人を捕まえるのに役に立ち、後で有罪判決のために使われます。スリなどの軽犯罪者も監視カメラの証拠で逮捕されます。どこに行こうとも、監視カメラは日々の行動を監視し記録しています。

A
Assertion (Conclusion)
主張

Overall, the benefits of surveillance cameras outweigh the drawbacks. Surveillance cameras can decrease crime in public places if they are used effectively. Therefore, I agree with installing surveillance cameras in all public places.

(198 words)

概して、監視カメラのメリットは、デメリットを上回ります。監視カメラは、効果的に使われれば、公共の場所の犯罪を減らします。そのため、すべての公共の場所に監視カメラを設置することに賛成です。

Against | 反対バージョン 10-❷

029

A
Assertion
主張

In many cities, the number of surveillance cameras in public places is increasing in order to reduce crime. However, some people are against this policy. I also disagree with installing surveillance cameras in all public places. I have two reasons for my opinion.

多くの都市で、犯罪を減らすために、公共の場所の監視カメラの数が増えています。しかし、この政策に反対する人がいます。私もすべての公共の場所に監視カメラを設置することに反対します。2つの理由があります。

R1
Reason
理由

First, surveillance cameras are used to monitor everyday activities. This could be considered an invasion of privacy.

第一に、監視カメラは毎日の行動を監視するために使われます。これは、プライバシーの侵害だとみなされます。

E1
Example
例

For instance, surveillance cameras are set up everywhere such as parks, stations, shopping malls, and so forth. All kinds of people visit these places. It's not necessary to monitor what we are doing and saying while there. Surveillance cameras record everyone regardless of their being a criminal or not. It's against the ideals of human rights and freedom.

例えば、監視カメラは、公園、駅、ショッピングモールなど至る所に設置されます。すべての人がこれらの場所を訪れます。そういう場所にいる間に、行動や発言すべてを監視する必要はありません。監視カメラは、罪を犯しているかどうかにかかわらず、すべての人を記録します。それは、人権や自由の理念に反します。

R2
Reason
理由

Second, it's troublesome to install a great number of surveillance cameras.

第二に、たくさんの監視カメラを設置することは厄介です。

E2
Example
例

For instance, it's costly to install them, and they require periodic maintenance. This is compounded by the fact that we have so many public places in Japan. Also, the image data from the surveillance cameras may be hacked and uploaded to the Internet. As a result, a great number of private images may be exposed to the public at large.

例えば、設置することは費用がかかり、定期的なメンテナンスを要します。これは、日本には非常に多くの公共の場所があるという事実が、状況を難しくしているのです。また、監視カメラの画像データは、不正侵入され、インターネットに流出するかもしれません。結果として、大量の個人画像が一般の目にさらされることになるかもしれません。

A
Assertion (Conclusion)
主張

Overall, it's true that surveillance cameras restrict our freedom and invade our privacy. It also makes it difficult to establish a culture of trust. Therefore, I disagree with installing surveillance cameras in all public places.

(224 words)

全体的に、監視カメラは、自由を制約しプライバシーを侵害します。信頼の文化を確立するのを難しくします。そのため、すべての公共の場所に監視カメラを設置することに反対します。

Words and Phrases

For

□ make efforts to	～する努力をする
□ install surveillance cameras in public places	公共の場所に監視カメラを設置する
□ ensure the safety of the society	社会の安全を確保する
□ in question	当該の、懸案の
□ be effective in	～において有効である
□ keep tabs on suspicious activities	不審な行動を監視する
□ criminal	犯罪者
□ commit a crime	罪を犯す
□ while under surveillance	監視下にいる間
□ strategically placed cameras	戦略的に配置されたカメラ
□ be a deterrent against criminal activity	犯罪活動に対して抑止力になる
□ be used as evidence in proving crimes	犯罪を証明する証拠として用いられる
□ camera image from crime scenes	犯罪現場のカメラ画像
□ catch a criminal	犯人を捕まえる
□ be used for one's conviction	有罪判決のために使われる
□ small-time criminals such as shoplifters	スリなどの軽犯罪者
□ get caught via evidence	証拠で逮捕される
□ monitor and record one's behavior	行動を監視し記録する
□ The benefits of surveillance cameras outweigh the drawbacks.	監視カメラのメリットはデメリットを上回る。
□ decrease crime	犯罪を減らす

Against

□ reduce crime	犯罪を減らす
□ be against this policy	この政策に反対する
□ invasion of privacy	プライバシーの侵害
□ and so forth	（具体例に続けて）など
□ regardless of ～ or not	～かどうかにかかわらず
□ It's against the ideals of human rights and freedom.	人権や自由の理念に反する。
□ it's troublesome to	～するのは厄介だ、面倒だ、難しい
□ require periodic maintenance	定期的なメンテナンスを必要とする
□ this is compounded by the fact that	～という事実で状況を悪化させる
□ image data	画像データ
□ be hacked and uploaded to the Internet	不正侵入され、インターネットに流出する
□ a great number of private images	大量の個人画像
□ be exposed to the public at large	一般の目に触れる、一般社会にさらされる
□ restrict one's freedom	個人の自由を制約する
□ invade one's privacy	個人のプライバシーを侵害する
□ establish a culture of trust	信頼の文化を確立する

Tips | 論理的に展開するためのキーフレーズ

根拠を示す②

❶ We have no more evidence.	もう証拠はありません。
❷ We have no more evidence for the existence of extraterrestrials.	宇宙人の生存を示す証拠は他にありません。
❸ There is no scientific evidence to support this theory.	この理論を裏付ける科学的な証拠はまったくありません。
❹ There is still no clear scientific explanation available about the accident.	事故について入手できる明白な科学的な説明はまだありません。
❺ Do you have any evidence to back up anything you say?	君の発言を裏付ける証拠は何かありますか。
❻ Do you have enough data to fully support your claim?	君の主張を全面的に裏付ける十分なデータはありますか。
❼ Do you have any proof to support your case?	主張を裏付ける証拠は何かありますか。
❽ There is no correlation between happiness and amount of money.	幸福とお金の量との相関関係はありません。

譲歩・逆接を示す②

❶ In spite of these problems, there is progress in many areas.	これらの問題にもかかわらず、多くの地域で進展があります。
❷ Despite many problems, there is a possibility of success.	多くの問題にもかかわらず、成功の可能性があります。
❸ Despite your efforts, we were unable to meet your expectations.	あなたの努力にもかかわらず、私たちはあなたの期待に応えることができませんでした。
❹ Regardless of age or sex, anyone can apply for the job.	年齢や性別にかかわらず、誰でも仕事に応募できます。
❺ Even though she can't cite ample evidence for her claim, she insists she's innocent.	主張を裏付ける十分な証拠がないけれども、彼女は、無実だと主張しています。

Should businesses be allowed to share facial images of suspected shoplifters?

万引き容疑者の顔写真を公開しても良いか？

背景知識とヒント

被害を受けた店には、万引き犯の顔を公開する権利があるか？

小売店にとって、万引きによる被害は経営に大きな打撃を与えるものです。近年、監視カメラに記録された万引き犯の画像を罪が確定しないうちに公開すべきか否かについて、賛否両論の議論が起きました。あるアンケート結果によると、90%以上が、画像の公開について妥当だと回答していました。

その被害額の多寡にかかわらず、万引きは犯罪行為だから公開はやむを得ないと主張する人がいます。一方、罪が確定していない時点での顔写真の画像の公開は名誉毀損に該当するので、適当でないと主張する人もいます。どちらの意見が支持されるべきでしょうか。

知っトク情報：頻出の関連トピック

Should names or photos of juvenile criminals be made public? / Is too much attention paid to the human rights of criminals?

コンセプトマップ

反対バージョンを参考にスピーチの土台となるコンセプトマップを作ってみましょう。

Assertion

I disagree with businesses sharing facial images of suspected shoplifters.

Reason 1

sensitive personal information

Reason 2

not reasonable to share facial images of suspected shoplifters

Example 1

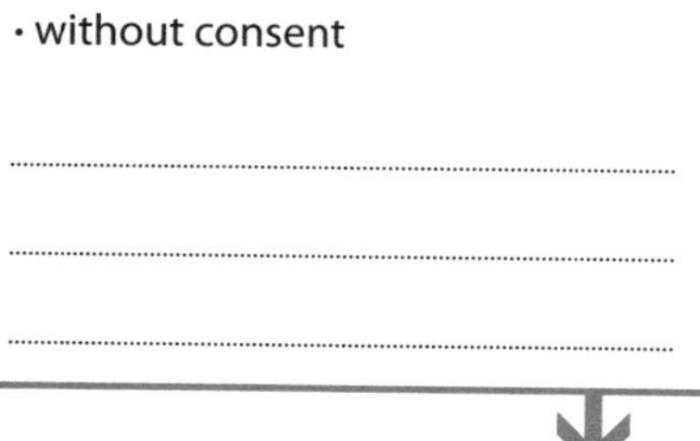

- not allowed to provide personal information
- without consent

Example 2

- suspects might sue the stores
- costly

Assertion (Conclusion)

I disagree with the idea of businesses sharing facial images of suspected shoplifters.

Speech | スピーチ

031

For | 賛成バージョン 11-❶

A Assertion 主張

Shoplifting is a serious problem, especially for small retail businesses. We have to handle this issue promptly. Therefore, I am strongly in favor of businesses sharing facial images of suspected shoplifters. I have two points to make.

特に小規模の小売業者にとって、万引きは深刻な問題です。速やかにこの問題に対処しなければいけません。そのため、小売業者が万引きの容疑者の顔の画像を公開することに賛成します。2つのポイントがあります。

R1 Reason 理由

First, the total financial damage due to shoplifting is huge.

第一に、万引きが原因の被害総額は莫大です。

E1 Example 例

One year, for example, this amount in damages once became the world's second largest. According to available data, shoplifting costs retailers several hundred billion yen annually in Japan. Even though it's a serious crime, some people look at shoplifting as no big deal. Therefore, many people start shoplifting without really thinking about it. However, shoplifting is a highly addictive form of crime. Regardless of age, once someone succeeds at shoplifting, they may continue to shoplift at stores until they get caught or even after getting caught.

例えば、1年間の被害総額は、世界で第2位になったことがありました。入手したデータによると、日本では、万引きは小売業者に年間数千億円の損失をもたらしています。重罪にもかかわらず、万引きは大したことではないという人がいます。そのため、軽い気持ちで万引きを始める人が多くいます。しかし、万引きは常習性の高い犯罪行為です。年齢にかかわらず、いったん万引きに成功すると、逮捕されるまで、または逮捕された後も万引きし続けるかもしれません。

R2
Reason 理由

Second, sharing facial images of suspected shoplifters is an effective way to enhance preventive measures.

第二に、万引きの容疑者の顔の画像を公開することは、予防対策を強化する効果的な方法です。

E2
Example 例

For example, if shoplifters are suspected of stealing at certain stores, their facial images are sent to other retailers. If their images are registered in a digital database, a warning is then issued to the staff at these other stores. Then, all the staff have to do is to wait for a person in the database to visit and carefully watch his or her actions.

例えば、もし万引き犯がある店で盗みが疑われると、顔の画像が他の小売店に送られます。その画像がデジタルデータベースに登録されると、それらの店のスタッフに警告が発せられます。ですので、データベースの当該人が来るのを待って、注意深くその人物の動きを注視しさえすればよいのです。

A
Assertion (Conclusion) 主張

In conclusion, shoplifting is a crime that causes significant financial damage. There is no acceptable crime, and preventive measures are crucial in curving criminal behavior. Furthermore, committing minor crimes many times potentially leads to serious ones in the future. To avoid such situations, proactive measures must be taken to prevent shoplifting now. Therefore, I am strongly in favor of businesses sharing facial images of suspected shoplifters.

(279 words)

結論として、万引きは経済的に大きな損害を与える犯罪です。受け入れられる犯罪などなく、犯罪行為を抑制するためには予防策が極めて重要です。さらに、軽犯罪を何度も犯すことは、いつか重大な犯罪につながる恐れがあります。そのような事態を避けるためにも、万引きを防ぐための積極的な対策を、今、講じるべきなのです。そのため、小売業者が万引きの容疑者の顔の画像を公開することに強く賛成します。

Against | 反対バージョン 11-❷

A
Assertion
主張

When a full-faced, direct digital image is taken, the rate of accurate facial recognition is 99.7% at best. But if the person in question looks down or looks to the side, the rate of accuracy declines tremendously. This could then potentially lead to cases of mistaken identity. Therefore, I disagree with businesses sharing facial images of suspected shoplifters. I have two points to make.

正面を向いたデジタル画像が撮られた場合でも、正確な顔認識率はよくて 99.7% です。しかし、もし当該者が下を向いていたり横を向いていたりすれば、その精度は著しく下がります。そうなると、人違いの可能性も出てきます。そのため、小売業者が万引きの容疑者の顔の画像を公開することに反対です。2 つのポイントがあります。

R1
Reason
理由

First, a facial image is very sensitive personal information. Without concrete evidence, it's not good to share such delicate images.

第一に、顔の画像は大変慎重に扱うべき個人情報です。具体的な証拠なしに、そのような扱いに注意が必要な画像を公開することはよくありません。

E1
Example
例

For example, under the law, we are not allowed to provide personal information to a third party without the second party's consent. Besides, once facial images are posted online, these images are easily reproduced and it's impossible to fully remove them from the Internet.

例えば、法の下では、本人の同意なく、第三者に個人情報を提供することは許されません。さらに、いったん、顔の画像がインターネット上で公開されれば、画像は簡単にコピーされてしまい、それらをインターネットから完全に取り除くことは不可能です。

R2
Reason
理由

Second, it's not reasonable to share facial images of suspected shoplifters. Being suspected shoplifters does not mean that they are actually true criminals. If they were falsely accused, then there would be big repercussions.

第二に、万引きの容疑者の顔の画像を共有することは、合理的ではありません。万引きの容疑者であることは、彼らが本当の犯罪者であるという意味ではありません。もし彼らがぬれぎぬを着せられたとしたら、大きな反動があるでしょう。

E2
Example
例

For example, the suspects might sue the stores for libel. Such mistakes by stores could end up being costlier than the damages caused by shoplifting itself.

例えば、容疑者は名誉毀損で店を訴えるかもしれません。店側によるそのような誤ちは、万引きそのものによって生じる損害よりも高くつく結果になるでしょう。

A
Assertion (Conclusion)
主張

In conclusion, it's too dangerous to share personal information on the Internet. Plus, facial images taken by security cameras are considered personal information. In fact, facial image sharing is also an invasion of privacy and a potential source of slander. Therefore, I disagree with the idea of businesses sharing facial images of suspected shoplifters.

(243 words)

結論として、インターネット上で個人情報を公開することはとても危険です。さらに防犯カメラで撮影された顔の映像は、個人情報だとみなされます。実際に、顔の画像の公開はプライバシーの侵害にもあたり、中傷の原因になりかねません。そのため、小売業者が万引きの容疑者の顔の画像を公開するという考えに反対です。

Words and Phrases

033

For

□ shoplifting	万引き
□ small retail business	小規模の小売業者
□ handle an issue	問題に対処する
□ the total financial damage	被害総額
□ according to available data	入手可能なデータによると
□ no big deal	大したことではない
□ highly addictive form of crime	常習性の高い犯罪行為
□ without really thinking about it	軽い気持ちで、それについて十分考えずに
□ regardless of age	年齢にかかわらず
□ succeeds at ~ing	~で成功する
□ get caught	逮捕される
□ enhance preventive measures	予防対策を強化する
□ be suspected of ~ing	~したのではないか疑われる
□ issue a warning	警告を発する
□ acceptable crime	容認できる犯罪
□ be crucial in	~するのに重要である
□ curve criminal behavior	犯罪行為を抑制する
□ commit minor crimes	軽犯罪を犯す
□ take proactive measures to	~するため積極的な対策を講じる

Against

□ rate of accurate facial recognition	正確な顔認識率
□ at best	せいぜい
□ look down	下を向く
□ look to the side	横を向く
□ rate of accuracy	精度
□ decline tremendously	著しく下がる
□ mistaken identity	人違い
□ sensitive personal information	取り扱いに注意すべき個人情報
□ without concrete evidence	具体的な証拠なしで
□ under the law	法律の下では
□ third party	第三者
□ without one's consent	~の同意なしで
□ post ~ online	~をインターネットで公開する
□ reproduce	~をコピーする、複製する
□ fully remove ~ from the Internet	~をインターネットから完全に取り除く
□ it's not reasonable to	~するのは合理的でない
□ be falsely accused	ぬれぎぬを着せられている
□ big repercussion	大きな反動
□ sue ~ for libel	~を名誉毀損で訴える
□ potential source of slander	中傷の原因となる可能性

Tips | 論理的に展開するためのキーフレーズ

根拠を示す③

1	According to an alarming report, it's difficult to stop drug smugglers from entering Japan.	憂慮すべき報告によると、麻薬の密輸業者が日本に入国するのを食い止めるのは困難です。
2	Survey results show many people support living in high-rise condominiums.	調査結果によると、多くの人が高層マンションに住むことを支持しています。
3	This indicates that the weather this year could cause serious damage to crops.	このことは、今年の天候が作物に深刻な被害をもたらす可能性を示しています。
4	This graph tells us that domestic sales this summer are in decline.	このグラフによれば、今年の夏の国内販売は下降しています。
5	Past studies suggest moderate exercise and proper diet lower mortality.	過去の研究では、適度な運動と適切な食事が死亡率を下げることが示唆されています。

追加を示す①

1	Furthermore, we tailor our products to specific markets.	さらに、製品を特定の市場に合わせて作ります。
2	Also, we have developed an efficient inventory control system.	また、効果的な在庫管理システムを開発しました。
3	Plus, we have established ourselves as a leading company of smartphone applications.	さらに、われわれはスマートフォンアプリのトップ企業としての地位を確立しました。
4	On top of that, we are devising a procedure to monitor all the costs and processes of a new project.	その上、新プロジェクトのすべてのコストとプロセスを監視する手順を考案しています。
5	Beyond that, some people get addicted to gambling and stop working.	その上、ギャンブルの中毒になって、働くことをやめる人がいます。

Should the death penalty be applied?

死刑制度は必要か？

背景知識とヒント

死刑制度の是非をめぐる議論

イギリスやフランスでは、死刑制度はすでに廃止されています。先進国の中で死刑制度があるのは、アメリカ合衆国と日本だけです。しかも、アメリカ合衆国では、23 の州で死刑が廃止されており、6 州が執行を停止しています。

しかし、日本では死刑制度を支持する声が根強く、80%を超える人が死刑を容認しているという世論調査のデータもあります。死刑制度の是非について、さらなる議論が必要です。

知っトク情報：頻出の関連トピック

Does the death penalty deter people from committing crimes? / Can the use of capital punishment be justified? / Should capital punishment be abolished?

コンセプトマップ

賛成バージョンを参考にスピーチの土台となるコンセプトマップを作ってみましょう。

Assertion

I agree with the idea of applying the death penalty.

Reason 1

save taxpayers' money

Reason 2

effective deterrent for major crimes

Example 1

- life without parole
- criminals stay in prison until the end of their lives
- money on food / health care / clothes

Example 2

- hesitant to commit crimes murder

Assertion (Conclusion)

I agree with the idea of applying the death penalty.

Speech | スピーチ

For | 賛成バージョン 12-❶

034

A
Assertion
主張

I know that there are people who oppose the death penalty under any circumstances. I believe the death penalty is a societal necessity. Therefore, I agree with the idea of applying the death penalty. I have two points to make.

いかなる場合でも、死刑に反対する人がいることは知っています。私は死刑が社会で不可欠なものだと信じます。そのため、死刑を適用するという考えに賛成です。2つのポイントがあります。

R1
Reason
理由

Firstly, the death penalty saves taxpayers' money.

第一に、死刑は納税者の負担を軽減します。

E1
Example
例

Take life without parole, for example. If the maximum punishment for major crimes is life without parole, such criminals will stay in prison until the end of their lives. It means that, in the long term, we will spend money on food, accommodations, healthcare, clothes, and so forth for such criminals. Today, every prison is filled to capacity. Long-term spending for people committing major crimes is a waste of money. Such money can be better used for the development of society and other positive things.

終身刑を例に挙げます。もし重大犯罪に対する最高刑が終身刑なら、その犯罪者たちは、死ぬまで刑務所で過ごします。長い目で見れば、その犯罪者たちの食事、収容設備、健康管理、衣服などに、私たちがお金を支出しなければならないのです。最近は、どの刑務所も満員です。重大な罪を犯した人に対する長期にわたる支出は、お金の無駄です。そのようなお金は、社会の発展やその他の良いことのために使われるべきなのです。

R2
Reason
理由

Secondly, the death penalty is an effective deterrent for major crimes.

第二に、死刑は重大犯罪への効果的な抑止力です。

E2
Example
例

For example, if criminals know that the punishment for major crimes is the death penalty, they will be hesitant to commit crimes like murder. Some say there is a risk of executing innocent people, but thanks to the power of scientific evidence, DNA greatly reduces the chance of punishing an innocent person.

例えば、もし犯罪者が、重大犯罪の罰は死刑だと知っていれば、殺人のような罪を犯すことをためらうでしょう。無実の人を処刑する危険性があるという人がいますが、科学的証拠の力のおかげで、DNAは無実の人を罰する可能性をかなり低くしてくれます。

A
Assertion (Conclusion)
主張

To sum up, I believe that the death penalty is the best way to control criminals, reduce government expenses and deter people from committing crimes. Therefore, I agree with the idea of applying the death penalty.

(232 words)

結論として、死刑は犯罪者をコントロールし、政府の経費を節減し、人が罪を犯すのを思いとどまらせる最善の方法です。そのため、死刑を適用するという考えに賛成です。

Against | 反対バージョン 12-❷

035

A
Assertion
主張

Some people believe that the death penalty is necessary to effectively maintain security in society, but the death penalty has negative aspects. Therefore, I disagree with the idea of applying the death penalty. I have two points to make.

社会の安全を効果的に維持するために、死刑は必要だと信じる人がいます。しかし死刑にはマイナス面があります。そのため、死刑を適用するという考えに反対です。2つのポイントがあります。

R1
Reason
理由

Firstly, nobody can prove 100% that criminals are guilty without a shadow of a doubt.

第一に、犯罪者が疑いもなく100%有罪であると、誰も証明できません。

E1
Example
例

Take DNA testing, for example. DNA can reduce the chance of punishing an innocent person, but we can't remove the chance completely. For example, what if the DNA found is that of an identical twin or someone not involved with the crime? Moreover, money talks in the justice system. In some cases, guilty people who can afford to hire experienced and competent lawyers may escape the death sentence. On the other hand, poor people can't afford to hire quality lawyers and may be found guilty even though innocent due to a poor defense.

DNAテストを例に挙げます。DNAは無実の人を罰する可能性を低くできます。しかしその可能性を完全には取り除けないのです。例えば、もし発見されたDNAが、一卵性双生児の片方のそれか、罪を犯していない誰かのものだったら、どうなるでしょうか。さらに、司法制度ではお金がモノを言います。場合によっては、経験豊富で有能な弁護士を雇う余裕がある罪人が、死刑を免れるかもしれません。一方で貧しい人が、有能な弁護士を雇うゆとりがなくて、下手な弁護が原因で、無罪であっても有罪を宣告されるかもしれません。

R2
Reason
理由

Secondly, it's reasonable to think that the death penalty is inhuman.

第二に、死刑が非人道的だと考えるのは妥当です。

E2
Example
例

Take the right to life, for example. Based on moral principles, we have no right to kill other people. The right to life is a fundamental right. In addition, the right to live with dignity is granted via our human rights policy. Plus, criminals often show remorse for their acts and repent. Even criminals deserve a second chance.

生存権を例にとってみましょう。道徳的原則に基づいて、他の人を殺す権利はありません。生存権は基本的権利の1つです。さらに、尊厳を持って生きる権利は、人権政策によって認められています。さらに、犯罪者がしばしば自分の行為に対する深い反省を示し、悔やむことがあります。犯罪者であっても、人生をやり直すチャンスが与えられるべきなのです。

A
Assertion (Conclusion)
主張

To sum up, although the death penalty has some advantages, I believe the death penalty isn't the best way to control criminals. This is because innocent people could be executed due to unfair sentences, and nobody can deny others a fundamental human right, that is, the right to life. Therefore, the death penalty is not the solution. For these reasons, I disagree with the idea of applying the death penalty.

(286 words)

結論として、死刑にはメリットがいくつかあるけれども、死刑が犯罪をコントロールする最善の方法だとは思いません。これは、無実の人が不公平な判決により処刑されかねないからです。そして、誰も他の人の基本的人権、つまり、生存権を否定できません。そのため、死刑は解決策ではありません。これらの理由で、死刑を適用するという考えに反対です。

Words and Phrases

036

For

□ under any circumstances	いかなる場合でも、状況でも
□ societal necessity	社会の不可欠なもの
□ save taxpayers' money	納税者の出費を抑える
□ life without parole	仮釈放のない終身刑
□ maximum punishment for major crimes	重大犯罪に対する最高刑
□ stay in prison	刑務所で過ごす
□ in the long term	長い目でみれば
□ accommodations	宿泊設備、収容設備
□ be filled to capacity	満員である
□ long-term spending	長期にわたる出費、支出
□ be an effective deterrent for	～の効果的な抑止力である
□ be hesitant to	～するのに気が進まない、ためらっている
□ there is a risk of	～のリスクがある
□ execute innocent people	無実の人を処刑する
□ thanks to the power of scientific evidence	科学的証拠の力のおかげで
□ reduce the chance of	～の可能性を低くする
□ be the best way to	～するための最善の方法である
□ reduce government expenses	政府の経費を節減する
□ deter ... from ~	…が～するのを阻止する

Against

□ have a negative aspect	マイナス面がある
□ guilty without a shadow of a doubt	疑いもなく有罪で
□ remove the chance	可能性を取り除く
□ identical twin	一卵性双生児の片方
□ what if	もし～だったらどうなるか
□ Money talks in the justice system.	司法制度ではお金がモノを言う。
□ in some cases	場合によっては
□ hire experienced and competent lawyers	経験豊富で有能な弁護士を雇う
□ quality lawyers	有能な弁護士
□ be found guilty	有罪を宣告される
□ due to a poor defense	下手な弁護のため
□ based on moral principles	道徳的原則に基づいて
□ fundamental right	基本的権利
□ right to live	生存権
□ with dignity	尊厳を持って、威厳ある態度で
□ grant	～を認める
□ via human rights policy	人権政策によって
□ show remorse for one's act	行為に対する深い反省を示す
□ repent	悔やむ
□ deserve a second chance	人生をやり直すチャンスが与えられる
□ be executed due to unfair sentences	不公平な判決により処刑される

Tips | 論理的に展開するためのキーフレーズ

根拠を示す④

❶	We can use video from a security camera as evidence.	監視カメラの映像を証拠として使うことができます。
❷	Fingerprints are used as evidence against him.	指紋は、彼に不利な証拠として使われます。
❸	Based on scientific evidence and data, I'm going to present you three ways to be happy.	科学的な証拠とデータに基づき、幸せになる３つの方法を提案します。
❹	Is this medical procedure supported by scientific evidence?	この医学の手法は、科学的な裏付けがあるのですか。
❺	Is there any evidence to prove that conclusion?	その結論を証明するために何か証拠がありますか。
❻	Do you have any proof to support your statement?	自分の意見を支持する証拠が何かありますか。
❼	Is the data sufficient to support your proposal?	自分の提案を支持する十分なデータがありますか。

問題を示す①

❶	The drop in oil prices is a big problem for OPEC.	原油価格の下落はOPECにとっては大きな問題です。
❷	Many companies face a problem in their approach to big data analysis.	多くの会社は、ビッグデータ分析の手法で問題に直面しています。
❸	Bad company management may cause big problems.	悪質な会社の経営により、大きな問題が起きるかもしれません。
❹	Another issue is that stolen USB has confidential information.	もう１つの問題は、盗まれたUSBには、機密情報が入っていることです。
❺	We have to work together to tackle this perplexing problem.	この複雑な問題に対応するために、協力して行動しなくてはいけません。

Should sex offenders be monitored using GPS technology?

性犯罪者はGPSで監視されるべきか？

背景知識とヒント

日本でも、性犯罪者に対する監視の検討を開始

性犯罪者、殺人、強盗などの重犯罪者に、GPS 端末の携帯を義務付けている国があります。対象者が GPS 端末を外すと警報が鳴る仕組みです。日本でも、特に性犯罪者に対して、GPS 端末携帯の義務化を議論し始めている自治体があります。というのも、性犯罪は被害者の心身に甚大な影響を及ぼすからです。

これには犯罪予防を目的とするという大義があるものの、一方で、犯罪者のプライバシーを侵害するという基本的人権の問題もあります。犯罪者への GPS 端末携帯の義務化について、どのように考えるべきでしょうか。

知っトク情報：頻出の関連トピック

Are the police doing enough to combat crime? / Prevention vs. cure in the battle against crime. / What type of crime most threatens society? / Should the Japanese government do more to promote human rights in other countries?

コンセプトマップ

賛成バージョンを参考にスピーチの土台となるコンセプトマップを作ってみましょう。

Assertion

I am strongly in favor of the idea of monitoring sex offenders using GPS.

Reason 1

way to help ensure the safety of the community

Reason 2

have a deterrent effect

Example 1

- track all sex offenders
- avoid them

Example 2

- sex offenders' recidivism rate was 14% in Korea
- the rate decreased to 1.7%

Assertion (Conclusion)

I agree with the idea of monitoring sex offenders using GPS.

Speech | スピーチ

037

For | 賛成バージョン 13-❶

A
Assertion
主張

I'm disgusted by sex offenders, especially pedophiles. I'm strongly in favor of the idea of monitoring sex offenders using GPS. I have two points to make.

性犯罪者、特に小児愛者に対して嫌悪感があります。性犯罪者をGPSで監視することに強く賛成です。2つのポイントがあります。

R1
Reason
理由

First, GPS monitoring is an excellent way to help ensure the safety of the community.

第一に、GPS監視は地域の安全を確保する優れた方法です。

E1
Example
例

For example, GPS could track all sex offenders so that parents can ensure their children avoid the locations where they may be. In addition, as taxpayers, we wouldn't have to spend money to keep sending offenders back to prison after repeatedly committing crimes. We and our children would be able to avoid having any contact with them.

例えば、GPSはすべての性犯罪者を追跡することができるので、親は自分の子どもが彼らのいるであろう場所を避けるようにすることができます。さらに、納税者として、何度も罪を犯した犯罪者を刑務所に送り続けるためにお金を使う必要がなくなります。私たちと子どもは、一切の接触を避けることができます。

R2
Reason
理由

Second, GPS monitoring has a deterrent effect on tracked sex offenders.

第二に、GPS監視は追跡される性犯罪者に対する抑止効果があります。

E2
Example
例

For instance, sex offenders' recidivism rate was 14% in South Korea in 2007. But ten years after introducing GPS monitoring, the rate decreased to 1.7%. It's important that they no longer commit violent crimes after being released. I believe GPS monitoring would encourage sex offenders to control their bad behavior.

例えば、2007年の韓国では性犯罪者の再犯率が14%でした。しかしGPS監視を導入した10年後、その割合が1.7%まで下がったのです。重要なのは、彼らが釈放された後、凶悪犯罪を二度と犯さないことです。GPSは彼らの悪い行動を抑制するのに効果があると確信しています。

A
Assertion (Conclusion)
主張

In the end, some people insist that monitoring the whereabouts of sex offenders using GPS is an invasion of privacy, but some of these offenders have even committed lewd acts on children under 16. We should put the community's safety first, not a sex offender's right to privacy. For these reasons, I agree with the idea of monitoring sex offenders using GPS.

(221 words)

最後に、GPSを使って性犯罪者の所在を監視することは、プライバシーの侵害だと主張する人がいますが、これらの犯罪者には、16歳未満の子どもたちにわいせつ行為を犯している人もいるのです。性犯罪者のプライバシーの権利ではなく、地域の安全を第一に考えるべきです。これらの理由で性犯罪者をGPSで監視することに賛成です。

Against | 反対バージョン 13-❷

 038

A
Assertion
主張

Whether they are sex offenders or not, all people should be treated equally under the law. Monitoring their whereabouts using GPS technology is an invasion of privacy and against the Constitution. I am not in favor of the idea of monitoring sex offenders using GPS. I have two points to make.

性犯罪者であろうとなかろうと、すべての人は法の下で平等に扱われるべきです。GPS を使って所在を監視するのは、プライバシーの侵害で、憲法に違反します。性犯罪者を GPS で監視するという考えに反対です。2 つのポイントがあります。

R1
Reason
理由

First, making sex offenders wear GPS devices could lead to prejudice and discrimination against them.

第一に、性犯罪者に GPS 端末を装着させることは、彼らに対する偏見や差別につながる恐れがあります。

E1
Example
例

For example, in South Korea, some sex offenders wearing GPS bracelets suffer from social withdrawal because they're scared of being seen. Even after completing their sentences in prison, they're still treated unfairly because of the GPS devices they have to wear.

例えば韓国では、GPS ブレスレットを装着した性犯罪者の中には、人目を気にして、社会的引きこもりに苦しむ人もいます。刑務所で刑期を終えた後も、GPS 端末を装着しているために不当な扱いを受けているのです。

R2 Reason 理由

Second, GPS monitoring is against the Constitution.

第二に、GPS で監視することは憲法に違反します。

E2 Example 例

For example, it's a violation of privacy. Criminals who have served their time in jail should be treated the same as other individuals after being released from prison. They have already paid for their crimes in prison and they shouldn't have to pay for their crimes again even after being released from prison. GPS monitoring may impact the social reintegration of convicted sex offenders into society.

例えば、プライバシーの侵害です。刑務所で服役した犯罪者でも、出所後は他の個人と同じく扱われるべきです。彼らは刑務所で罪を償ったのです。出所後まで、再びその罪を償う必要はありません。GPS で監視することは、有罪判決を受けた性犯罪者の社会復帰に影響を与えるかもしれません。

A Assertion (Conclusion) 主張

In the end, all people should be treated equally under the Constitution. As I mentioned earlier, wearing GPS bracelets could lead to withdrawal. Furthermore, they have already paid for their crimes by serving their time in jail. For these reasons, I disagree with the idea of monitoring sex offenders using GPS.

(231 words)

最後に、すべての人は、憲法の下では平等に扱われるべきなのです。先に述べたように、GPS ブレスレットをつけると引きこもりになる恐れがあります。しかも、服役することによって罪をすでに償っています。これらの理由で、性犯罪者を GPS で監視するという考えに反対です。

Words and Phrases

For

□ be disgusted by	～に嫌悪感を持っている、うんざりである
□ sex offender	性犯罪者
□ pedophile	小児愛者
□ monitor ～ using GPS	～を GPS で監視する
□ excellent way to ensure the safety of the community	地域の安全を確保する優れた方法
□ track	～を追跡する
□ taxpayer	納税者
□ offender	犯罪者
□ commit crimes	罪を犯す
□ sex offenders' recidivism rate	性犯罪者の再犯率
□ violent crimes	凶悪犯罪
□ be released	釈放される
□ encourage ～ to ...	～を…するよう促す
□ control one's bad behavior	悪い行動を抑制する
□ have a deterrent effect on	～に対する抑制効果がある
□ in the end	結局
□ monitor the whereabouts of	～の所在を監視する
□ invasion of privacy	プライバシーの侵害
□ commit lewd acts	わいせつ行為を犯す
□ for these reasons	これらの理由で

Against

□ whether ～ or not	～であろうがなかろうが
□ be treated equally	平等に扱われる
□ against the Constitution	憲法に違反して
□ GPS device	GPS 端末
□ prejudice and discrimination	偏見と差別
□ suffer from social withdrawal	社会的引きこもりに苦しむ
□ complete one's sentence	刑期を終える
□ be treated unfairly	不公平に扱われる
□ violation of privacy	プライバシーの侵害
□ serve time in jail	刑務所で服役する
□ pay for one's crimes in prison	刑務所で罪を償う
□ social reintegration of convicted sex offenders into society	有罪判決を受けた性犯罪者の社会復帰

Tips | 論理的に展開するためのキーフレーズ

効果を示す

1	The revised rule could have a deterrent effect on teenagers.	改正されたルールには、ティーンエイジャーに対する抑止効果があります。
2	Researchers found no evidence of a deterrent effect of surveillance cameras on crimes.	研究者は、犯罪に対する監視カメラの抑止効果について、何も証拠を見つけていません。
3	Video surveillance is helpful in deterring street crimes.	ビデオ監視は路上での犯罪を抑止するのに役に立っています。
4	Capital punishment is a strong deterrent to violent crimes.	死刑は、凶悪犯罪に高い抑止力があります。
5	Strategically placed cameras can be deterrents against criminal activities.	戦略的に配置したカメラは犯罪行為に対して抑止効果があります。
6	Do such decisions have a restraining effect on the development of nuclear weapons?	そのような決定は、核兵器の配備に対して抑止効果がありますか。

例を示す①

1	I've heard about some terrible accidents. For instance, some parents left their kids in the car in the hot summer.	悲惨な事故について耳にしました。例えば、暑い夏、車内に子どもを置き去りにした両親がいました。
2	Take watches, for example. If they are both high-quality and low-priced, many people would want to buy them.	時計を例にとります。それらが高品質で低価格なら、多くの人が欲しがるでしょう。
3	Their skill is often used in ballet, figure skating and gymnastics, just to name a few examples.	彼らの技術は、いくつか例を挙げるだけでも、バレエ、フィギュアスケートや体操で使われています。
4	This prepaid electronic money would be convenient for multiple purposes. For example, commuting, shopping, and the like.	このプリペイド式電子マネーは、多目的に使えて便利です。例えば、通勤や買い物などです。
5	Your salary depends on your skills, such as computers, communication skills and so forth.	あなたの給料は、コンピュータ、コミュニケーション力のようなスキル次第です。

Should animals be kept in zoos?

動物は動物園で飼われるべきか？

背景知識とヒント

動物園の功罪を考える

動物園には、「種の保存」、「教育・環境教育」、「調査・研究」、「レクリエーション」という４つの役割があるとされています。来園者の楽しみを提供するだけではなく、絶滅の危機にある野生生物を保全する役割も担っているのです。

一方、飼育されている動物は、自然とは異なる環境で、自由を制限された状態で過ごすことになります。動物にとって動物園はどうあるべきなのでしょうか。

知っトク情報：頻出の関連トピック

Are scientific efforts to bring back extinct species a waste of time? / Is enough being done to protect the world's wilderness areas? / Can keeping animals in captivity be justified? / Agree or disagree: Zoos do more harm than good. / Is the extinction of some plant and animal species inevitable? / Can animal testing be justified?

コンセプトマップ

反対バージョンを参考にスピーチの土台となるコンセプトマップを作ってみましょう。

Assertion

I am opposed to the idea of keeping animals in zoos.

Reason 1

hardly have any privacy

Reason 2

living conditions are terrible

Example 1

- watched by visitors
- no freedom
- lead stressful daily lives

Example 2

- spaces are limited
- overweight
- lose their natural instincts

Assertion (Conclusion)

I am opposed to the idea of keeping animals in zoos.

Speech | スピーチ

For | 賛成バージョン 14-❶

040

A
Assertion
主張

Lots of people like to take their kids to the zoo on holidays. It's a very popular way of spending family time. On the whole , zoos play important roles in education about endangered species. I'm all for the idea of keeping animals in zoos. I have two points to make.

休日に子どもを動物園に連れて行くのが好きな人は多くいます。家族の時間を過ごす、人気の高い方法です。全体として、動物園は、絶滅危惧種の教育に重要な役割を果たしています。私は、動物園で動物を飼うことに賛成です。2つのポイントがあります。

R1
Reason
理由

Firstly, zoos play an educational role.

第一に、動物園は教育的な役割を果たしています。

E1
Example
例

For example, it's a lot of fun and very educational to see many rare animals, such as gorillas, giraffes, elephants, and hippos, all in one place. Furthermore, visitors can actually touch and feed the less aggressive, less dangerous animals. Therefore, teachers often plan excursions to zoos because they provide educational experiences. Also, zoos provide information about endangered species. Visitors can learn more about the lives of such animals and how to protect them.

例えば、ゴリラやキリン、象やカバなど、多くの珍しい動物を1か所で見ることは楽しく、教育的です。さらに、攻撃的でなく危険でない動物には、来場者が実際に触れたり餌をやったりすることができます。そのため、教育的な経験を提供してくれるので、教師は動物園への遠足をしばしば計画するのです。さらに、動物園は絶滅危惧種に関する情報を提供してくれます。来場者はそのような動物の生態や保護する方法について学ぶことができます。

R2
Reason
理由

Secondly, zoos provide animals safe places to live, and the animals themselves are carefully taken care of.

第二に、動物園は、動物に安全な生活の場を提供します。そして動物は大切に世話されます。

E2
Example
例

For example, they don't have to find food on their own. They are regularly fed balanced meals by their zoo keepers. Plus, these zoo keepers are making every effort to protect and breed endangered animals. Outside zoos, many poachers kill lots of animals for their valuable parts, such as the ivory tusks of elephants, and they also smuggle live rare animals abroad. To make matters worse, some of these animals are in danger of extinction! We need to save endangered species by keeping them safe in zoos.

例えば、動物は自分で餌を見つける必要がありません。動物園の飼育員によって、定期的にバランスの取れた餌を与えられます。また、これらの動物園の飼育員は、絶滅の危機に瀕した動物の保護と繁殖のためにあらゆる努力をしています。動物園の外では、多くの密猟者が貴重な部位を求めて多くの動物を殺しています。例えば、象の象牙などです。そして、希少動物を海外へ密輸しています。さらに悪いことには、その中には、絶滅の危機に瀕している動物がいるのです！　それらの動物を動物園で飼うことで、絶滅危惧種を救う必要があります。

A
Assertion (Conclusion)
主張

For these reasons, I'm all for the idea of keeping animals in zoos. Zoos may not be their natural habitat, but animals are much safer in zoos. When they are sick or endangered, they can be treated immediately and protected. Moreover, zoos educate us about animals and their needs, which enables us to take every possible step to save all animal species.

(295 words)

これらの理由で、動物園で動物を飼うことに賛成です。動物園は自然の生息地ではないかもしれませんが、動物は動物園ではかなり安全です。病気になったり、危険にさらされたりしたときには、すぐに治療され、保護されます。さらに動物園は、動物や動物が必要としていることについて啓発します。それにより私たちはすべての動物の種を救うために、あらゆる手段を講じることが可能になります。

Against | 反対バージョン 14-❷

041

A
Assertion
主張

On TV, have you ever seen a sleek cheetah running as swift as the wind on the Serengeti Plain of Africa? They seem so happy to be free. I am opposed to the idea of keeping animals in zoos. They are endlessly displayed in front of visitors and kept in small enclosures. I have two points to make.

アフリカのセレンゲティ草原を風のように速く走っている流線型のチーターをテレビで見たことがありますか。彼らは自由で幸せそうに見えます。私は動物園で動物を飼うことに反対です。動物は来場者の前に絶えず展示され、小さな囲いの中に入れられています。2つのポイントがあります。

R1
Reason
理由

Firstly, zoo animals hardly have any privacy.

第一に、動物園の動物には、ほとんどプライバシーがありません。

E1
Example
例

For example, they are almost always being watched by visitors. Every day, many visitors come near the cages; some even shout at the animals and tease them! If these animals were in their natural habitats, they could freely move to a private, quieter, more peaceful place. However, the prison-like zoo cages don't allow them such freedom. Zoo animals lead very stressful daily lives.

例えば、動物はほとんどいつも来場者によって見られています。毎日多くの来場者が檻の近くまで来ます。動物に向かって叫んだりからかったりする人もいます！　もしこれらの動物が自然の生息地にいれば、プライベートで、より静かで、より穏やかな場所へ自由に移動することができるのです。しかし、動物園の檻は刑務所のようで、動物にそのような自由は許しません。動物園の動物は、大変ストレスを感じる日常生活を送っています。

R2
Reason
理由

Secondly, the living conditions of zoo animals are almost always terrible.

第二に、動物園の動物の生活環境は、ほとんどいつも悲惨です。

E2
Example
例

For example, their living spaces are very limited compared to where they used to live. Because they can't get enough exercise, many animals become overweight. In addition, some people say we should save endangered species in zoos, but animals kept for a long time in captivity usually lose their natural instincts for hunting, self-preservation and so forth. Animals need their natural habitat to properly develop.

例えば、生活する空間は、かつて暮らしていた場所と比べて、大変限られています。動物は十分な運動ができないので、多くの動物は太りすぎてしまいます。さらに、動物園で絶滅危惧種を救うべきだという人がいます。しかし、長い間檻の中で飼われた動物は、元来備わっている狩りや自衛といった本能を失ってしまうものです。動物には適切に成長するための、自然の生息地が必要なのです。

A
Assertion (Conclusion)
主張

For these reasons, I am opposed to the idea of keeping animals in zoos. Animals should live in their usual natural environment. There, they are much healthier and happier. Though some people say zoos protect animals from poachers, it would be better if instead we took drastic steps to get rid of poachers. All we have to do is to arrest and punish them severely.

(269 words)

これらの理由で、動物園で動物を飼うという考えに反対です。動物は通常の自然環境で生きるべきなのです。そこで動物は、より健康でより幸せになれます。動物園が動物を密猟者から保護しているという人がいますが、その代わりに、密猟者を一掃するために思い切った手段をとったほうが良いのです。私たちがしなければいけないことは密猟者を逮捕し厳しく罰することなのです。

Words and Phrases

 042

For

□ play an important role in	～において重要な役割を果たす
□ education about endangered species	絶滅危惧種についての教育
□ I'm all for	～に全面的に賛成である
□ gorillas, giraffes, elephants and hippos	ゴリラ、キリン、象やカバ
□ furthermore	さらに
□ feed	～に餌を与える
□ provide an educational experience	教育的体験を提供する
□ regularly	定期的に
□ zoo keeper	動物園の飼育員
□ make every effort to	～するために最大限の努力をする
□ breed	～を繁殖させる
□ poacher	密猟者；侵入者
□ ivory tusks of elephants	象の象牙
□ smuggle	～を密輸する
□ to make matters worse	さらに悪いことには
□ be in danger of extinction	絶滅の危機に瀕している
□ natural habitat	自然の生息地
□ be endangered	危機にさらされる
□ enable ~ to ...	～が…するのを可能にする
□ take every possible step to	～するためあらゆる手段を講じる

Against

□ sleek cheetah	流線型のチーター
□ as swift as the wind	風のように速く
□ the Serengeti Plain of Africa	アフリカのセレンゲティ草原
□ I am opposed to	～に反対である
□ endlessly	際限なく
□ enclosure	囲い
□ cage	檻
□ tease	～をからかう
□ compared to	～と比較すると
□ become overweight	太りすぎる
□ in addition	さらに
□ in captivity	拘束されて、囚われて
□ lose one's natural instinct	備わっている本能を失う
□ self-preservation	自衛本能
□ and so forth	（具体例に続けて）など
□ instead	代わりに
□ take a drastic step to	～するために思い切った手段をとる
□ get rid of	～を一掃する、取り除く
□ arrest	～を逮捕する
□ punish	～を罰する

Tips | 論理的に展開するためのキーフレーズ

程度を示す

1	In general, customers' questions and complaints are of great value to us.	一般的に、顧客の質問や苦情は、私たちにとって、非常に価値があります。
2	Generally, we have wrong impressions about some countries owing to false information on the Internet.	一般的に、インターネット上の誤った情報によって、私たちはいくつかの国々について間違った印象を持っています。
3	On the whole, we have a shortage of funds to start a new business.	全体的に、新しいビジネスを始めるのに資金が不足しています。
4	Overall, the project is progressing better than originally expected.	全体的に、当初予定したよりも、その計画はうまく進んでいます。
5	As a rule, it's important to monitor economic trends before making the next move.	原則として、次の一手を打つ前に、経済動向を注視することが重要です。

反論を示す②

1	I disagree with your idea of renting new facilities.	新しい施設を貸し出すという考えに反対です。
2	I can't agree with any restrictions on social media.	SNSのいかなる規制にも賛成できません。
3	I can't accept your opinion on this matter.	この件に関しては、君の意見を受け入れることができません。
4	I can't back you up on this issue.	この件に関しては、君を支持できません。
5	I have a different opinion on this subject.	この件に関しては、意見が違います。
6	I can't go along with your idea concerning employee benefits.	従業員の福利厚生に関しての君の考えには賛成できません。

Should nuclear power plants be abolished?

原子力発電所を廃止すべきか？

背景知識とヒント

資源に乏しい日本の選択は？

福島の原子力発電所の事故のあと、ドイツでは2023年に、最後の原子力発電所の稼働を完全に停止しました。原子力発電所の事故をコントロールできないというリスクが主な要因です。原子力発電所は、大容量の電気を安く安定して供給でき、発電時に二酸化炭素を排出しないなどのメリットがあります。一方、いったん事故が起きれば、そのリスクはコントロールできません。廃炉に膨大な時間と費用がかかるなどの問題もあります。エネルギー資源の乏しい日本は、今後どのように考えるべきなのでしょうか。

知っトク情報：頻出の関連トピック

Is solar power the energy of the future? / Is Japan doing enough to ensure its energy security? / Will renewable energy sources ever completely replace fossil fuels?

コンセプトマップ

賛成バージョンを参考にスピーチの土台となるコンセプトマップを作ってみましょう。

Assertion

I agree with the idea of abolishing nuclear power plants.

Reason 1

not always safe

Reason 2

costs of a meltdown are very high

Example 1

- nuclear disasters
- Chernobyl and Fukushima disasters
- health risks

Example 2

- financial compensation
- money-consuming and time-consuming
- costly in human life

Assertion (Conclusion)

I agree with the idea of abolishing nuclear power plants.

Speech | スピーチ

For | 賛成バージョン 15-❶

A
Assertion
主張

After the most recent powerful earthquake and tsunami disasters, many people have become worried about the possible problems caused by nearby nuclear power plants. In fact, Switzerland has already decided to abolish all the nuclear power plants it has in the not-too-distant future. I agree with the idea of abolishing nuclear power plants. I have two points to make.

最近の大地震と津波の災害の後、多くの人は近くの原子力発電所によって起こりうる問題について心配しています。実際に、スイスでは、そう遠くない将来にすべての原子力発電所を廃炉にすることをすでに決定しています。原子力発電所を廃炉にする考えに賛成です。2つのポイントがあります。

R1
Reason
理由

First, nuclear power is not always safe.

第一に、原子力はいつも安全とは限りません。

E1
Example
例

For example, we have faced unprecedented nuclear disasters, such as the Chernobyl and Fukushima disasters, due to human error and natural forces. In fact, we are still experiencing the effects of these nuclear disasters. Once such an accident occurs, it takes many years to eliminate the resulting radioactivity and consequent health risks. Besides, nuclear power plants could be targets of terrorism.

例えば、チョルノービリや福島の災害のように、人的ミスや自然の力によって前代未聞の原子力災害に直面しています。実際、これらの原子力災害の影響をいまだに受けています。いったん事故が起きると、結果として生じる放射能と、それに起因する健康上のリスクを取り除くために、多くの年数がかかります。さらに、原子力発電所がテロのターゲットになる可能性もあります。

R2
Reason
理由

Second, when it comes to the disadvantages of nuclear power plants, the overall costs of a meltdown are astronomical.

第二に、原子力発電所のデメリットに関して言えば、メルトダウンの全体のコストは、天文学的になります。

E2
Example
例

For example, a huge amount of financial compensation has to be guaranteed by the energy company and the government. It's almost impossible to estimate the total amount needed for compensation, waste removal and so on. Plus, it takes an enormous amount of time to dispose of nuclear waste and reconstruct a disaster area. In other words, such nuclear disasters are money-consuming and time-consuming, not to mention costly in terms of human life itself.

例えば、巨額の補償金は、エネルギー会社と政府によって保証されなければなりません。補償金、廃棄物の除去などに必要な総額を見積もることは、ほぼ不可能に近いのです。しかも、放射性廃棄物を処理したり、被災地を復興させたりするのに膨大な時間がかかります。言い換えると、そのような原子力被害は、人命という点で犠牲が大きいのは言うまでもなく、お金がかかり、時間もかかるのです。

A
Assertion (Conclusion)
主張

In conclusion, Japan is a quake-prone country, so nobody can ensure the safety of such energy plants. Also, in the case of a meltdown, the cost is significantly huge. Once again, I agree with the idea of abolishing nuclear power plants.

(260 words)

結論として、日本は、地震多発国家ですから、誰もそのエネルギープラントの安全を保障することはできません。また、メルトダウンした場合には、そのコストは莫大なものになります。もう一度繰り返しますが、原子力発電所の廃炉に賛成です。

Against | 反対バージョン 15-❷

044

A
Assertion
主張

After the most recent earthquake and tsunami disasters, many people say we should abolish nuclear power plants, but I oppose that idea. I have two points to make.

最近の地震と津波の災害のあと、多くの人は、原子力発電所を廃炉にすべきだと言いますが、私はその考えに反対です。２つのポイントがあります。

R1
Reason
理由

First, regarding energy, Japan's energy self-sufficiency ratio is very low. Now Japan is over-dependent on the Middle East and Australia for imports of oil and natural gas. It's very dangerous for us to depend only on our limited energy sources.

第一に、エネルギーに関して、日本の自給率は、極めて低いです。今、日本は石油や天然ガスの輸入を中東やオーストラリアに過度に依存しています。限られたエネルギー源だけに頼るのは大変危険です。

E1
Example
例

For example, in the 1970s, we experienced a terrible oil shortage twice. Both times, it was because we depended on the Middle East for most of the oil we used. These shortages greatly affected our daily lives. We should not depend on such limited sources of energy that are beyond our control.

例えば1970年代、日本は深刻な石油不足を２度経験しました。いずれも、使う石油のほとんどを中東に頼っていたためです。これらの不足は、日常生活に大きな影響を与えました。自分の手に負えないような限られたエネルギー源に頼るべきではないのです。

R2
Reason
理由

Second, carbon dioxide causes a lot of problems.

第二に、二酸化炭素は多くの問題を引き起こします。

E2
Example
例

For example, a lot of carbon dioxide is produced by burning fossil fuels, and this is a major factor behind global warming. Global warming, in turn, leads to a lot of environmental problems like melting glaciers and rising sea levels. Rising sea levels may even cause islands and coastal land to submerge. Therefore , we have to stop global warming. Nuclear power generation is one effective way to slow down global warming, since it's not directly related to this environmental problem.

例えば、多くの二酸化炭素が、化石燃料を燃やすことによって作り出されます。そして、これが地球温暖化の主な原因です。地球温暖化は、氷河の溶解や海面上昇といった多くの環境問題を次々と引き起こします。海面が上昇すると、島や沿岸の土地が水没する可能性さえあるのです。そのため、地球温暖化を止めなければなりません。原子力発電は、この環境問題と直接関係していないので、地球温暖化を抑える効果的な手段です。

A
Assertion (Conclusion)
主張

In conclusion, nuclear power plants are the most cost-efficient, eco-friendly sources of power. Plus, we can ensure a stable energy supply through nuclear power. It's a great alternative to fossil fuels. Therefore, I oppose abolishing nuclear power plants.

(246 words)

結論として、原子力発電が最も費用効率が高く、環境にやさしいエネルギー源です。さらに、原子力発電を通して、安定したエネルギー供給を確保できます。化石燃料に代わる素晴らしい選択肢です。そのため、原子力発電所を廃炉にすることには反対です。

Words and Phrases

045

For

□ earthquake and tsunami disasters	地震や津波の災害
□ in the not-too-distant future	そう遠くない将来に
□ face unprecedented nuclear disasters	前代未聞の原子力災害に直面する
□ Chernobyl	チョルノービリ
□ due to human error and natural forces	人的ミスと自然の力によって
□ eliminate the resulting radioactivity	結果として生じた放射能を取り除く
□ consequent	結果として起きる
□ astronomical	天文学的な、けた違いに大きい
□ a huge amount of financial compensation	巨額の補償金
□ waste removal	廃棄物の除去
□ dispose of	～を処理する
□ nuclear waste	放射性廃棄物
□ enormous amount of time	膨大な時間
□ reconstruct a disaster area	被災地を復興させる
□ money-consuming and time-consuming	お金がかかり、時間がかかる
□ costly in terms of human life itself	人命という点では犠牲が大きい
□ quake-prone country	地震多発国
□ ensure the safety of	～の安全を確保する

Against

□ self-sufficiency ratio	自給率
□ be over-dependent on the Middle East and Australia	中東やオーストラリアに過度に依存している
□ natural gas	天然ガス
□ limited energy source	限られたエネルギー源
□ experience a terrible oil shortage	深刻な石油不足を経験する
□ affect one's daily lives	日常生活に影響を与える
□ beyond one's control	不可抗力の、手に負えない
□ carbon dioxide	二酸化炭素
□ burn fossil fuels	化石燃料を燃やす
□ a major factor behind global warming	地球温暖化の主な要因
□ melting glaciers and rising sea levels	氷河の溶解と海面上昇
□ coastal land	沿岸陸地
□ submerge	水没する
□ be directly related to	～と直接関係している
□ cost-efficient	費用効率の高い
□ eco-friendly sources of power	環境にやさしいエネルギー源
□ stable energy supply	安定したエネルギーの供給
□ it's a great alternative to	～に代わる素晴らしい選択肢である

Tips | 論理的に展開するためのキーフレーズ

観点を示す①

1	When it comes to money, he can't be trusted.	お金のこととなると、彼は信用できません。
2	I've had good and bad memories when it comes to studying abroad.	留学に関しては、私には楽しい思い出と不愉快な思い出があります。
3	Our company is excellent in terms of product quality, reliability, and customer satisfaction.	当社は、製品の品質、信頼性、顧客満足度において優れています。
4	As to business in our office, we have various perspectives.	私たちのオフィスでの仕事については、さまざまな意見があります。
5	With respect to your work, I can't help you at all.	あなたの仕事に関しては、まったく助けることができません。

結論・結果を示す

1	This apartment is bigger and therefore more comfortable than mine.	このマンションは広く、そのため、私のマンションより快適です。
2	We are not that rich. Therefore, we cannot afford to buy a fancy sports car.	私たちはそれほどお金持ちではありません。そのため、高級スポーツカーを買う余裕はありません。
3	College students are too busy with their part-time jobs. After all, they can't secure enough time for studying.	大学の学生はアルバイトで忙しくしています。結局、勉強のため十分な時間が確保できません。
4	He lost both his parents in a car accident. For that reason, he has no one to depend on.	彼は自動車事故で両親を二人とも亡くしました。そういう理由で、彼には頼る人が誰もいません。
5	Consequently, it was difficult to pinpoint the cause of the explosion.	結果として、その爆発の原因を特定することは難しかったのです。

Should homeowners install solar panels in homes for a sustainable Earth?

持続可能な地球のために自宅にソーラーパネルを設置すべきか？

背景知識とヒント

太陽光発電の普及が SDGs 達成に貢献

国際連合が 2015 年に採択した SDGs（Sustainable Development Goals：持続可能な開発目標）に、「エネルギーをみんなに、そしてクリーンに」「気候変動に具体的な対策を」という目標があります。その達成には太陽光発電の普及が必要不可欠ですが、個人住宅での太陽光パネル設置は、費用や維持費の問題もあり、思うように進んでいない現状があります。日本では電力の約 8 割を化石燃料に依存しており、太陽光発電のさらなる普及が求められています。

知っトク情報：頻出の関連トピック

Agree or disagree: Solar power is the key energy of the future. / Agree or disagree: Renewable energy sources should completely replace fossil fuels in the near future. / Agree or disagree: All nuclear power plants should be shut down.

コンセプトマップ

賛成バージョンを参考にスピーチの土台となるコンセプトマップを作ってみましょう。

Assertion

I think homeowners should install solar panels.

Reason 1

densely populated countries / produce clean energy

Reason 2

can save money

Example 1

- fossil fuels
- tackle global warming and environmental pollution

Example 2

- generate their own electricity
- sell surplus electricity

Assertion (Conclusion)

I support the idea of homeowners installing solar panels.

Speech | スピーチ

For 賛成バージョン 16-❶

A Assertion 主張

We are currently facing critical environmental problems, such as massive floods and wildfires around the world. This is mainly because burning fossil fuels has caused global warming. Therefore, I think homeowners should install solar panels to address this issue. I have two main reasons.

現在、世界中で大規模な洪水や山火事など、危機的な環境問題に直面しています。これは主に化石燃料の燃焼が地球温暖化を引き起こしているためです。そのため、私は住宅所有者がこの問題に対処するために太陽光パネルを設置すべきだと考えています。私には2つの主な理由があります。

R1 Reason 理由

First, densely populated countries need to take proactive steps toward producing clean energy.

第一に、人口密度の高い国は、クリーンエネルギーの生産に向けて積極的な対策を講じる必要があります。

E1 Example 例

For instance, Japan has a population of more than 120 million. Therefore, it is necessary to burn a significant amount of fossil fuels, such as coal, gas, and oil, to sustain modern comfortable lives for the Japanese. When these fuels are burned, they release greenhouse gases such as carbon dioxide. As a result, greenhouse gases remain in the atmosphere, trapping heat from the sun and warming the earth. However, homeowners can help tackle global warming and environmental pollution by installing solar panels.

例えば、日本は1億2,000万人以上の人口を抱えています。したがって、日本で現代の快適な生活を維持するためには、石炭やガス、石油などの化石燃料をかなりの量燃焼させる必要があります。これらの燃料を燃焼させると、二酸化炭素などの温室効果ガスが放出されます。その結果、温室効果ガスは大気中にとどまり、太陽からの熱を閉じ込めて地球を温めます。しかし、住宅所有者は太陽光パネルを設置することで、地球温暖化や環境汚染に対処するのに役立つことができます。

R2
Reason
理由

Second, homeowners can save money on electricity bills by installing solar panels.

次に、太陽光パネルを設置することで、住宅所有者は電気料金を節約することができます。

E2
Example
例

For example, homeowners could turn their private homes into small power stations with the installation of solar panels. Then, they can generate their own electricity with solar energy systems. In some cases, they can even sell surplus electricity back to the power companies. Moreover, homes equipped with solar panels tend to increase in value in the real estate market.

例えば、住宅所有者は太陽光エネルギーシステムで自分の家を小さな発電所に変えることができます。そして、太陽エネルギーを使用して自家発電することができます。場合によっては、余剰電力を電力会社に売ることさえできます。さらに、太陽光パネルを備えた家は不動産市場での価値が高まる傾向があります。

A
Assertion (Conclusion)
主張

In conclusion, homeowners have a responsibility to reduce their carbon footprint. Installing solar panels is an investment in a sustainable future, both environmentally and economically. Therefore, I support the idea of homeowners installing solar panels.

(245 words)

結論として、住宅所有者には自らの二酸化炭素排出量を減らす責任があります。太陽光パネルの設置は、環境的にも経済的にも持続可能な未来への投資です。そのため、私は住宅所有者が太陽光パネルを設置する考えを支持しています。

Against | 反対バージョン 16-❷

A
Assertion
主張

Solar panels are often regarded as a clean and renewable energy source. However, there are significant drawbacks to consider when it comes to installing them in homes. Therefore, I oppose homeowners installing solar panels in homes. I have two reasons.

太陽光パネルはしばしば、クリーンで再生可能なエネルギー源と見なされます。しかし、住まいに設置する際に考慮すべき重要な欠点があります。そのため、私は自宅に太陽光パネルを設置することに反対します。その理由は２つあります。

R1
Reason
理由

First, solar panels are costly to install, even with government financial aid.

まず、太陽光パネルの設置費用が高額です。政府の補助金を受けても、高額な投資が必要です。

E1
Example
例

For example, it can cost more than two million yen upfront for a regular home solar setup. It's a financial burden for many homeowners, especially for those with low incomes. Moreover, the lifespan of solar panels is approximately 20 years, so they need to be replaced every 20 years after this period. The initial financial burden can deter many homeowners from installing solar panels in homes. These significant costs make it impractical for homeowners.

例えば、通常の家庭用太陽光設備の設置には、最初に200万円以上かかることがあります。これは多くの住宅所有者にとって財政的な負担となります。特に低所得者にとってはなおさらです。また、太陽光パネルの寿命は約20年であり、この期間が過ぎると20年ごとに交換する必要があります。このような初期費用の負担が、多くの住宅所有者を太陽光パネルの設置から遠ざけています。これらの高額な費用は、住宅所有者にとって実用的ではありません。

R2
Reason
理由

Second, compared to nuclear energy and fossil fuels, solar panels lack stability in terms of generating electricity.

次に、原子力エネルギーや化石燃料と比較して、太陽光パネルは、発電するという点で安定性に欠けています。

E2
Example
例

For example, solar power generation relies heavily on weather conditions, particularly sunlight. It's evident that solar panels cannot produce electricity during the night or on cloudy days. Therefore, homeowners need to buy large-scale batteries to store energy for use at night. Batteries of these kinds cost more than one or two million yen. This is also extremely costly.

例えば、太陽光発電は主に天候条件、特に日光に依存しています。夜間や曇りの日に太陽光パネルが電気を作れないことは明らかです。そのため、住宅所有者は夜間に使用するために大規模なバッテリーを購入する必要があります。この種のバッテリーは200万円以上かかることもあります。これもまた非常に高価です。

A
Assertion
(Conclusion)
主張

In conclusion, solar panels appear to be a good solution for clean energy, but they are expensive to install and their energy output is dependent on the weather. Therefore, they are impractical and unpredictable for the production of electricity in homes. Until these issues are resolved, other energy options might be better for homeowners. For these reasons, I cannot support installing solar panels in homes.

(266 words)

結論として、太陽光パネルはクリーンなエネルギーのための良い解決策のように見えますが、設置費用が高額であり、そのエネルギー出力は天候に依存しています。したがって、家庭で電力を生産するには太陽光パネルは非現実的で、予測不可能と言えます。これらの問題が解決されるまで、住宅所有者は他のエネルギーを選択するほうが良いかもしれません。このような理由から、私は住まいに太陽光パネルを設置することを支持することができません。

Words and Phrases

For

□ face critical environmental problems	危機的な環境問題に直面する
□ massive floods and wildfires	大規模な洪水と山火事
□ burning fossil fuels	化石燃料の燃焼
□ cause global warming	地球の温暖化をもたらす
□ install solar panels	太陽光パネルを設置する
□ address this issue	この問題に対処する
□ densely populated countries	人口密度の高い国々
□ take proactive steps toward	～に対して積極的な対策を講じる
□ sustain modern comfortable lives	現代的で快適な生活を維持する
□ release greenhouse gases	温室効果ガスを放出する
□ carbon dioxide	二酸化炭素
□ atmosphere	大気
□ trap heat from the sun	太陽からの熱を閉じ込める
□ save money on electricity bills	電気代金を節約する
□ power station	発電所
□ with the installation of	～の設置で
□ generate electricity	電気を発電させる
□ sell surplus electricity	電力の余剰分を売る
□ be equipped with	～の設置で
□ real estate market	不動産市場
□ have a responsibility to	～をする責任がある
□ carbon footprint	カーボンフットプリント（個人・企業が日常的に出す二酸化炭素排出量）

Against

□ be regarded as	～と見なされる
□ clean and renewable energy source	クリーンで再生可能なエネルギー
□ drawback	欠点
□ when it comes to	～に関して言えば
□ costly	費用のかかる
□ government financial aid	政府の財政支援
□ upfront	先行投資で
□ initial financial burden	初期の財政負担
□ deter … from ～ing	…が～するのを阻止する
□ impractical	実現不可能な
□ compared to	～と比較すると
□ lack stability	安定性に欠ける
□ in terms of	～の観点で
□ rely heavily on	～に大きく依存する
□ buy large-scale batteries	大型電池を買う
□ store energy for use at night	夜間使用するためのエネルギーを蓄える
□ be a good solution for	～の良い解決法である
□ be dependent on	～に左右される
□ unpredictable	予測不可能な
□ resolve an issue	課題を解決する

Tips | 論理的に展開するためのキーフレーズ

理由を示す②

❶	This is because I am against capital punishment.	これは、私が死刑に反対しているからです。
❷	This is because I'm totally indifferent to this matter.	これは、私がこの件に関して、まったく無関心だからです。
❸	There are several reasons why I'm optimistic about the future.	私が将来について楽観的な理由がいくつかあります。
❹	I have several reasons for taking this stance.	このスタンスをとるいくつかの理由があります。
❺	That's the reason why I don't agree with this statement.	それが、私がこの意見に同意しない理由です。
❻	That's the reason why I can't back you up on this matter.	それが、私がこの件についてあなたを支持しない理由です。

強調を示す②

❶	Such damages are quite common, in particular, in car accidents.	そのような損害は極めて普通です。特に、自動車事故では。
❷	If there is something in particular you are looking for, please let us know.	もし特に何か探し物があれば、私たちにお知らせください。
❸	As a matter of fact, it's not easy to get detailed information about that.	実を言うと、それについての詳細な情報を入手するのは簡単じゃありません。
❹	Definitely, it's difficult to evaluate the risk of investing in the stock market.	間違いなく、株式市場に投資するリスクを評価するのは難しいです。
❺	Certainly, net sales are increasing every year.	確かに、毎年、純売上高が伸びています。
❻	It's evident that security cameras are a must to protect your property.	監視カメラは財産を保護するのに必須だということは明らかです。
❼	Apparently, the number of foreign tourists is higher than usual.	明らかに、外国人旅行者の数が、通常より多いです。

Should high school graduates take a gap year?

高校卒業後にギャップイヤーを取るべきか？

背景知識とヒント

東京大学もギャップイヤーを導入

ギャップイヤーとは、高校と大学、大学と大学院との間に学生が自主的に取得する休学期間のことです。イギリスで始まった習慣で、日本ではまだなじみのない制度ですが、欧米の大学では広く普及しています。

東京大学では、新入生の希望者を対象にして、1年間休学して社会経験を積む制度としてギャップイヤーを導入し、注目を集めました。自主的にボランティア活動、インターンシップ、留学、海外旅行などの目標や計画を立てて、チャレンジすることが求められ、特に内容には指定がありません。ギャップイヤーを取得することには、どんなメリットやデメリットがあるのでしょうか。

知っトク情報：頻出の関連トピック

Does a college education prepare people for work? / Are young adults today less independent than in the past?

コンセプトマップ

賛成バージョンを参考にスピーチの土台となるコンセプトマップを作ってみましょう。

Assertion

I agree with the idea of taking a gap year.

Reason 1

more free time to explore in depth

Reason 2

work experience

Example 1

- travel around the world
- meet a lot of new people
- try new things
- improve foreign language skills

Example 2

- work as part-time employees
- interns
- earn money
- people skills

Assertion (Conclusion)

I agree with the idea of taking a gap year.

Speech | スピーチ

For | 賛成バージョン 17-❶

A
Assertion
主張

It's popular for some students to take a year off before entering university. It's a good chance for them to become better prepared both academically and socially for university. Therefore, I agree with the idea of taking a gap year. I have two points to make.

大学に入学する前に1年間休むことが、一部の学生にとっては人気があります。大学生活に向けて学問的にも社会的にも、しっかりと準備を整える良いチャンスです。そのため、ギャップイヤーを取るという考えに賛成します。2つのポイントがあります。

R1
Reason
理由

Firstly, a gap year gives students more free time to explore anything they'd like in depth.

第一に、ギャップイヤーを取ると、学生は物事を深く追究する多くの自由時間が得られます。

E1
Example
例

For instance, they can travel around the world and learn about different countries and cultures while doing so. They can also meet a lot of new people as well as try new things. Moreover, students can learn to be more self-organized through planning their itinerary, keeping track of their money, taking care of their health, and so on while traveling. Besides, they can improve their foreign language skills.

例えば、世界一周旅行をして、さまざまな国や文化について学べます。また、新しいことに挑戦するだけではなく、多くの人との新しい出会いがあります。さらに、旅行中に旅程を計画したり、お金の出入りを把握したり健康管理をしたりすることなどを通して、より自立することを学べます。その上、外国語のスキルを向上させることもできます。

R2
Reason
理由

Secondly, a gap year can give students work experience. By working, they can broaden their horizons as well as develop their character through diligent work.

第二に、ギャップイヤーを通して、職業体験ができます。働くことで、勤労を通して人格を成長させるだけでなく、視野を広げることができます。

E2
Example
例

For instance, they can work as part-time employees, interns, and so forth. This hands-on work experience is a good way to explore difficult career choices for their future. In addition, they will learn the value of earning money and attain people skills.

例えば、パートタイム従業員やインターンなどとして働くことができます。この実務経験は、将来の難しいキャリア選択を検討するのに良い方法です。その上彼らは、お金を稼ぐことの意義や社会性を身につけます。

A
Assertion (Conclusion)
主張

In conclusion, they will have enough free time to further broaden their horizons by taking a gap year. From a more practical point of view, they can gain special experience that will stand out on a curriculum vitae or resume. Once again, I agree with the idea of taking a gap year.

(249 words)

結論として、学生は、ギャップイヤーを取ることにより、視野をさらに広げるための十分な自由時間がもてるでしょう。より実用的観点から見ると、履歴書で目立つ特別な経験を積むことができます。もう一度言いますが、ギャップイヤーを取るという考えに賛成です。

Against | 反対バージョン 17-❷

A
Assertion
主張

A gap year might be welcomed by some students. On the other hand, it would be rather frustrating for most students. I disagree with the idea of taking a gap year. I have two points to make.

ギャップイヤーは一部の学生に歓迎されるかもしれません。一方、ほとんどの学生に挫折感を与えることでしょう。ギャップイヤーを取るという考えには反対です。2つのポイントがあります。

R1
Reason
理由

Firstly, there is a risk in taking a gap year.

第一に、ギャップイヤーを取ることにはリスクがあります。

E1
Example
例

For example, knowledge rapidly fades. Students spent many years acquiring knowledge through continuous study at school. However, during a gap year, they may forget much of what they learned in high school. Plus, students could lose good study habits as well as the motivation to study. Moreover, they may fall both academically and socially behind their peers by taking a gap year.

例えば、知識は急速に消えていきます。学生は学校で継続した学習を通じて、何年もかけて知識を身につけてきました。しかし、ギャップイヤーの間に、高校で学んだことの多くを忘れるかもしれません。さらに、勉強するための意欲だけでなく、良い学習習慣をなくすかもしれません。しかも、ギャップイヤーを取ることで、学問的にも社会的にも同輩から遅れをとるかもしれません。

R2
Reason
理由

Secondly, taking a gap year may cause the loss of something precious.

第二に、ギャップイヤーを取ることで、何か貴重なものを失うかもしれません。

E2
Example
例

For example, students may waste time and money. They must pay their own travel expenses and hotel fees. Besides, if they aren't organized and don't have clear gap year goals, they may end up doing nothing but playing video games all year long. Time is fleeting and money is hard-earned.

例えば、学生は時間やお金を浪費します。旅行の費用やホテルの宿泊費を支払わなければなりません。さらに、もし彼らが計画的でなく、ギャップイヤーの明確な目標を持っていなければ、一年中テレビゲームだけで終わることになるかもしれません。時間はあっという間に過ぎます。そしてお金は苦労して稼ぐものです。

A
Assertion
(Conclusion)
主張

In conclusion, students don't have to rush to take a gap year right after high school. As an alternative, it's possible to be an intern, work in a foreign country, or study abroad during a long vacation, such as the summer holidays. Once again, I disagree with the idea of taking a gap year.

(226 words)

結論として、学生は高校卒業後すぐにあわててギャップイヤーを取る必要はありません。代替案として、夏休みなどの長期休暇期間中に、インターンをしたり、外国で働いたり、留学したりすることが可能です。もう一度言いますが、私はギャップイヤーを取ることに反対です。

Words and Phrases

051

For

□ take a year off	1年間休む
□ become better prepared both academically and socially	学問的に、社会的にもより良く準備が整う
□ explore ~ in depth	~を詳しく検討する
□ travel around the world	世界旅行をする
□ be self-organized	自立している
□ plan one's itinerary	~の旅程を立てる
□ keep track of money	お金の出入りを記録する、把握する
□ take care of one's health	健康を管理する
□ broaden one's horizons	視野を広げる、見聞を広める
□ develop one's character	人格を成長させる
□ diligent work	勤労、勤勉
□ part-time employee	パートタイム従業員
□ intern	インターン
□ hands-on work experience	実務経験
□ career choice for one's future	将来のキャリア選択
□ people skills	社会性、人との接し方
□ have enough free time to	~をする十分な自由時間がある
□ from a more practical point of view	より実用的観点から見ると
□ stand out on a curriculum vitae (CV)	履歴書で目立つ
□ resume	履歴書

Against

□ be welcomed by	~に歓迎される
□ frustrating	挫折感を起こさせる
□ there is a risk in	~にはリスクがある
□ rapidly fade	急速に衰える、消えていく
□ continuous	継続した
□ plus	さらに
□ lose good study habits	良い学習習慣をなくす
□ motivation	意欲、動機付け
□ fall behind	遅れをとる、脱落する
□ peer	同輩、同級生
□ travel expenses	旅費
□ hotel fees	ホテル宿泊料金
□ organized	系統的な、計画的な
□ end up ~ing	結局~になる
□ nothing but	~の他は何もない
□ all year long	一年中
□ time is fleeting	時間はあっという間に過ぎる
□ money is hard-earned	お金は苦労して稼ぐものである
□ rush to	大急ぎで~する

Tips | 論理的に展開するためのキーフレーズ

観点を示す②

❶ From a scientific point of view, it's important to review all the evidence we've acquired.	科学的な観点からすると、入手したすべての証拠を再検証することが大切です。
❷ From the point of view of consumers, inexpensive quality products are still lacking.	消費者の立場からすると、低価格で良質品がいまだに不足しています。
❸ From a broader point of view, it's a must to improve global security.	より広い視点から見れば、世界規模の安全保障を高めることが必要です。
❹ From another point of view, can you see this is all a trick?	観点を変えれば、これがすべてトリックだとわかりますか。
❺ From an artistic point of view, what is so great about Edward Munch?	芸術的観点からは、エドヴァルド・ムンクの何がすごいのですか？

代替を示す①

❶ Do you have an alternative solution to this problem?	この問題への代替案がありますか。
❷ Do you agree with a substitute proposal?	代替案に賛成ですか。
❸ Why do you need a backup plan?	なぜ代替案が必要なのですか。
❹ The ruling party doesn't have a good counter-plan to replace it.	与党には、その代わりとなるよい対抗策がないのです。
❺ It's better to consider an alternative approach.	代替方法を検討しておいたほうが良いです。

Speech 18

Should students study abroad?

海外留学するべきか？

背景知識とヒント

留学のメリットとデメリット

若者の留学離れが懸念される昨今、政府は留学を支援するためのさまざまな施策を講じています。「実践的な英語力が身につく」、「何事も１人でやることになるので自立する」、「異国文化を体験することで、国際理解を深め、視野を広げられる」など、海外留学にはもちろん多くのメリットがあります。

一方、デメリットとして、「日本と比べ、高い学費を払う」、「食生活や環境の変化による体調不良の可能性がある」、「コミュニケーション能力が低いと、孤独な生活が待っている」などが挙げられます。日本で十分な準備をせずに、メリットだけを期待して海外留学しても、成果が十分に得られない可能性があります。

知っトク情報：頻出の関連トピック

Should large companies in Japan make English their official language? / Do the strengths of multicultural societies outweigh the weaknesses? / Has the influence of Western values weakened Japanese identity?

コンセプトマップ

反対バージョンを参考にスピーチの土台となるコンセプトマップを作ってみましょう。

Assertion

I disagree with the idea of studying abroad.

Reason 1

feel stressed

Reason 2

there is no royal road to learning a language

Example 1

- meet new people
- new environment
- different cultures
- communication barriers
- become homesick

Example 2

- make great efforts
- improve English skills
- need time and effort

Assertion (Conclusion)

I disagree with the idea of studying abroad.

Speech | スピーチ

For | 賛成バージョン 18-❶

052

A
Assertion
主張

We can experience many things, whether successes or failures, through studying abroad. Such experience is priceless and can't be measured. Through it, we can experience success and failure and learn how to effectively deal with both. I agree with the idea of studying abroad. I have two points to make.

成功しても失敗しても、海外留学によってたくさんのことが経験できます。そのような経験は貴重で、かけがえのないものです。留学を通して成功や失敗を経験し、その両方に効果的に対処する方法を学ぶことができます。留学するという考えに賛成です。2つのポイントがあります。

R1
Reason
理由

First, it's easier and faster to learn a foreign language while abroad because we are immersed in the language.

第一に、その国の言語にどっぷり漬かるので、留学中は外国語の習得がずっと簡単で早いです。

E1
Example
例

For example, during a homestay in the U.S.A., we are required to interact with our host family in English. Moreover, we need to use the target language for every task from A to Z.

例えば、アメリカでのホームステイ期間には、ホストファミリーと英語で交流することが求められます。さらに、すべての課題に最初から最後まで英語を使わなければなりません。

R2
Reason 理由

Second, we can broaden our horizons when studying abroad.

第二に、留学中に視野を広げられます。

E2
Example 例

For example, we can interact with people of different backgrounds and perspectives from our own. Through such interaction, we can then form lasting friendships. As a result, we will become more internationally open-minded people.

例えば、自分とは違う背景や視点を持つ人と交流できます。そのような交流を通して、長く続く友情を築けます。結果として、偏見のない国際人になるでしょう。

A
Assertion (Conclusion) 主張

To sum up, we can broaden our horizons through the formation of long-lasting international friendships. And our overseas experience will lead to more job opportunities because of our acquired English abilities and our more cosmopolitan way of thinking. In addition, we can add our study abroad experience to our resume. This is why I agree with the idea of studying abroad.

(207 words)

要約すれば、長く続く国境を越えた友情を通して、視野を広げることができます。そして、海外での経験は、獲得した英語力や国際感覚のおかげで、より多くの雇用の機会につながるでしょう。さらに、海外経験を履歴書に加えることができます。こういうわけで、留学するという考えに賛成です。

Against | 反対バージョン 18-❷

053

A
Assertion
主張

Studying abroad is tough. We don't have the safety net of our family nearby. Without great effort, we are bound to stumble. I disagree with the idea of studying abroad. I have two points to make.

海外留学は厳しいです。近くに住む自分の家族という、セーフティネットがありません。努力しなければ、失敗する運命にあります。海外留学するという考えに反対です。2つのポイントがあります。

R1
Reason
理由

First, we feel stressed while studying abroad.

第一に、留学中にストレスを感じます。

E1
Example
例

For example, we have to meet new people in a new environment. Moreover, we will be exposed to different cultures and face communication barriers. Furthermore, we may not be good enough to make ourselves understood in English. As a result, we'll become homesick and then lose our motivation to study.

例えば、新しい環境で新しい人に会わなくてはなりません。さらに、異文化にさらされ、コミュニケーションの壁にぶつかります。また、英語で自分を理解してもらうには能力不足かもしれません。結果としてホームシックになり、学ぶ意欲をなくしてしまいます。

R2
Reason
理由

Second, there is no royal road to learning a language. In other words, studying abroad does not mean we learn English by magic.

第二に、言葉を習得するのに王道はありません。言い換えると、海外留学は、魔法のように英語を習得することを意味するわけではありません。

E2
Example
例

Let me show you an example of two students who studied abroad. One made great efforts and returned with greatly improved English skills, while the other did not. Even if we study abroad, we will not improve our English skills unless we try to communicate in English. Simply stated language learning requires time and effort.

例えば、2人の学生が1年間海外に留学しました。1人は大変な努力をして、英語がかなり上達して帰ってきました。もう1人は、努力も上達もしませんでした。たとえ海外留学しても、英語でコミュニケーションしようとしなければ、英語力は向上しません。簡単にいうと、言語を学ぶには時間と努力を必要とするのです。

A
Assertion (Conclusion)
主張

To sum up, there are also a number of key disadvantages we should keep in mind. Severe homesickness is a risk, and without effort, foreign language learning will fail. Besides, it costs a lot of money to study abroad. This is why I disagree with the idea of studying abroad.

(219 words)

要約すれば、肝に銘じておかなければならない多くの重要なデメリットがあるのです。重度のホームシックはリスクです。努力なしには外国語習得は失敗します。さらに留学するには、たくさんの費用がかかります。こういうわけで、海外留学するという考えに反対です。

Words and Phrases

For

□ whether successes or failures	成功しようが、失敗しようが
□ priceless	貴重な
□ can't be measured	ものさしでは測れない、かけがえのない
□ experience success and failure	成功や失敗の体験をする
□ effectively deal with	効果的に対処する
□ be immersed in	～にどっぷり漬かる、浸る
□ be required to	～することが求められる
□ interact with	～と情報を交換する、～と対話する
□ for every task from A to Z	すべての課題
□ broaden one's horizons	～の視野を広げる
□ with people of different backgrounds and perspectives	違う背景や視点を持った人々と
□ form lasting friendships	いつまでも続く友情を築く
□ open-minded	心の広い、偏見のない
□ long-lasting international friendships	長く続く国境を越えた友情
□ job opportunity	雇用の機会
□ cosmopolitan way of thinking	国際感覚
□ add ~ to …	～を … に加える
□ resume = curriculum vitae (CV)	履歴書
□ this is why	こういうわけで～

Against

□ tough	つらい、厳しい
□ have the safety net of	～の安全網を持つ
□ without great effort	苦労せず、努力しないで
□ be bound to stumble	つまずく運命にある、失敗する運命にある
□ feel stressed	ストレスを感じる
□ be exposed to different cultures	異文化に触れる
□ face communication barriers	コミュニケーションの壁にぶつかる、直面する
□ make oneself understood in English	英語で自分を理解させる、英語が通じる
□ become homesick	ホームシックになる
□ lose one's motivation to	～する意欲をなくす
□ There is no royal road to learning a language.	言語を習得するのに王道なし。
□ in other words	言い換えると
□ simply stated	簡単にいうと
□ require time and effort	時間と努力を要する
□ there are a number of key disadvantages	たくさんの重要なデメリットがある
□ keep in mind	留意する、肝に銘じる
□ severe homesickness	重度のホームシック
□ besides	さらに

Tips | 論理的に展開するためのキーフレーズ

追加を示す②

1	I lost my wallet in London. On top of that, I got lost there.	ロンドンで財布をなくしました。その上、そこで道に迷いました。
2	In big cities, there are lots of things to do like going to a concert and a musical. Besides, there are lots of chances to work.	大都市では、コンサートやミュージカルに行くなどたくさんの楽しみがあります。さらに働く機会が多いです。
3	In big cities, trains are crowded. Moreover, there is less nature there.	大都市では、電車が混んでいます。さらに自然が少ないです。
4	Casinos create places for businesses like hotels and shopping malls. In addition, casinos attract lots of tourists from all over the world.	カジノは、ホテル、ショッピングモールなど働く場所を創ります。さらに、カジノは、世界中からたくさんの旅行者を引き寄せます。

言い換えを示す②

1	The population of Japan is declining; that is to say, there is a possibility that the Japanese economy will slow down.	日本の人口は、減少しています。つまり、日本経済が減速する可能性があります。
2	I am so busy I don't have any free time, I mean, I want to cut my workload.	忙しくて、自由時間がとれません。つまり、仕事量を減らしたいです。
3	This gymnasium is so hot and humid that we can't move anymore. To put it simply, we need to cancel all the activities today.	この体育館はあまりに蒸し暑いので、もう動けません。簡単に言うと、今日の活動をすべてキャンセルする必要があります。
4	If other stores change their prices, we will adjust our prices promptly. More simply put, prices and availability can change in the blink of an eye.	もし他の店が価格を変えたら、すぐに価格を合わせます。簡単にいうと、値段と納期は、瞬時にして変わります。
5	Personal data is confidential. More simply put, personal data including name, address, telephone number, and email address will only be used to contact you.	個人情報は機密扱いです。簡単にいうと、氏名、住所、電話番号やメールアドレスを含む個人情報は、お客様と連絡を取るためだけに使われます。

Speech 19

Should university tuition be made free?

大学の授業料は無料にすべきか？

背景知識とヒント

大学無償化は、日本でも必要なのか？

日本では2025年度から、扶養する子どもが3人以上いる世帯に対して、大学の授業料などを無償化する方針が定められました。すでに年収380万円未満の世帯では授業料を減免するなどの制度がありますが、少子化対策の一環として、対象世帯に所得制限を設けない大幅な拡充です。

少子化対策は喫緊の課題であり、政府内では授業料の無償化が先行していますが、大学の質の低下の可能性など、本来十分に議論されるべき点が議論されていないようです。

知っトク情報：頻出の関連トピック

Should university education be free for everyone? / Agree or disagree: A university degree is necessary for success. / Does university education prepare young people for real life? / Should English be included in university entrance exams in Japan?

コンセプトマップ

反対バージョンを参考にスピーチの土台となるコンセプトマップを作ってみましょう。

Assertion

I disagree with making university tuition free.

Reason 1

Japan has a large debt

Reason 2

the quality of education would get worse

Example 1

- debt is 1,100 trillion yen
- 9 million yen per person

Example 2

- anybody could enter such universities
- quality of education

Assertion (Conclusion)

I disagree with making university tuition free.

Speech | スピーチ

For | 賛成バージョン 19-❶

055

A
Assertion
主張

University education has become very important in life today. Certain positions within each field require certain qualifications. In other words, without a university degree, we will not be qualified for particular jobs. However, some people don't have enough money to pay tuition for higher education and give up on their dream of advancing to university. Therefore, I agree with making university tuition free. I have two points to make.

大学教育は、今日、人生において大変重要になってきています。それぞれの分野における特定のポジションには、特定の資格が求められます。言い換えれば、大学の学位がなければ、特定の仕事につく資格がないのです。しかし、高等教育の学費を払うことができずに大学へ進学するという夢を諦める人がいます。そのため、私は大学の無償化について賛成です。2つのポイントがあります。

R1
Reason
理由

First, free university education means advancing the world for all.

第一に、大学の無償化はみんなのために世界を前進させることを意味します。

E1
Example
例

For example, some people give up advancing to higher education due to their financial situation. Among such people, there may be some with exceptional talent, but they don't have the opportunity to develop these talents further at university. By going on to higher education, they have the chance to fulfill their potential. Therefore, increasing access to higher education enhances the potential for further improvement and innovation.

例えば、経済的な事情で高等教育に進学することを諦める人がいます。そんな人の中には、たぐいまれな才能を持っている人がいるかもしれません。しかし彼らには、これらの才能を大学で開花させるチャンスがないのです。高等教育へ進むことで、彼らはその可能性を発揮するチャンスが得られます。そのため、高等教育を受ける機会が増えれば、さらなる進歩や革新の可能性が広がるのです。

R2
Reason
理由

Second, free university education leads to equality among people.

第二に、大学の無償化は人々に公平さをもたらします。

E2
Example
例

For example, the tuition in the faculty of literature at many universities costs an estimated 1 million yen per year. Even some people who are accepted at a university can't afford it. For them and many others, the present system is unequal and unfair. If free university education is realized, whether rich or poor, students can concentrate on their studies in depth. As a result, more and more people will be able to attain whatever academic credentials they desire.

例えば、多くの大学の文学部の教育費は、1年につきおよそ100万円かかります。大学に合格した人でさえ、払う余裕がない人がいます。彼らや多くの他の人にとって、現在の制度は不平等で不公正です。もし大学無償化が実現されれば、お金のある人もない人も、学生は学問に徹底的に集中できます。結果として、より多くの人が、必要とするどんな学位でも取得することができるでしょう。

A
Assertion (Conclusion)
主張

To conclude, with free university education, students will get equal opportunities to pursue higher level studies. More and more talented people will work toward further improvement and innovation. This, in turn, will result in the rise of competitiveness and help to build an even stronger nation. Therefore, I agree with making university tuition free.

(287 words)

結論として、大学の無償化で、学生はより高いレベルの学問を追求する平等なチャンスを得ることができます。ますます多くの才能ある人が、さらなる進歩と革新に向けて働けるでしょう。このことが競争力を生み、さらに強い国を作ることにつながっていくのです。そのため、大学の無償化には賛成です。

Against | 反対バージョン 19-❷

056

A
Assertion
主張

University tuition fees are escalating. The policy of tuition-free university has already been agreed upon. It is targeted at households with three or more children, with the aim of increasing the number of households with many children. The content of the policy does not extend to all students. Therefore, I disagree with making university tuition free. I have two points to make.

大学の授業料がだんだん上昇しています。授業料無料の政策はすでに合意されています。この政策は、3人以上の子どもがいる世帯を対象としており、多子世帯の数を増やすことを目的としています。この政策の内容はすべての学生に適用されるわけではありません。したがって、私は大学の授業料を無料にすることは反対です。私の意見は次の2つです。

R1
Reason
理由

First, Japan is burdened with a large debt.

第一に、日本は巨額の負債を背負っています。

E1
Example
例

For example, the national debt in Japan is about 1.1 quadrillion yen. This means the government has a debt of over 9 million yen per person. If university tuition were made free, the budget of Japan would most likely become extremely strained. Japan has no reliable source of revenue for the proposal at present. The remaining potential source of finance is taxes and similar sources. Therefore, if we introduced a tuition-free university system, such expenditures would increase greatly and people, especially younger adults, would suffer from increasing economic burdens.

例えば、日本の国債は、およそ1,100兆円です。これは、国民1人当たり900万円を超える借金が政府にあるということです。もし大学の授業料が無償化されれば、日本の予算は、十中八九、大きくひずみます。日本には、現在その提案のための確実な財源がありません。残る可能性のある財源は税金や類似の収入源です。そのため、もし大学の無償化制度を導入すれば、こうした支出は大幅に増加し、人々、特に若い成人はさらなる経済的負担で苦しむでしょう。

R2
Assertion 主張

Second, the quality of higher education would get worse.

第二に、高等教育の質が悪化します。

E2
Reason 理由

For example, even now, there are universities that fall short of their recruiting targets. Anybody who has a minimal academic level can enter such universities. If higher education were free, students would likely take their university studies less seriously. As a result, there would be a drastic drop in academic levels and quality of education. Besides, not all high school graduates necessarily advance to university.

例えば、今でさえ、定員割れを起こしている大学があります。わずかな学力があれば誰でも、そのような大学に進学することが可能です。もし高等教育が無償化になれば、学生は、おそらく大学の学問をあまり真剣に受け止めないでしょう。結果として、学問のレベルや教育の質がかなり低下することになります。さらに、すべての高校の卒業生が必ずしも大学へ進学するわけではないのです。

A
Assertion (Conclusion) 主張

To conclude, it is not reasonable for Japan to make university education free for everyone considering the many disadvantages mentioned earlier. Therefore, I disagree with making university tuition free.

(262 words)

結論として、日本にとって、先に述べた多くの欠点を考慮すると、大学教育を無償化することは合理的でありません。そのため、大学の無償化に反対です。

Words and Phrases

For

□ require a certain qualification	ある資格を必要とする
□ university degree	大学の学位
□ be qualified for	～のための資格がある；能力がある
□ pay tuition	授業料を払う
□ advance to university	大学へ進学する
□ financial situation	財政状態、家計の状況
□ exceptional talent	たぐいまれな才能
□ enhance the potential for	～の可能性を高める
□ lead to equality	公平さにつながる
□ faculty of literature	文学部
□ cost an estimated 1 million yen	およそ100万円かかる
□ can't afford	～する余裕がない
□ whether rich or poor	お金のある人もない人も
□ concentrate on	～に集中する
□ in depth	徹底的に；すっかり
□ attain academic credentials	学位を取る
□ pursue higher level studies	より高いレベルの学問を追求する
□ competitiveness	競争力

Against

□ escalate	段階的に増大する
□ household with three or more children	3人以上の子どもがいる世帯
□ extend to ～	～にまで及ぶ
□ be burdened with a large debt	巨額の負債を背負う
□ national debt	国債
□ 1.1 quadrillion (=1,100 trillion) yen	1,100兆円
□ have a debt of over 9 million yen per person	1人当たり900万円を超える借金がある
□ most likely	十中八九
□ extremely strained	大きくひずんだ、苦しい
□ have no reliable source of revenue for	～のための確実な財源がない
□ remaining potential	残る可能性のある
□ source of finance	資金源
□ tuition-free	授業料が無料の
□ increasing economic burdens	拡大する経済的負担
□ a minimal academic level	最低限の学力
□ take ～ less seriously	～をあまり真剣に受け取らない
□ a drastic drop in	～における低下、激減
□ not all ～	すべてが～というわけではない
□ it's not reasonable for … to ～	…が～するのは合理的でない、妥当でない

Tips | 論理的に展開するためのキーフレーズ

原因を示す

❶	Due to legalizing casinos, new businesses and more jobs will be created.	カジノの合法化により、新しい事業や仕事が創出されるでしょう。
❷	Due to flight delays, many passengers may miss their connection to their next destination.	飛行機が遅れたため、多くの乗客が次の目的地への乗り継ぎ便に間に合わないかもしれません。
❸	I made a terrible mistake because of a lack of experience.	経験不足のため、ひどい間違いをしました。
❹	It was on account of traffic congestion that I missed my flight to New York.	ニューヨーク行きの飛行機に乗り遅れたのは、交通渋滞のせいでした。
❺	Owing to overeating, people are at high risk of becoming obese.	食べすぎのため、人は肥満になるリスクが高いです。

部分否定を示す

❶	Not all students believe such a story.	すべての学生がそんな話を信じているわけではありません。
❷	Not all people behave the same way.	すべての人が、同じように振る舞うわけではありません。
❸	Winning the lottery doesn't necessarily bring happiness.	宝くじに当たることが、必ずしも幸せをもたらすとは限りません。
❹	I don't necessarily agree with you, but I support your decision.	必ずしもあなたに賛成していませんが、あなたの決意は支持します。
❺	Even the richest people can't always get what they want in life.	金持ちでさえ、人生で欲しいものがいつも手に入るわけではありません。

Is the organ donation system necessary?

臓器提供制度は必要か？

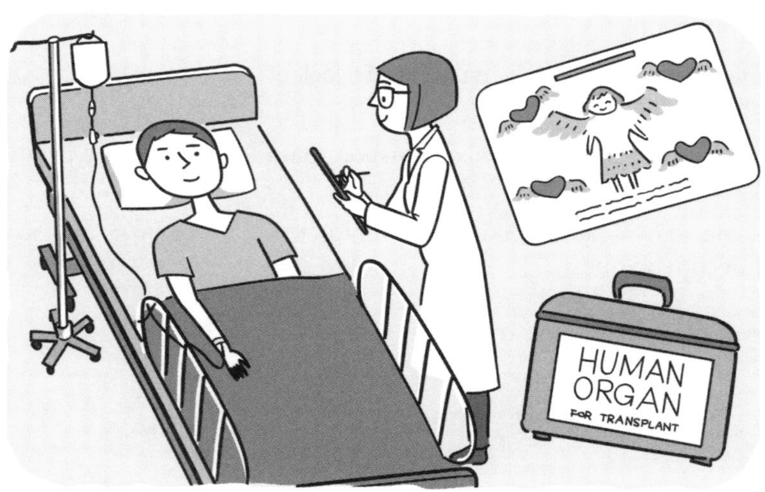

背景知識とヒント

臓器提供の光と影

臓器移植とは、事故や病気のため臓器が十分に機能しなくなった患者に対して、脳死状態や心停止後の患者の健康な臓器を移植する医療行為です。

臓器提供は、本人の臓器提供意思表示カードと家族の承諾があれば、基本的に可能です。しかし、脳死状態では心臓が鼓動しており、体温もあるため、そのような状態を死としてみなすことに異論を唱える人もいます。また、心停止後の移植でも、遺族にとっては簡単に受け入れられることではありません。

知っトク情報：頻出の関連トピック

Should organ transplants be made more available in Japan? / Would I be willing to donate my organs after death?

コンセプトマップ

賛成バージョンを参考にスピーチの土台となるコンセプトマップを作ってみましょう。

Assertion

I strongly believe that the organ donation system is necessary.

Reason 1

saves lives or improves the quality of life

Reason 2

contributes to medical advancement

Example 1

- donate liver, kidneys, heart and lungs

Example 2

- essential for educating medical students

Assertion (Conclusion)

I strongly believe that the organ donation system is necessary.

Speech | スピーチ

058

For | 賛成バージョン 20-❶

A Assertion 主張

Over hundreds of thousands of people are on the waiting list for an organ transplant. Some of these people can be saved if we register as organ donors. Therefore, I strongly believe that the organ donation system is necessary. I have two points to make.

数十万人を超える人々が、臓器移植のために順番を待っています。もし臓器のドナー登録をすれば、救われる人がいます。そのため、臓器提供制度は必要だと強く思います。2つのポイントがあります。

R1 Reason 理由

Firstly, donating organs can save lives or improve the quality of life for a number of people who need organs. It's important to note that many organs can be donated.

第一に、臓器提供すれば、臓器を必要としている多くの人の命を救ったり、生活の質を向上させたりできます。多くの臓器が提供できると気づくことが重要です。

E1 Example 例

For instance, we can donate our liver, kidneys, pancreas, heart, and lungs. Not only that, we can also donate body tissues like skin, heart valves, and so on. Organs are used for people with serious diseases and defects. As for tissues, they are used for people with severe burns and such.

例えば、肝臓、腎臓、膵臓（すいぞう）、心臓や肺を提供できます。それだけでなく、肌や心臓の弁などのような体内組織も提供できます。臓器は重大な病気や不具合がある人に用いられます。組織は、ひどいやけどなどを負った人に用いられます。

R2
Reason 理由

Secondly, whole-body donation greatly contributes to medical advancement.

第二に、献体は医療の進歩に貢献します。

E2
Example 例

For example, medical schools are in need of cadavers. Cadavers are essential for educating medical students. In other words, having whole-bodies to examine may help medical students to become great doctors in the future.

例えば、医学部には解剖用の遺体が必要です。解剖用の遺体は医学生の教育に欠かせません。言い換えると、献体を調べてもらうことで、医学生が将来偉大な医師になるのに貢献するかもしれません。

A
Assertion (Conclusion) 主張

To sum up, organ donation can save precious lives. Moreover, whole-body donation can greatly assist medical students during their training period. For these reasons, I strongly believe that the organ donation system is necessary.

(202 words)

要約すれば、臓器提供は貴重な命を救います。さらに献体すれば、医学生の研修期間に大いに役立ちます。これらの理由で、臓器提供制度が必要だと強く思います。

Against | 反対バージョン 20-❷

059

A
Assertion
主張

Almost anyone can become a donor if they meet certain criteria, but organ donation is a controversial subject and carries negative effects. Therefore, I oppose the notion that the organ donation system is necessary. I have two points to make.

ほとんど誰でも、ある基準を満たしていればドナーになれます。しかし、臓器提供は物議を醸すテーマであり、よくない影響をもたらします。そのため、臓器提供制度が必要だという考えに反対です。2つのポイントがあります。

R1
Reason
理由

Firstly, the idea of a deceased family member's organs being removed can traumatize their families. This is because the majority of donations only take place after someone who is a registered donor has an untimely and early death. It's a big concern.

第一に、亡くなった家族の臓器が摘出されるということは、その家族にトラウマを与える可能性があります。というのも、臓器提供の大半は、ドナー登録をしている人が早すぎる死を遂げた後にしか行われないからです。これは大きな懸念事項です。

E1
Example
例

For example, car accidents or other disasters can be both sudden and shocking for families. In such cases, families may be too overwhelmed to consider organ donation. At this time, the families of the deceased are often completely shocked and traumatized. Families may feel further distress and emotional pain even if they already know that using their organs for donation is what their family member would have wanted.

例えば、交通事故やその他の災害は、家族にとって突然かつ、衝撃的なことです。このような場合、遺族はあまりに打ちのめされて臓器提供を考えることができないかもしれません。この時、遺族は完全にショックを受け、心に傷を負っていることが多いのです。臓器提供は本人が望んでいたことだとわかっていても、家族はさらなる悲しみや精神的苦痛を感じるかもしれません。

R2
Reason
理由

Secondly, all surgery carries the risk of medical error, infection and even death.

第二に、すべての手術には、医療ミス、感染症や死にいたるリスクがあります。

E2
Example
例

For example, people sometimes donate organs, such as a kidney or a portion of a liver, lung, intestine or pancreas, while they are still alive. Both the donor and the recipient are at risk here. What's more, there are cases where serious complication of organ rejection by a recipient's body happens a few minutes after a transplant, or even a few weeks to months later. Even with careful preparation, there is always some risk during and after surgery.

例えば、生存中に腎臓、肝臓の一部、肺、腸や膵臓などの臓器を提供することもあります。ドナーにもレシピエントにもリスクがあります。さらに、手術の数分後や数週間、数か月後に、臓器の提供を受けた人に臓器拒絶反応の深刻な合併症が起こる場合があります。周到な準備をしても、手術中、手術後に絶えずリスクがあるのです。

A
Assertion (Conclusion)
主張

To sum up, the organ donation system could cause recently bereaved family members to be further traumatized and upset. What's worse, there is the risk of medical error and death. For these reasons, I oppose the notion that the organ donation system is necessary.

(285 words)

要約すれば、臓器提供制度は遺族にさらなるトラウマと動揺を与える可能性があります。さらに悪いことに、医療ミスや死のリスクがあります。これらの理由から、臓器ドナーとして登録することに反対です。

Words and Phrases

For

□ on the waiting list	順番を待って；キャンセル待ちで
□ organ transplant	臓器移植
□ organ donation system	臓器提供制度
□ I strongly believe that	～を確信する
□ improve the quality of life	生活の質を向上させる
□ a number of people	たくさんの人
□ it's important to note that	～だということに気づくことは重要である
□ liver, kidneys, pancreas, heart and lungs	肝臓、腎臓、膵臓、心臓と肺
□ body tissue	体内組織
□ heart valves	心臓の弁
□ disease and defect	病気や欠陥
□ severe burns	ひどいやけど
□ and such	（具体例に続けて）など
□ contribute to medical advancement	医学の進歩に貢献する
□ be in need of	～を必要としている
□ cadaver	解剖用の遺体
□ medical student	医学生
□ to sum up	要約すれば
□ during one's training period	研修期間に

Against

□ meet certain criteria	ある基準を満たす
□ controversial subject	物議を醸すテーマ
□ (a) deceased family member	亡くなった家族（の一員）
□ remove an organ	臓器を摘出する
□ traumatize	～に精神的ショックを与える
□ take place	（事故などが）起こる
□ registered donor	登録ドナー
□ feel distress (at)	（～に）心を痛める
□ emotional pain	心の痛み
□ medical error	医療ミス
□ infection	感染症
□ a portion of	～の一部
□ intestine or pancreas	腸や膵臓
□ recipient	レシピエント（臓器移植を受ける人）
□ serious complication	深刻な合併症
□ organ rejection	臓器拒絶反応
□ transplant	移植
□ after surgery	手術後

Tips | 論理的に展開するためのキーフレーズ

観点を示す③

1	As for adults, it's important to apply sunscreen lotion to exposed areas of skin.	大人に関しては、肌の露出部分に日焼け止めローションを塗ることが大切です。
2	Concerning this topic, we should discuss how to handle this in more detail at the next meeting.	このトピックに関しては、扱い方について、次の会議で詳しく議論すべきです。
3	With respect to your proposal, we are sorry to say that we can't agree to it.	あなたの提案については、賛成できないと言わざるを得ません。
4	Regarding cooking, he doesn't stick to procedure if tastes are good.	料理に関しては、もし味がよければ、彼は手順にこだわりません。
5	Speaking of spring, what's the weather like here?	春と言えば、ここはどんな天気ですか。

問題を示す②

1	Air pollution used to be a big concern in China.	中国では、空気汚染は以前大きな関心事でした。
2	Another concern is that tipping at restaurants is not a common practice for Japanese.	もう１つの懸念は、レストランでのチップ制は、日本人にとって習慣化されていないことです。
3	Food safety is another big concern.	食の安全はもう１つの大きな関心事です。
4	I worry about the tax payment on the assets after I inherit from my father.	父の遺産を相続後、税の支払いを心配しています。
5	I'm deeply concerned about the result of medical checkup.	健康診断の結果について、憂慮しています。
6	I'm concerned that no effective method is available to control black hackers.	悪意あるハッカーをコントロールする効果的な方法がないことを懸念しています。

Should a smoking ban be introduced?

禁煙を推進すべきか?

背景知識とヒント

禁煙をめぐり、議論が活発化

第 32 回夏季オリンピック競技会が東京で開催されることをきっかけの 1 つとして、飲食店や駅、空港構内などの原則禁煙化をめぐる議論が活発になり、東京都受動喫煙防止条例が施行されました。他人の吸っているタバコの煙を吸ってしまう受動喫煙を防ぐことが、大きな目的です。

ファミリーレストランや居酒屋でも、条件に合った喫煙所がなければタバコを吸うことができず、喫煙者の肩身はますます狭くなっています。喫煙者の喫煙する権利や、非喫煙者の受動喫煙を避ける権利などについて、十分に議論する必要があります。

知っトク情報：頻出の関連トピック

Should cigarette advertisements be banned? / Agree or disagree: Alcohol is more damaging to society than tobacco. / Should the sale of tobacco products be made illegal? / Is the Japanese healthcare system a good model for other countries?

コンセプトマップ 反対バージョンを参考にスピーチの土台となるコンセプトマップを作ってみましょう。

Assertion

I disagree with introducing a smoking ban.

……………………………………

……………………………………

……………………………………

Reason 1

smoking is legal

……………………………………

……………………………………

……………………………………

Reason 2

there are some other harmful activities

……………………………………

……………………………………

……………………………………

Example 1

- prohibited in certain areas
- medical facilities
- school grounds
- government offices

……………………………………

……………………………………

……………………………………

Example 2

- drinking alcohol
- eating fatty foods

……………………………………

……………………………………

……………………………………

Assertion (Conclusion)

I disagree with introducing a smoking ban.

……………………………………

……………………………………

……………………………………

Speech | スピーチ

For | 賛成バージョン 21-❶

A
Assertion
主張

Every year, a large number of people die from smoking-related diseases, such as lung cancer, heart disease, and stroke. Therefore, I agree with introducing a smoking ban. I have two points to make.

毎年、非常にたくさんの人が、肺ガン、心臓病、脳卒中などの喫煙関連の病気で亡くなっています。そのため、禁煙条例を導入することに賛成です。２つのポイントがあります。

R1
Reason
理由

First, a smoking ban is good for nonsmokers.

第一に、禁煙条例は非喫煙者にとって良いことです。

E1
Example
例

For example, now people have to smoke in designated areas in public places like restaurants, parks, shopping malls, and streets. However, this smoke is more harmful and dangerous for nonsmokers because they inhale the smoke directly without a cigarette filter. As such, smoking can be detrimental to the health of nonsmokers. Nonsmokers can't feasibly avoid such harmful smoke if people smoke around them. Furthermore, smoke may smell good to smokers; nonsmokers, however, can't stand the smell of smoke.

例えば現在、レストラン、公園、ショッピングモールや道路のような公共の場所では、指定された場所でタバコを吸わなくてはいけません。しかし、非喫煙者はタバコのフィルターを通さずに直接煙を吸うことになるので、この煙は非常に有害で危険です。そのため、喫煙は非喫煙者の健康にとって致命傷となるのです。もし、喫煙者が周りでタバコを吸えば、非喫煙者はその有害な煙をうまく避けられません。さらに煙は、喫煙者にとってはよい香りがするかもしれませんが、非喫煙者はその煙の臭いに耐えられないのです。

R2
Reason 理由

Second, a smoking ban is a cost-saving policy.

第二に、禁煙条例は、経費節約の政策です。

E2
Example 例

For example, smoking itself is an expensive habit. A pack of cigarettes costs about 600 yen. If you smoke a pack of cigarettes every day, it will cost you 219,000 yen in one year. A smoking ban would also encourage smokers to quit smoking. At the same time, it would discourage nonsmokers from starting to smoke. Saved money can be spent on more healthy habits.

例えば、喫煙はお金がかかる習慣です。1箱のタバコは約600円します。もし毎日1箱のタバコを吸えば、1年で21万9千円かかります。禁煙条例は喫煙者の禁煙を促すことになるでしょう。同時に、非喫煙者が喫煙を始めるのを抑制することにもなるでしょう。節約したお金は、より健康的な習慣に使えます。

A
Assertion (Conclusion) 主張

In conclusion, while smokers may insist on the right to smoke, they violate the rights of nonsmokers when doing so in public. What's worse, they can endanger the health of nonsmokers. Therefore, I agree with introducing a smoking ban.

(231 words)

結論として、喫煙者はタバコを吸う権利を主張するかもしれませんが、彼らは人前でタバコを吸って、非喫煙者の権利を侵害しています。さらに悪いことには、非喫煙者の健康も危険にさらしているのです。そのため、禁煙条例を導入することに賛成です。

Against 反対バージョン 21-❷

062

A
Assertion
主張

Smoking is harmful and unpleasant for nonsmokers. However, it's not acceptable to deny smokers' rights. Therefore, I disagree with introducing a smoking ban. I have two points to make.

喫煙は非喫煙者にとって有害で不快です。しかし、喫煙者の権利を無視することは容認できません。そのため、禁煙条例を導入することに反対です。2つのポイントがあります。

R1
Reason
理由

First, smoking is legal in general and yet it is prohibited to smoke in many places.

第一に、一般的に喫煙は合法であるのにかかわらず、多くの場所では喫煙が禁じられています。

E1
Example
例

For example, smoking is prohibited by law in certain designated areas, like on the premises of medical facilities, school grounds from the elementary to senior high level, and government offices, to name a few. Smokers who violate the law get fined. Why do smokers have to face such difficulties?

例えば、喫煙は、ある指定された場所では法律によって禁止されています。2、3例を挙げれば、医療施設の敷地内、小学校から高校などの学校の敷地や役所などです。法律を破る喫煙者は、罰金を科せられます。どうして喫煙者は、そのように苦労しなければいけないのでしょうか。

R2
Reason
理由

Second, there are some other harmful activities that have not been banned or have only been limited in some small way.

第二に、禁止されていないか、あるいはわずかな制限にとどまっている有害な行為がいくつか他にもあります。

E2
Example
例

For example, drinking alcohol, eating fatty foods and so forth are also harmful if done in excess. It's okay to drink alcohol on public transportation. As for the intake of high cholesterol or fatty foods, it can lead to life-threatening diseases such as heart disease, obesity, and other critical diseases. However, such foods are not designated as harmful. Why do smokers have to be treated as if they are committing an illegal act?

例えば、飲酒や脂っこい食事なども、限度を過ぎれば有害です。公共交通機関での飲酒は認められています。高コレステロールや脂っこいものの摂取に関しては、心臓病、肥満や他の重症疾患などの命に関わる病気につながります。しかし、それらの食べ物は、有害なものとして指定されていません。なぜ喫煙者は、まるで違法行為を犯しているかのような扱いを受けなければならないのでしょうか。

A
Assertion (Conclusion)
主張

In conclusion, regulations and contradictory laws make it difficult for smokers to find a place to enjoy their legal habit. Not being able to do so violates their rights. Therefore, I disagree with introducing a smoking ban.

(225 words)

結論として、規則と矛盾した法律のせいで、喫煙者が法律で認められた習慣を楽しむための場所を見つけるのが難しくなっています。喫煙ができないことは、喫煙者の権利を侵害しています。そのため、禁煙条例を導入することに反対です。

Words and Phrases

For

□ a large number of	非常に多くの〜
□ die from smoking-related diseases	喫煙関連の病気で死ぬ
□ such as lung cancer, heart disease, and stroke	例えば、肺がん、心臓病、脳卒中など
□ in designated areas	指定された場所で
□ inhale the smoke directly	直接煙を吸う
□ without a cigarette filter	タバコのフィルターを通さないで
□ as such	それゆえ：同様に
□ be detrimental to	〜にとって有害になる、致命傷となる
□ feasibly avoid such harmful smoke	そんな有害な煙をうまく避ける
□ can't stand the smell of smoke	煙の臭いに耐えられない
□ cost-saving policy	経費節約の政策
□ a pack of cigarettes	1箱のタバコ
□ encourage ~ to quit …	〜に…をやめることを促す
□ discourage ~ from starting to …	〜に…し始めることを抑制する
□ insist on the right to	〜する権利を主張する
□ violate the rights of	〜の権利を侵害する
□ what's worse	さらに悪いことには
□ endanger the health of	〜の健康を危険にさらす

Against

□ be harmful and unpleasant for	〜にとって有害で不快である
□ be acceptable to	〜することを容認できる
□ deny one's rights	〜の権利を無視する、否定する
□ legal	法律で認められた
□ be prohibited to	〜することを禁じられる
□ on the premises of medical facilities	医療施設の敷地内に
□ to name a few	2、3例を挙げると
□ get fined	罰金を科される
□ eat fatty foods	脂っこいものを食べる
□ do in excess	過剰に行う
□ public transportation	公共交通機関
□ as for	〜に関しては
□ intake of high cholesterol	高コレステロールの摂取
□ lead to life-threatening diseases	命に関わる病気につながる
□ critical diseases	重症疾患
□ commit an illegal act	違法行為を犯す
□ in conclusion	結論として
□ regulations and contradictory laws	規則と矛盾した法律
□ legal habit	法律で認められた習慣

Tips | 論理的に展開するためのキーフレーズ

問題を示す③

1	Such chemicals are harmful to the environment.	そのような化学薬品は環境に有害です。
2	The contents are legal but harmful to youth. They must be controlled by laws.	内容は合法ですが、若者には害があります。それらは法律で管理されるべきです。
3	Food additives could be hazardous to human health.	食品添加物は人間の健康に害になる可能性があります。
4	Lack of sleep has a negative impact on work performance.	睡眠不足は、仕事の能率にマイナスの影響を与えます。
5	Sexual content on the Web has a negative impact on teenagers.	ウェブ上の性的描写は、10 代の若者にマイナスの影響を与えます。

禁止を示す

1	False and misleading advertisements are prohibited.	虚偽の誇大広告は禁じられています。
2	Smoking in public places must be strictly prohibited by law.	公共の場での喫煙は法律により厳しく禁止されなければなりません。
3	The use of smartphones is not allowed during the meeting.	スマートフォンの利用は、会議中は許可されません。
4	Cellular phone use should be banned in public places.	携帯電話の使用は公共の場では禁止されるべきです。
5	Bad-mannered driving should be punished severely.	悪いマナーの運転は厳しく罰せられるべきです。

Speech 22 Should printed books be replaced with e-books?

紙の本を電子書籍に切り替えるべきか？

背景知識とヒント

電子書籍を選ぶか、紙の本を選ぶか

電子書籍が登場してから年数が経ち、スマートフォンやタブレットで読書をする人が増えています。一方、子どものころの絵本に始まり、教科書など勉強の一環としても使われてきた紙の本には、根強い支持者もいます。

値段が手頃で、いつでもどこでもダウンロードできる電子書籍と、子どものころから使い慣れている紙の本では、今後、どちらがより多くの支持を集めるのでしょうか。

知っトク情報：頻出の関連トピック

Are books in danger of becoming obsolete? /Are printed books and newspapers destined to die out? / Will books eventually be replaced by electronic media?

コンセプトマップ

反対バージョンを参考にスピーチの土台となるコンセプトマップを作ってみましょう。

Assertion

I disagree with replacing printed books with e-books.

Reason 1

digital device has adverse effects on our health

Reason 2

is prone to technical problems

Example 1

- near-sighted because of excessive close work
- read from screens all day long while working

Example 2

- not durable
- worry about battery life

Assertion (Conclusion)

I disagree with replacing printed books with e-books.

Speech | スピーチ

For | 賛成バージョン 22-❶

064

A
Assertion
主張

There are lots of advantages to e-books, such as portability and lower cost. There are too many advantages to describe. Therefore, I agree with replacing printed books with e-books. I have two reasons to support my opinion.

電子書籍には、携帯性や低コストなどのたくさんの利点があります。すべての利点は言い尽くせません。そのため、紙の本を電子書籍に変えることに賛成します。意見を支持する2つの理由があります。

R1
Reason
理由

First, e-books are eco-friendly.

第一に、電子書籍は環境にやさしいです。

E1
Example
例

For example, we need a lot of electricity, water, and trees to publish printed books. However, by replacing printed books with e-books, it's not necessary for us to cut down a lot of trees, or to waste water or energy. More and more, e-books will lead us toward a paperless and eco-friendly society.

例えば、印刷された本を出版するには、たくさんの電気や水、木材が必要です。しかし、紙の本を電子書籍に変えることにより、たくさんの木を伐採したり、水またはエネルギーを浪費したりする必要がなくなります。電子書籍はペーパーレスで環境にやさしい社会へ、どんどんと導いてくれます。

R2
Reason
理由

Second, e-books are extremely convenient.

第二に、電子書籍はとても便利です。

E2
Example
例

For example, e-book devices are as thin and light as a smartphone, and are therefore highly portable. In addition, we can carry thousands of books in a single e-book device. We can also easily search for particular content within a book using the device. We don't have to turn page after page to find the information. Moreover, electronic text on such devices may be copied and pasted with some limits.

例えば、電子書籍端末はスマートフォンのように薄くて軽く、そのため運びやすいのです。さらに、1つの電子書籍端末の中に、何千冊もの本を運ぶことができます。また、その端末機器を使って、本の中の特定の情報を簡単に探せます。情報を見つけるために次々にページをめくる必要がありません。さらに、そのような機器では、電子テキストは一定の制限下でコピペすることが可能です。

A
Assertion (Conclusion)
主張

In conclusion, it's possible to carry thousands of books in a single e-book device. Putting it differently, we can carry our own personalized library in our pocket. We won't have to go to bookstores anymore. We can download e-books directly from the Internet. Our reading and research will also be eco-friendly, and require less time and money. The advantages far outweigh the disadvantages. Therefore, I agree with replacing printed books with e-books.

(241 words)

結論として、1つの電子書籍端末の中に何千冊もの本を運ぶことが可能です。言い換えれば、ポケットの中に個人用の図書館を運ぶことができるのです。もはや書店に行く必要がありません。インターネットから直接電子書籍をダウンロードできるのです。私たちの読書や調査は環境にやさしくなり、時間もお金も少なくてすみます。欠点よりも利点の方がはるかに多いのです。そのため、紙の本を電子書籍に変えることに賛成です。

Against | 反対バージョン 22-❷

065

A
Assertion
主張

E-books are publications in digital form. It's possible to read them on computers or e-book devices. Some people agree that e-books should replace printed books. However, I disagree with this idea. I have two reasons to support my opinion.

電子書籍は、デジタル化された出版物です。コンピュータや電子書籍端末でそれらを読むことができます。電子書籍は紙の本に取って代わるべきだと同意する人もいます。しかし、私はこの考えに反対です。意見を支持する２つの理由があります。

R1
Reason
理由

First, reading on a digital device has adverse effects on our health.

第一に、デジタル機器で読むことは、健康に悪影響を及ぼします。

E1
Example
例

For example, more and more people are becoming near-sighted because of excessive close work on handheld devices. Moreover, many people use smartphones or read from electronic screens all day long while working. They usually read books for pleasure. For those who read from electronic screens all day long, reading e-books for pleasure is the last thing they will want to do.

例えば、携帯用端末に極度に目を近づける作業が原因で、ますます多くの人が近視になっています。さらには、多くの人が、働いている間ずっとスマートフォンを使うか、電子画面で読んでいます。通常は、娯楽のために本を読みます。一日中、電子画面で読んでいる人にとっては、娯楽のために電子書籍を読むことは、やりたくないことです。

R2
Reason
理由

Second, every machine is prone to technical problems.

第二に、どの機械も技術的な問題に陥りやすいものです。

E2
Example
例

For example, e-book devices are fragile information technology hardware. In other words, e-book devices are not durable. Therefore, we can't treat them nearly as roughly as printed books. We also have to worry about the e-book device's battery life.

例えば、電子書籍端末は壊れやすい情報技術のハードウェアです。言い換えれば、電子書籍端末は、耐久性がないのです。そのため、電子機器を紙の本のように、雑に扱うことはできません。電子書籍の電池の寿命も心配しなくてはいけません。

A
Assertion (Conclusion)
主張

In conclusion, I'm sure there are some advantages to e-books; however, there are definitely some serious problems too. Reading from electronic screens all day long is not good for our health. In addition, e-book devices are fragile. More disturbingly, dead batteries mean dead devices. To reiterate, I disagree with replacing printed books with e-books.

(213 words)

結論として、電子書籍にはいくつかの利点はあります。しかし、明らかにいくつかの深刻な問題があります。一日中電子画面で読むことは、健康によくありません。さらに、電子書籍端末は壊れやすいのです。気がかりなことに、電池切れとは機器が壊れたことを意味するのです。繰り返し言いますが、紙の本を電子書籍に変えることには反対です。

Words and Phrases

For

□ portability	携帯性
□ lower cost	安いコスト
□ There are too many advantages to describe.	利点が多すぎて言い尽くせない。
□ replace ～ with…	～を…に置き換える
□ eco-friendly	環境にやさしい
□ it's not necessary for… to ～	～することは必要でない
□ paperless society	ペーパーレス社会
□ extremely convenient	とても便利
□ e-book device	電子書籍端末
□ as thin and light as	～と同じくらい薄く軽い
□ highly portable	携帯性の高い
□ turn page after page	次々にページをめくる
□ electronic text	電子テキスト
□ copy and paste	コピペをする
□ to put it differently	言い換えると
□ personalized library	個人用図書館
□ download e-books directly from the Internet	インターネットから直接電子書籍をダウンロードする
□ The advantages far outweigh the disadvantages.	欠点よりも利点の方がはるかに多い。

Against

□ publications in digital form	デジタル化された出版物
□ digital device	デジタル機器
□ have adverse effects on	～に悪影響を与える
□ become near-sighted	近視になる
□ because of	～のため
□ excessive close work	極度に目を近づける作業
□ handheld devices	携帯用端末
□ for pleasure	娯楽のため
□ all day long	一日中
□ be the last thing	～は最も嫌なことである
□ be prone to ～	～しがちである、～する傾向がある
□ fragile information technology hardware	壊れやすい情報技術のハードウェア
□ durable	耐久性のある
□ roughly	乱暴に、雑に
□ battery life	電池の寿命
□ definitely	確かに、疑いなく
□ be not good for	～にとってよくない
□ more disturbingly	気がかりなことに
□ dead battery	電池切れ
□ to reiterate	繰り返し言うが

Tips | 論理的に展開するためのキーフレーズ

連結語②

❶ Zero emission cars are eco-friendly.	無公害車は、環境にやさしいです。
❷ Is our website customer-friendly?	私たちのウェブサイトは、顧客の立場を考えていますか。
❸ This restaurant is kid-friendly.	このレストランは、子ども向けです。
❹ I'm satisfied with this hotel because of its budget-friendly service.	財布にやさしいサービスのため、このホテルに満足しています。
❺ You are requested to make user-friendly proposals.	利用者にとって使いやすい提案をすることが求められています。

代替を示す②

❶ Prepaid cards may take the place of cash.	プリペイドカードが、キャッシュにとって代わるかもしれません。
❷ Robots may take the place of current staff.	ロボットが、現在のスタッフの代わりをするかもしれません。
❸ Cats cannot substitute for dogs.	猫が、犬の代役を務めることはできません。
❹ Security cameras can replace guards.	監視カメラは、警備員の代わりになりえます。
❺ Human beings will be replaced by artificial intelligence robots.	人間は、人工知能ロボットに取って代わられるでしょう。

Should the Internet be censored by the government?

インターネットを検閲するべきか？

背景知識とヒント

スマートフォンの普及とインターネット検閲の必要性

「インターネットの検閲」とは、SNS を含め、インターネット上の情報を対象とした政府機関による検閲を指します。例えば映画には、セックスや暴力の描写により R18 や R15 などの年齢指定があります。政府があらかじめ、未成年が視聴できないように規制しているのです。

一方、インターネットには、そのような指定や規制がありません。検閲の議論が活発化している背景には、スマートフォンの普及により、本来 R15 や R18 に指定されるべきものでも、未成年者が視聴できてしまうという問題があります。

知っトク情報：頻出の関連トピック

Can government censorship ever be justified? / Can censorship be justified in a democratic society? / Agree or disagree: The Internet should be free from censorship. / Should there be restrictions on Internet content?

コンセプトマップ

賛成バージョンを参考にスピーチの土台となるコンセプトマップを作ってみましょう。

Assertion

I agree with Internet censorship.

Reason 1

some dangerous activities on the Internet

Reason 2

some harmful information on the Internet

Example 1

- recruiting for criminal groups
- hacking
- remain anonymous

Example 2

- sex or violence
- hard to monitor online activities

Assertion (Conclusion)

I agree with Internet censorship.

Speech | スピーチ

For | 賛成バージョン 23-❶

A
Assertion
主張

We live in a world where accessing the Internet is indispensable. We can't escape it. Therefore, we have to learn to distinguish good content from bad. But I have found it difficult to do so. I agree with Internet censorship. I have two points to make.

私たちは、インターネットにアクセスすることが不可欠な世界に住んでいます。それから逃れることができません。そのため、良いコンテンツと悪いコンテンツを識別する方法を学ばなくてはいけません。しかし、それが難しいことはわかっています。私はインターネットの検閲に賛成です。2つのポイントがあります。

R1
Reason
理由

Firstly, some activities on the Internet are dangerous.

第一に、インターネット上の活動には危険なものがあります。

E1
Example
例

For example, recruiting for criminal groups and hacking in general for identity theft can ruin people's lives. At the moment, it's also very hard to trace such suspects or criminals because the Internet allows them to remain anonymous. I'm certain that Internet censorship can prevent such illicit and criminal activities by limiting their online communication.

例えば、犯罪集団への勧誘や、個人情報を盗むためのよくあるハッキングは、人の人生を狂わせます。現在、そのような容疑者や犯罪者を追跡することも難しいのです。というのは、インターネットでは、匿名のままでいることが許されるからです。インターネット検閲は、オンライン上でのやり取りを制限することで、このような不法行為や犯罪活動を防ぐことができると確信しています。

R2
Reason
理由

Secondly, some information on the Internet is harmful.

第二に、インターネット上の情報には、有害なものがあります。

E2
Example
例

For example, some video clips contain indecent and inappropriate scenes for children, such as sex or violence. Today's children grow up using the Internet. Because they are curious and mischievous, they may search for certain inappropriate images. Furthermore, children are so proficient in using the Internet that adults around them don't have the know-how to stop them from accessing sites with bad content. On top of that, it's very difficult to monitor their online activities. Sexual and violent video clips have a harmful influence on both children and adults. We already have a kind of censorship system for movies. For instance, some movies receive an R or PG-13 rating due to violence, sex, and profanity. We should introduce a similar but stricter censorship system for the Internet.

例えば、セックスや暴力といった、子どもにはわいせつで不適切なシーンを含む動画があります。今日の子どもはインターネットを使って育っています。彼らは好奇心が強くいたずら好きなので、特定の不適切な画像を検索するかもしれません。さらに、大人は悪いコンテンツのあるサイトへアクセスさせないための専門知識を持っていないのに、子どもはインターネットを使うことにとても堪能です。その上、彼らのネット上の活動を監視するのは難しいのです。性的・暴力的な動画は子どもにも大人にも有害です。映画には、すでにある種の検閲制度があります。例えば、暴力やセックス、みだらな言葉のせいでR指定やPG13指定を受けている映画があります。同様の、より厳しい検閲制度をインターネットには導入すべきです。

A
Assertion (Conclusion)
主張

To sum up, censorship is the best way to limit and decrease illegal and criminal activities on the Internet. I agree with Internet censorship.

(268 words)

要約すれば、検閲は不法な犯罪活動を制限したり、減らしたりするには最善の方法です。私は、インターネット検閲には賛成です。

Against | 反対バージョン 23-❷

068

A
Assertion
主張

We use the Internet 24/7 to obtain information and communicate with other people. It's a very convenient service. It's unthinkable and impossible to censor the Internet. I disagree with Internet censorship. I have two points to make.

私たちは、情報を収集したり人とコミュニケーションをとったりするために、24 時間インターネットを使っています。大変便利なサービスです。インターネットを検閲するなんて、想像もできないし不可能です。インターネット検閲に反対です。2つのポイントがあります。

R1
Reason
理由

Firstly, the Internet is not only a place to gather information but also a place where people enjoy expressing their ideas and opinions nowadays.

第一に、今や、インターネットは情報を収集する場所であるだけではなく、人が考えや意見を表現することを楽しむ場所なのです。

E1
Example
例

For instance, writing novels on the Internet is very popular. Some such novels become so popular that they are even published into books and then made into movies. If the Internet is censored by the government, fewer and fewer people will post attractive and creative stories. Furthermore, freedom of expression is a basic and inalienable human right. It should not be taken away on the Internet.

例えば、インターネット上で小説を書くことは、大変人気があります。非常に人気が出たので本として出版されたり、映画化されたりした小説もあります。インターネットが政府に検閲されれば、魅力的で創造的な物語を投稿する人はどんどん減っていくでしょう。さらに、表現の自由は、人間の基本的で不可侵の権利です。その権利は、インターネットから取り上げられるべきではありません。

R2
Reason
理由

Secondly, it's very difficult to decide what to restrict and what to allow on the Internet.

第二に、インターネット上で、何を制限し、何を許可するかを決めるのはとても困難です。

E2
Example
例

For example, there are all kinds of opinions on the Internet; some are biased, harmful, and offensive. Even so, our values differ from each other and so should our opinions. Moreover, it may be true that some information is questionable, but it's not up to the government, but the individual, to decide what content to read, post and ignore.

例えば、インターネット上にはあらゆる種類の意見があります。偏見がある意見もあれば、有害なもの、不愉快なものがあります。それでも、価値観はお互いに違いますし、意見も違うべきです。さらに、疑わしい情報もあるのは事実ですが、どのコンテンツを読み、投稿し、無視するかを決めるのは、政府ではなく個人なのです。

A
Assertion (Conclusion)
主張

To sum up, the Internet is one of the most helpful inventions for gathering information. It's not up to the government, but us, to decide what content is important and what is not. I disagree with Internet censorship.

(240 words)

要約すれば、インターネットは、情報を収集するための最も役に立つ発明のうちの１つです。どの情報が重要で、どの情報が重要でないかを決めるのは、政府でなく私たちなのです。インターネットの検閲に反対します。

Words and Phrases

For

□ indispensable	必須の、不可欠の
□ Internet censorship	インターネットの検閲
□ hack for identity theft	個人情報を盗むため不正侵入する
□ at the moment	現在
□ trace suspects or criminals	容疑者や犯罪者を追跡する
□ remain anonymous	匿名のままでいる
□ prevent illicit and criminal activities	不法行為や犯罪を防ぐ
□ contain inappropriate scenes	不適切なシーンを含む
□ mischievous	いたずら好きな
□ be proficient in	～に堪能である
□ have the know-how to	～する専門知識がある
□ stop … from ~ing	…に～させない
□ on top of that	それに加えて
□ monitor	～を監視する
□ have a harmful influence on	～に有害な影響を及ぼす
□ R or PG-13 rating	R 指定や PG13 指定の
□ profanity	みだらな言葉；不敬
□ to sum up	要約すれば
□ limit illegal activities	不法な活動を制限する

Against

□ use 24/7	24 時間年中使う
□ unthinkable	想像もできない
□ gather information	情報を収集する
□ novel	小説
□ post attractive and creative stories	魅力的で創造的な物語を投稿する
□ freedom of expression	表現の自由
□ basic and inalienable human right	人間の基本的で不可侵の権利
□ take away	～を取り上げる
□ what to restrict and what to allow	何を制限し、何を許可するか
□ biased, harmful and offensive	偏見があり、有害で、不愉快な
□ values differ from each other	価値観はお互いに異なる
□ it may be true that	～は本当かもしれない
□ questionable	疑わしい
□ it's not up to the government but the individual to	～するのは政府でなく個人である
□ helpful	役に立つ

Tips | 論理的に展開するためのキーフレーズ

譲歩・逆接を示す③

❶	It may be true, but the problem is more profound than that.	それは本当かもしれないですが、問題はそれよりもっと深いのです。
❷	It may be right, but the drug is effective for some people.	そうかもしれませんが、その薬は、一部の人には効き目があるのです。
❸	You have a good point, but I don't agree with your opinion.	いいところをついていますが、あなたの意見には賛成しません。
❹	You are partially right, but it doesn't hold true for all customers.	一部は正しいですが、それはすべての顧客には当てはまりません。
❺	Indeed smartphones have made our lives easier, but excessive use of them can lead to addiction.	スマートフォンは私たちの生活を楽にしてくれましたが、使いすぎは中毒になります。
❻	What you said may be true, but it doesn't apply to every single person.	あなたの言っていることは正しいかもしれませんが、それが一人一人に適用されるわけではありません。

確信を示す

❶	I'm 100% sure it's important to feature new products in advance.	事前に新商品を特集することが大切だと確信しています。
❷	I'm absolutely certain my colleagues will support my opinion in this situation.	この状況で、同僚が私の意見を支持してくれると確信しています。
❸	I'm confident my boss would support the decision as a right move.	私の上司がその決定を妥当な措置だと支持してくれることを確信しています。
❹	I'm fully confident that I can manage both work and study at the same time.	仕事と勉強を両立できる自信があります。
❺	I'm not convinced that you got all the necessary information on your PhD studies.	私は、あなたが博士号の研究に必要なすべての情報を集めたとは納得していません。

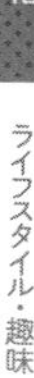

Speech 24

Is the Internet harmful to children?

インターネットは子どもに有害か？

背景知識とヒント

子どもたちへのインターネットの影響とは

インターネットは、現代の生活にとって必需品です。インターネットには、無料のゲーム、自分の考えを書き込めるブログ、知らない人と交流できるSNSなど、子どもが楽しめるコンテンツがあふれています。

一方、インターネットには、ネットいじめ、自殺サイト、成人向け画像など危険なコンテンツもあふれています。いつ、どのようにして、インターネットを子どもに教えていけばよいのでしょうか。

知っトク情報：頻出の関連トピック

Is the Internet destroying family communication? / Should Internet crime be taken more seriously? / Is the Internet harmful to children?

コンセプトマップ

反対バージョンを参考にスピーチの土台となるコンセプトマップを作ってみましょう。

Assertion

I disagree with the idea that the Internet is harmful to children.

Reason 1

learning opportunities

Reason 2

enjoy their lives

Example 1

- English conversation lessons
- obtain a bachelor's degrees

Example 2

- keep in touch with friends
- same hobbies and interests

Assertion (Conclusion)

I disagree with the idea that the Internet is harmful to children.

Speech | スピーチ

For | 賛成バージョン 24-❶

070

A
Assertion
主張

Almost every day, I use the Internet with a smartphone. This is because it's useful; in other words, the Internet helps me a lot. However, when it comes to children, that's a different story. I agree with the idea that the Internet is harmful to children. I have two points to make.

ほとんど毎日、私はスマートフォンでインターネットを使います。これは、インターネットが役に立つからです。言い換えると、インターネットにかなり助けられています。しかし、子どものこととなると、それは話が違います。インターネットが子どもにとって有害であるという考えに賛成です。２つの理由があります。

R1
Reason
理由

Firstly, it's difficult for children to handle the Internet responsibly.

第一に、子どもがインターネットを責任を持って扱うのは難しいです。

E1
Example
例

For example, children can get addicted to the Internet very easily because it's interesting to watch unique videos and read informative articles on the Internet. They can also play exciting online games for free. Moreover, children may start staying at home all the time because they can do everything they need to do on the Internet, such as chatting, playing games, shopping, and so on. What's worse, children may even stop talking with their family members. As a result, they then find it difficult to communicate with others.

例えば、子どもは、簡単にインターネット中毒になります。なぜならば、インターネットで面白い動画を見たり情報記事を読んだりするのは、興味深いからです。子どもは刺激的なオンラインゲームを無料で楽しむこともできます。さらに、彼らは常時家にこもり始めるかもしれません。というのは、チャットやゲーム、買い物など、必要なことはインターネットですべてできるからです。さらに悪いことには、家族と話すこともやめるかもしれません。結果として、他の人とコミュニケーションをとるのが難しくなります。

R2
Reason 理由

Secondly, the Internet has a lot of potential dangers.

第二に、インターネットには多くの潜在的危険があります。

E2
Example 例

For example, children tend to post their personal information on the Internet without realizing the risks. Once they post a photo on the Internet, such as a photo of two people kissing, it may go viral and they can't delete it. Such pictures tend to spread over the Internet by copying, pasting, and sharing. What's more, on the Internet, users can remain anonymous. It means people sometimes pretend to be someone else. These people can create fake profiles, for example, as young girls and try to contact children of similar ages from the information they find on the Internet. As a result, children can fall victim to sexual crimes at any time.

例えば子どもは、リスクに気づかずに、インターネットに個人情報を投稿しがちです。いったんインターネットに写真を投稿したら、例えば、2人がキスしている写真などは、急速に広まって、消すことができません。そのような写真はインターネット上でコピペと共有により広まります。さらに、インターネット上では、ユーザーは匿名でいられます。つまり誰か他の人になりすますことができるのです。例えば若い女の子として偽のプロフィールを作り、見つけた情報から、そのうその年齢と同じくらいの年の子どもと接触しようとします。結果として、子どもはいつでも性犯罪の被害者になりえます。

A
Assertion (Conclusion) 主張

In conclusion, with or without intent, any child could become involved in Internet-related problems. Therefore, I'm convinced parents and schools should take the necessary actions to prevent this from happening. Once again, I agree with the idea that the Internet is harmful to children.

(315 words)

結論として、意図があってもなくても、どの子どももインターネット関連の問題に巻き込まれる可能性があります。そのため、親や学校は問題が起こるのを防ぐために必要な行動をとるべきです。繰り返しますが、インターネットが子どもにとって有害であるという考えに賛成です。

Against | 反対バージョン 24-❷

A
Assertion
主張

It's true that the Internet is not always beneficial to children, but I'm sure that the benefits of the Internet outweigh the negatives. As such, I disagree with the idea that the Internet is harmful to children. I have two reasons why I think so.

インターネットが子どもにとって常に有益であるとは限らないということは本当です。しかし、インターネットのプラス面の方がマイナス面の方を上回るということを確信しています。そのため、インターネットが子どもに有害であるという考えに反対です。2つの理由があります。

R1
Reason
理由

Firstly, the Internet gives children learning opportunities. Learning is possible anytime and anywhere on the Internet.

第一に、インターネットが子どもに学習の機会を与えてくれます。学習はいつでもどこでもインターネットで可能です。

E1
Example
例

For example, if children have questions about a certain subject, they can easily answer them by accessing a wide range of information almost instantly. Recently, even English conversation lessons are available on the Internet. In fact, children can learn English from native speakers of English through such online lessons. In many cases, online school services are available 24 hours a day. In addition, school tuition fees are often very cheap. Plus, for older children, many colleges offer not only basic classes but also classes to obtain a bachelor's degree. Sometimes it's even possible to get an online master's degree!

例えば、子どもがある題材について疑問があれば、幅広い情報にアクセスすることによって、すぐに答えてくれます。最近では、英会話のレッスンでさえ、インターネットで利用できます。実際に、インターネットで子どもがネイティブスピーカーから英語を学ぶことができます。多くの場合、オンラインスクールサービスは24時間利用できます。さらに、授業料は大変安いことが多いです。また、年長の子どものために、多くの大学が基本的な授業を提供しているだけでなく、実際にオンラインで学士号を取得するための授業を実施している大学さえあります。修士号の取得が可能なことだってあるのです！

R2
Reason
理由

Secondly, the Internet gives children advantages that can help them to enjoy their lives more.

第二に、インターネットには、子どもがより生活を楽しむためのメリットがあります。

E2
Example
例

For example, children are connected with friends on social media. Social media platforms are great Internet tools to keep in touch with friends, even after graduating or moving to a new home. Moreover, there are lots of Internet groups, catering to people with the same hobbies and interests. Once online, they can chat in depth about the things they like. In fact, it's a great way for them to meet people sharing the same interests! In addition, children can then learn a variety of perspectives from their new friends and deepen their friendships even more.

例えば、子どもはSNSで友達とつながっていられます。SNSは、卒業したあとや新居へ引っ越ししたあとでさえ、友達と連絡を取るための主要なインターネットのツールです。さらにたくさんのインターネット上のグループがあり、同じ趣味や興味を持っている人に応えています。いったんオンラインでつながれば、好きなことについて踏み込んで話ができます。実際に、同じ趣味を持つ人と会うのに素晴らしい方法です。さらに、子どもは新しい友人からさまざまな視点を学んだり、友情を深めたりできます。

A
Assertion (Conclusion)
主張

In conclusion, it's clear that, though the Internet has some risks, its pros far outweigh its cons. It's possible for parents and schools to protect children from such online risks by using child safety tools. The biggest risk, however, is to risk nothing at all. Once again, I disagree with the idea that the Internet is harmful to children.

(329 words)

結論として、インターネットにはリスクがいくつかありますが、メリットがデメリットをかなり上回ります。親や学校は、子ども用安全ツールを使って、そのようなインターネットのリスクから子どもを守ることは可能です。しかし、最大のリスクは、何も危険を冒さないことです。繰り返しますが、インターネットが子どもに有害であるという考えに反対です。

Words and Phrases

For

□ this is because	これは～のためである
□ When it comes to ～, that's a different story.	～のこととなると、それは別の話です。
□ handle ～ responsibly	～を責任を持って扱う
□ get addicted to	～の中毒になる
□ read informative articles	情報記事を読む
□ what's worse	さらに悪いことには
□ as a result	結果として
□ have a lot of potential dangers	多くの潜在的危険がある
□ post one's personal information	個人情報を投稿する
□ go viral	インターネットや口コミで急速に広まる
□ spread over the Internet by copying, pasting, and sharing	コピペと共有でネット上に広まる
□ remain anonymous	匿名のままでいる
□ pretend to be someone else	誰か他の人になりすます
□ create fake profiles	偽のプロフィールを作る
□ fall victim to sexual crimes	性犯罪の被害者になる
□ at any time	いつでも
□ with or without intent	意図があってもなくても
□ become involved in Internet-related problem	インターネット関連の問題に巻き込まれる
□ take necessary actions to prevent this from happening	これが起こるのを防ぐために必要な行動をとる

Against

□ be beneficial to	～にとって有益である、役に立つ
□ The benefits of the Internet outweigh the negatives.	インターネットのプラス面の方がマイナス面を上回る。
□ as such	それゆえ、だから
□ learning opportunities	学習の機会
□ access a wide range of information	幅広い情報にアクセスする
□ be available on the Internet	インターネットで利用できる、入手できる
□ be available 24 hours a day	24 時間利用できる、入手できる
□ tuition fee	授業料
□ obtain	～を取得する
□ bachelor's degree	学士号
□ master's degree	修士号
□ be connected with friends on social media	SNS で友達とつながっている
□ keep in touch with	～と連絡をとる、接触する
□ cater to	～に応じる、応える
□ chat in depth about	～について一歩踏み込んだおしゃべりをする
□ learn a variety of perspectives	さまざまな視点を学ぶ
□ Its pros far outweigh its cons.	メリットがデメリットをかなり上回る。
□ The biggest risk is to risk nothing at all.	最大の危険は、何も危険を冒さないことである。

Tips | 論理的に展開するためのキーフレーズ

傾向を示す①

1	We are prone to make mistakes when we are tired.	私たちは疲れると間違いを犯しがちです。
2	We are apt to criticize something new and different.	私たちは、何か新しく違うものを非難する傾向にあります。
3	It is likely that everyone will choose new gadgets.	みんな新しい機器を選ぶ傾向にあります。
4	It is likely that hosting the Olympics will bring economic benefits.	オリンピックを開催することにより、経済効果がもたらされる傾向にあります。
5	The elderly are more likely to choose talking robots.	高齢者はおしゃべりロボットを選ぶ傾向にあります。

問題を示す④

1	Most smokers have big risks of getting cancer.	ほとんどの喫煙者はガンになる大きなリスクがあります。
2	Investing in the market carries some risk.	株式に投資するにはリスクが伴います。
3	The only way to gain something is to take a risk at something.	何かを得ようとすれば、何か危険を冒さなければいけません。
4	Some people take illegal drugs to improve their athletic performance. Such behavior is dangerous to their health.	運動能力を向上させようとして、違法な薬物に手を出す人がいます。そのような行為は健康にとって危険です。
5	Using a smartphone while walking on the street is very dangerous.	道を歩きながらスマートフォンを使うのは大変危険です。

Is there value in meeting people through social media?

SNS を通じた出会いに価値はある？

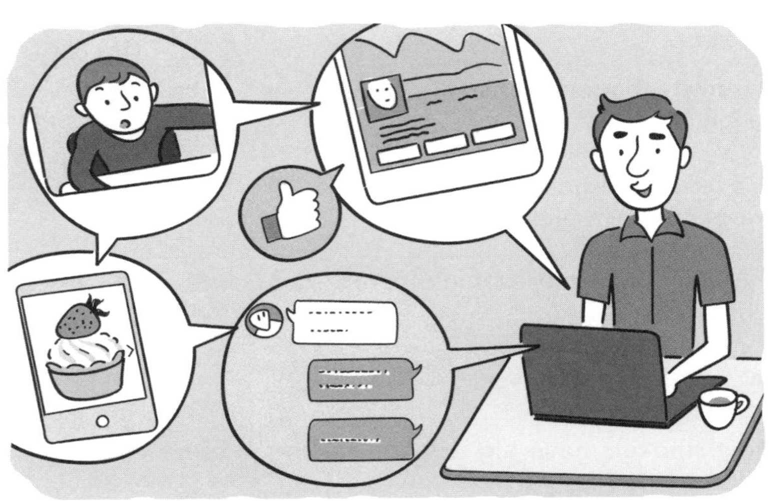

背景知識とヒント

SNS 上での出会いの是非を考える

近年、SNS は人と出会うためのツールとして活用されています。賛否両論ありますが、「SNS でやりとりを続けていくうちに共通点が見出せた」、「同じ趣味や目的を持った人のコミュニティで知り合って親しくなった」などの好意的な意見も聞かれます。出会うきっかけにこだわらない人にとっては、性別、世代や地域を超えたさまざまな出会いが魅力なのでしょう。

しかし、ネット上ならではのトラブルや見逃せない問題点もあります。SNS を通したコミュニケーションのあり方については、今後も時代に即した議論が必要です。

知っトク情報：頻出の関連トピック

Agree or disagree: Social media do more harm than good. / Does the Internet encourage people to express extreme attitudes? / Agree or disagree: Internet advertising is effective.

コンセプトマップ

賛成バージョンを参考にスピーチの土台となるコンセプトマップを作ってみましょう。

Assertion

I agree there is value in meeting people through social media.

Reason 1

connect and interact with others

Reason 2

easy to share files and data online

Example 1

- meet romantic partners
- build business connections

Example 2

- after special events, share photos and videos
- exchange information in real time

Assertion (Conclusion)

I agree there is value in meeting people through social media.

Speech | スピーチ

For | 賛成バージョン 25-❶

073

A
Assertion
主張

I agree there is value in meeting people through social media. It's a service widely used in modern times because it provides big benefits to individuals as well as society. I have two points to make.

SNSを通した人との出会いに、価値があることに同意します。SNSは、社会だけでなく個人にとっても大きなメリットがあるので、現代では広く利用されているサービスです。2つのポイントがあります。

R1
Reason
理由

Firstly, social media allows us to connect and interact with others over the Internet.

第一に、SNSはインターネットを通して、他の人とつながって対話できるようになります。

E1
Example
例

For instance, we can meet romantic partners or build business connections. Sometimes places to meet people are limited nowadays, and so social media is the best way for people to do so. It's also possible to screen social media profiles, including the interests of potential partners before meeting.

例えば、恋人に出会ったり、取引関係を築いたりできます。最近では、人と出会う場所が限られることもあります。そのため、SNSは人が出会うための最高の方法なのです。パートナー候補の興味を含めて、SNSのプロフィールを事前にチェックすることも可能です。

R2
Reason
理由

Secondly, once we establish connections, it's easy to share files and data online.

第二に、いったん関係を築いたら、ネット上でファイルやデータを共有することが簡単です。

E2
Example
例

For instance, after special events, we can share photos and videos through social media. It's really quick. All we have to do is post photos, videos, and stories of what we witnessed. It's like a dream to share pictures taken all over the earth. Furthermore, this helps us save time and effort. What's more, using chat rooms or online conferencing, we can exchange information in real time.

例えば、特別なイベントの後に、SNS で写真や動画を共有できます。あっという間です。写真や映像、目にしたことを投稿するだけでよいのです。世界中で撮影された写真を共有できるなんて夢のようです。さらに、時間と手間を省けます。また、チャットルームやオンライン会議を使って、リアルタイムで情報を交換できます。

A
Assertion (Conclusion)
主張

In conclusion, there are many positive aspects, like worldwide connectivity, real-time information sharing and so on. I'm confident the pros outweigh the cons. For these reasons, I agree there is value in meeting people through social media.

(215 words)

結論として、世界とのつながり、リアルタイムの情報交換などのように、多くのメリットがあります。メリットがデメリットを上回ることに自信があります。これらの理由で、SNS を通して人と出会う価値があるということに同意します。

Against | 反対バージョン 25-❷

074

A
Assertion
主張

Many people fervently utilize social media because it allows us to connect with each other, create personal websites, share information and so on. But there are lots of other concerns to consider. I disagree there is value in meeting people through social media. I have two points to make.

SNSがお互いをつなげたり、個人のウェブサイトを作ったり、情報を共有することなどを可能にするので、多くの人がSNSを熱心に利用しています。しかし、他に検討すべきたくさんの懸念があります。SNSを通して人と出会う価値があるということに反対します。2つのポイントがあります。

R1
Reason
理由

Firstly, we spend too much time on social media. This hinders us a lot.

第一に、SNSにあまりにも長い時間を使っています。それが私たちの妨げとなります。

E1
Example
例

For instance, we don't get enough true person-to-person interaction. To make matters worse, the time spent on social media often occurs during working hours. Whether at work, on the train, at the movies, or along the street, people are almost constantly accessing social media. Also, they are paying no attention to either the people or the activities going on around them. Therefore, some people bump into others or fall off the train platform while online.

例えば、本当の意味での人と人との交流が足りていません。さらに悪いことには、SNSに費やす時間は、勤務時間中に発生することもよくあるのです。仕事中でも、電車に乗っていても、映画を見ていても、道を歩いていても、人は、絶えずSNSにアクセスしています。また、身の回りの人や起きていることにまったく注意を払っていません。そのため、オンライン中に、人とぶつかったり、駅のプラットフォームから落ちたりする人もいます。

R2
Reason 理由

Secondly, social media causes a lot of problems.

第二に、SNS は多くの問題を引き起こします。

E2
Example 例

For instance, cyberbullying is a big problem now. By using social media, it's easy to harass others by posting mean or slanderous things. Harassing messages and indecent images can be broadcast to the entire cyberworld. It can happen anytime around the clock. It can also be done anonymously. In this way, social media can be a sinister venue for unacceptable behavior like cyberbullying.

例えば、ネットいじめは、今大きな問題です。SNS を使って、意地悪で中傷的なものを投稿することで、他の人に簡単に嫌がらせができます。嫌がらせのメッセージやわいせつな画像はネット上で拡散されます。24 時間いつでも起こりえます。そしてこれは匿名で行われます。このように SNS は、ネットいじめなどの受け入れがたい行動の悪質な場となりえます。

A
Assertion (Conclusion) 主張

In conclusion, although I often only hear about the good aspects of social media, such as worldwide connectivity and real-time information sharing, I think we should not underestimate the current and potential problems of social media. We need to use caution and be vigilant. For these reasons, I disagree there is value in meeting people through social media.

(260 words)

結論としては、世界とのつながりやリアルタイムでの情報共有といった、SNS の良い面ばかりをよく耳にしますが、現在の潜在的な問題を軽視するべきではないと思います。用心に用心を重ねる必要があります。これらの理由で、SNS を通して人と出会う価値があるということに反対します。

Words and Phrases

075

For

□ social media	SNS
□ service widely used in modern times	現代では幅広く使われているサービス
□ connect and interact with others	つながって他の人と対話する
□ meet romantic partners	恋人に出会う
□ build business connections	取引関係を築く
□ It's possible to screen social media profiles.	SNSのプロフィールを確認することが可能である。
□ establish connections	関係を築く
□ share files and data online	オンラインでファイルやデータを共有する
□ for instance	例えば
□ witness	目撃する
□ it's like a dream to	～するのは夢のようである
□ save time and effort	時間と手間を省く
□ what's more	さらに
□ use chat rooms	チャットルームを使う
□ online conferencing	オンライン会議
□ exchange information in real time	リアルタイムで情報を交換する
□ worldwide connectivity	世界とのつながり
□ real-time information sharing	リアルタイムの情報交換
□ I'm confident the pros outweigh the cons.	メリットがデメリットを上回ることに自信がある。

Against

□ fervently utilize social media	SNSを熱心に利用する
□ There are lots of other concerns to consider.	検討すべきたくさんの他の懸念がある。
□ hinder	～を妨げる
□ true person-to-person interaction	人と人との本物の交流
□ to make matters worse	さらに悪いことには
□ occur during working hours	勤務時間中に起こる
□ constantly access social media	絶えずSNSにアクセスする
□ pay no attention to	～に全く注意を払わない
□ bump into	～に衝突する
□ fall off the train platform	駅のプラットフォームから落ちる
□ Cyberbullying is a big problem now.	ネットいじめは今大きな問題である。
□ harass	～に嫌がらせをする
□ mean	意地悪な
□ slanderous	中傷的な
□ harassing messages and indecent images	嫌がらせのメッセージとわいせつな画像
□ be broadcast to	～に拡散される、言いふらされる
□ around the clock	一日中、24時間ぶっ通しで
□ sinister venue	悪質な場所
□ underestimate the current and potential problems	現在ある潜在的な問題を軽視する
□ use caution and be vigilant	用心に用心を重ねる

Tips | 論理的に展開するためのキーフレーズ

比較・対照を示す①

❶	I believe the benefits outweigh the costs.	メリットがコストを上回ると信じます。
❷	The cons outweigh the pros.	デメリットがメリットに勝っています。
❸	The advantages outweigh the disadvantages.	メリットがデメリットに勝っています。
❹	The negative effects outweigh the benefits.	マイナス効果がプラス面に勝っています。
❺	The plusses far outweigh the minuses.	プラス面がはるかにマイナス面を上回ります。
❻	A fund-raising dinner has more advantages than disadvantages.	チャリティーディナーには、デメリットよりかなり多くのメリットがあります。
❼	The benefits of surveillance cameras outweigh the drawbacks.	監視カメラの長所が欠点に勝ります。
❽	The overall problems outweigh the benefits.	全体的な問題が、長所を上回ります。

追加を示す③

❶	She is not a good singer. What's worse, she can't dance well.	彼女は良い歌手ではありません。さらに悪いことには、ダンスもうまく踊れません。
❷	The new American teacher is good at teaching, and to put the icing on the cake, she is charming.	新しいアメリカ人の先生は教え方が上手です。さらに良いことには、可愛いです。
❸	The rooms are available even during peak seasons, what's more, prices are unbelievingly low.	部屋は最も混む時期なのに空いています。さらに値段も信じられないほど安いです。
❹	A travel company went bankrupt. Not only that, some executives at the company disappeared.	ある旅行代理店が倒産しました。それだけでなく、会社の重役が行方不明になりました。
❺	I got stuck in a traffic accident. To make matters worse, I missed an important meeting.	交通事故で動けなくなりました。さらに悪いことには、重要な会議を欠席しました。

Speech 26

Should we keep a pet?

ペットを飼うべきか？

背景知識とヒント

人間とペットのより良い関係のために

猫や犬、ヘビ、サル、ワニまで、たくさんの種類の動物たちが、人のペットとして飼育されています。犬のように、狩猟などで人間のよきパートナーとして、昔から活躍してきた動物もいます。

しかし時には、アライグマのように、ペットの始末に困り、捨てられて、野生化してしまう動物もいます。ペットを飼う前に動物が健康で快適に暮らせるようにするなど、飼い主としてのモラルとマナーが必要です。

知っトク情報：頻出の関連トピック

The roles that pets play in our lives. / Do modern societies spend too much money on pets? / Can the use of animals for medical research be justified? / Controversy surrounding the use of animals in experiments.

コンセプトマップ

賛成バージョンを参考にスピーチの土台となるコンセプトマップを作ってみましょう。

Assertion

I agree with keeping pets.

Reason 1

help us stay in shape

Reason 2

can be our dearest companions

Example 1

- dogs need lots of exercise
- walk the dog in the morning

Example 2

- dogs are man's best friend
- loyal and intelligent

Assertion (Conclusion)

I agree with the idea of keeping pets.

Speech | スピーチ

For | 賛成バージョン 26-❶

076

A
Assertion
主張

Many people want to keep pets, such as dogs, cats, even snakes and the like. Keeping pets is beneficial to our bodies and our health. Therefore, I agree with keeping pets. I have two points to make.

多くの人が、ペットを飼いたいと思うものです。例えば、犬、猫、さらにヘビなどです。ペットを飼うことは、人間の身体や健康に有益です。そのため、ペットを飼うことに賛成です。2つのポイントがあります。

R1
Reason
理由

First, keeping pets helps us stay in shape.

第一に、ペットを飼うことで健康を保てます。

E1
Example
例

Take dogs, for example. Dogs need lots of exercise to keep them fit and healthy. For that reason, together with our dogs, we have a routine schedule. Walk the dog at 7 in the morning and at 6 in the evening. If we forget this routine, our dog lets us know it's time for our walk together. We need to walk our dog even in the rain. In this respect, pets help keep us active and healthy.

犬を例にとってみましょう。犬は、元気で健康でいるためには、たくさんの運動を必要とします。そのため、愛犬と一緒に、日々決まったスケジュールを立てます。犬の散歩は朝7時と夕方6時。この日課を忘れると、犬が一緒に散歩する時間だと教えてくれます。雨天時でさえ、散歩する必要があるのです。この点で、ペットは私たちが活動的かつ健康的でいる手助けをしてくれます。

R2
Reason
理由

Second, pets can be our dearest companions.

第二に、ペットは最愛の友になりえます。

E2
Example
例

For example, it's often said that dogs are man's best friend. Dogs are very loyal and intelligent animals. Some experts say pets of all kinds have therapeutic effects on humans and they can even prolong our lives. Pets are considered especially useful for the elderly, the widowed, and those living alone.

例えば、「犬は人間の一番の友です」とよく言われます。犬は大変忠誠心が強く、知性がある動物です。あらゆる種類のペットには、人間に対する癒やし効果があり、寿命を延ばしさえすると言う専門家もいます。ペットは、年配者、つれあいを亡くした人や一人暮らしの人のために、特に役に立つと考えられています。

A
Assertion (Conclusion)
主張

To conclude, as I mentioned earlier, keeping pets brings us many benefits. Moreover, dogs, in particular, could save us in emergency situations, such as a fire, an accident, a break-in, and the like. Taking these benefits into account, I agree with keeping pets.

(223 words)

結論として、これまで述べたように、ペットを飼うことは多くの長所をもたらします。さらに、特に犬は、火事、事故、窃盗などの緊急時に助けてくれます。これらの利益を考慮して、ペットを飼うことに賛成です。

Against | 反対バージョン 26-❷

A
Assertion
主張

There are some pros and cons to keeping pets. However, for a number of people, keeping pets can be problematic. Therefore, I disagree with keeping pets. I have two points to make.

ペットを飼うことには良い点と悪い点があります。しかし、多くの人にとって、ペットは問題となりえます。そのため、ペットを飼うことに反対します。2つのポイントがあります。

R1
Reason
理由

First, pets can be troublesome and dangerous.

第一に、ペットは煩わしく、危険です。

E1
Example
例

For example, dog hair and cat fur can be the root cause of allergy symptoms, sometimes life-threatening ones. As such, we have to clean our rooms very carefully every day. In addition, dogs tend to bark at unfamiliar visitors and strangers constantly. Moreover, after keeping a pet for a while, often a strange and lingering pet odor may begin to greatly annoy us.

例えば、犬の毛や猫の毛はアレルギー症状の根本的原因になりえます。生命を脅かすこともあります。そのため、毎日部屋をしっかり掃除しなければなりません。さらに、犬は見知らぬ訪問者やよそから来た人に向かって、吠え続ける傾向にあります。さらに、しばらくペットを飼っていると、奇妙でなかなか消えないペットの嫌な臭いが、私たちを大いに悩ませるようになるかもしれません。

R2
Reason
理由

Second, keeping pets involves a lot of responsibilities.

第二に、ペットを飼うことにはたくさんの責任が伴います。

E2
Example
例

For example, we have to feed pets properly. We have to take them outside for exercise. We also need to shoulder some extra costs like medical treatment as well as yearly vaccinations. Moreover, when we plan a trip for summer break, it's necessary to make arrangements for the pets' needs and care.

例えば、きちんとペットに餌を与えなければいけません。運動のために外に連れていかなければなりません。また、毎年の予防接種や治療など、追加でかかる費用を負担する必要があります。さらに、夏休みのために旅行を計画するときには、ペットに必要なことや世話の準備をしなくてはなりません。

A
Assertion (Conclusion)
主張

To conclude, keeping pets can be troublesome due to their barking and shedding hair. Sometimes, they can even endanger our lives. They also demand a lot of care and attention, like being walked and taken for medical treatment. Taking everything into account, I disagree with keeping pets.

(209 words)

結論として、吠えたり毛が抜けたりすることが原因で、ペットを飼うことは煩わしくなります。私たちの命さえ脅かすこともあります。散歩に連れていったり、治療に連れていったり、ペットは多くのケアと注意を要求します。すべてを考慮して、ペットを飼うことに反対です。

Words and Phrases

078

For

□ snake	蛇
□ be beneficial to	～にとって役に立つ、有益である
□ stay in shape	健康を保つ
□ take ～ , for example	～を例にとってみる
□ keep ～ fit and healthy	元気で健康に保つ
□ for that reason	その理由で
□ have a routine schedule	決まりきったスケジュールがある
□ walk a dog	犬を散歩させる
□ active	活動的で
□ dearest companions	最愛の友
□ loyal and intelligent	忠誠心があり、知性がある
□ have therapeutic effects on	～に癒やし効果がある
□ prolong one's life	寿命を延ばす
□ be useful for	～に役立つ
□ to conclude	結論として
□ in particular	特に
□ in emergency situations	緊急の状況では
□ break-in	窃盗
□ taking these benefits into account	これらの利益を考慮すると

Against

□ there are some pros and cons to	～には良い点と悪い点がある
□ a number of people	たくさんの人々
□ problematic	問題のある
□ fur	毛
□ the root cause of allergy symptoms	アレルギー症状の根本的原因
□ life-threatening	生命を脅かす
□ bark at unfamiliar visitors constantly	よく知らない訪問者に絶えず吠える
□ for a while	しばらくの間
□ lingering pet odor	なかなか消えないペットの嫌な臭い
□ annoy	～をイライラさせる
□ feed pets properly	ペットに適切に餌をやる
□ shoulder extra costs	別料金を負担する
□ medical treatment	治療
□ yearly vaccinations	年１回の予防接種
□ make arrangements for	～の準備をする
□ shedding hair	抜ける毛
□ endanger one's life	命を危険にさらす
□ demand a lot of care and attention	多くのケアと注意を要求する

Tips | 論理的に展開するためのキーフレーズ

ことわざ・根拠を示す

※ことわざは Assertion をサポートするための根拠として使う

1	There is a famous saying, "When in Rome, do as the Romans do."	「郷に入っては、郷に従え」という有名なことわざがあります。
2	It is often said that love does not consist of looking at each other but looking in the same direction.	「愛とはお互いを見つめ合うことではなくて、同じ方向を見ることだ」とよく言われます。
3	As the proverb goes, "Boys be ambitious."	「少年よ、大志を抱け」とことわざにあります。
4	He once quoted, "No pain, no gain."	彼はかつて、「苦労なくして、得るものはない」という引用をしました。
5	As the proverb goes, "You see trees but not a mountain."	「木を見て森を見ず」ということわざがあります。
6	Hunger is the best sauce.	空腹にまずいものなし／空腹は最高の調味料
7	Nothing ventured, nothing gained.	冒険しなければ何も得られない。（虎穴に入らずんば虎児を得ず）
8	Money can't buy everything.	お金ですべてのものが買えるわけではない。

要約・結論・結果を示す①

1	To sum up today's lecture, I'd like to point out two things.	今日の講義をまとめるために、2つ指摘したいと思います。
2	As a result, I completely agree with your suggestion.	結果として、あなたの提案にまったく異論はありません。
3	In sum, the agenda is as follows. First, we'll discuss our monthly sales quota. Then, we'll review our budget.	要約すると、議題は次の通りです。最初に1か月の販売ノルマについて話し合います。次に、予算を見直します。
4	In conclusion, there are some reasons why it doesn't work.	結論として、それがなぜうまくいかないのか、いくつかの理由があります。
5	To conclude, it's essential for business people to get to know each other.	結論として、実業家にとってお互いに知り合うことは、とても大切です。

Are big cities really the best places to live?

都会は本当に住みやすい？

背景知識とヒント

地方に暮らすか都会に暮らすか

　都会から地方への移住を希望する人がいます。地方自治体も支援制度などを設けて積極的に移住者を募っています。

　確かに地方は自然環境が豊かで、新鮮な野菜が安く手に入りやすいこともありますが、商業施設や娯楽施設へのアクセスが悪い地域も少なくありません。一方都会は、仕事や子どもの教育、交通の利便性などを考えると便利ですが、住宅や土地代が高く、ストレスもたまります。地方の暮らしと都会の暮らし、どちらが良いのでしょうか。

知っトク情報：頻出の関連トピック

Is it possible to make large cities more environmentally friendly? / The pros and cons of ongoing urbanization. / Urbanization in Japan: Is there a crisis?

コンセプトマップ 賛成バージョンを参考にスピーチの土台となるコンセプトマップを作ってみましょう。

Assertion

I support the idea that big cities are the best places to live in.

Reason 1

provide many convenient facilities

Reason 2

more opportunities for both business and pleasure

Example 1

- education
- lots of schools, private and public schools
- public transportation, well developed

Example 2

- government, industry
- sales, trade, and finance
- concert, musical

Assertion (Conclusion)

I support the idea that big cities are the best place to live in.

Speech | スピーチ

For | 賛成バージョン 27-❶

A
Assertion
主張

The places where we live can influence our lives greatly. Therefore, we can't be too careful when choosing where we live. There are several benefits to living in a big city. I support the idea that big cities are the best places to live. I have two points to make.

住む場所は、人生に大いに影響する可能性があります。そのため、私たちはどこに住むかを選ぶのに、いくら注意しても、しすぎることはありません。大都市に住むことにはいくつかのメリットがあります。私は大都市が住むのに最も良い場所だという考えに賛成します。2つポイントがあります。

R1
Reason
理由

My first reason is that big cities provide many convenient facilities. They are everywhere!

1つ目の理由は、大都市には多くの便利な施設があるということです。至る所にあるのです！

E1
Example
例

Take education, for example. There are lots of schools including private and public ones from prestigious to vocational. What is more, public transportation is well developed in urban areas. As such, transit services are available until midnight every day. It's very convenient to educate and take care of children, and a number of facilities are even within walking distance. Also, big cities have lots of hospitals and qualified doctors.

教育を例にとります。名門校から専門学校まで、私立学校や公立学校を含めて、たくさんの学校があります。さらに、都市部では、公共交通機関がとても発達しています。そのため、毎日夜中まで交通機関を利用できます。子どもを教育し、養育することも大変便利です。そして、たくさんの施設が徒歩圏内にあります。また、大都市には多くの病院と有能な医者がいます。

R2
Reason
理由

My second reason is that big cities have more opportunities for both business and pleasure. This being the case, it's much easier to find a job in a big city.

2つ目の理由は、大都市には、仕事や娯楽のための多くのチャンスがあるということです。そのため、大都市では、仕事を探すことがより簡単です。

E2
Example
例

For instance, we can find a variety of suitable jobs in government, industry, sales, trade, and finance. Plus, after work, there are many things to do like going to a pub, a concert, or a musical and the like.

例えば、役所、製造業、営業、貿易、金融でさまざまな自分に合う職業を見つけられます。さらに、仕事が終わってから、パブ、コンサート、ミュージカルに行くことなど、たくさんやることがあります。

A
Assertion (Conclusion)
主張

To put it simply, it's clear that big cities are the best places to live. They have not only many convenient facilities but also a variety of opportunities. Once again, I agree with the idea that big cities are the best places to live.

(246 words)

簡単に言えば、大都市が住むのに最適の場所だということは明白です。多くの便利な施設だけでなく、さまざまなチャンスにも恵まれています。もう一度言います。都会が住むのに最も適した場所だという考えに賛成です。

Against | 反対バージョン 27-❷

080

A
Assertion
主張

I know that, in big cities, we have many facilities, such as spacious parks, cinemas, libraries and so on. But there are several drawbacks to believing that big cities are the best places to live. I disagree with the idea that big cities are the best places to live. I have two points to make.

私は、大都市には広々とした公園、映画館、図書館などの多くの施設があることを知っています。しかし、大都市が住むのに最も良い場所だと信じるには、いくつかの欠点があります。大都市が住むのに最も良い場所だという考えには反対です。２つポイントがあります。

R1
Reason
理由

My first reason is that living in big cities is very stressful. This is because life there is very busy and competitive.

第一の理由は、大都市に住むことは、大変ストレスを感じるということです。これは、そこでの生活が大変せわしなく、競争が激しいからです。

E1
Example
例

Take commuting, for example. Generally speaking, we spend an hour or more on crowded trains. Or, we have to endure rush-hour traffic on our way to and from work. Moreover, in big cities, there is less nature. Big cities are full of buildings and pavements. Therefore, we can neither slow down nor relax.

通勤を例にとります。一般的に言って、私たちは、１時間かそれ以上、満員電車に乗ります。または、仕事への行き帰りでラッシュアワーの交通渋滞を我慢しなければいけません。さらに、大都市では、自然が少ないのです。都市は、建物や舗装道路でいっぱいです。そのため、私たちはゆっくりしたりリラックスしたりできません。

R2
Reason
理由

My second reason is that everything is expensive in big cities.

第二の理由は、大都市ではすべてが高額だということです。

E2
Example
例

For example, daily living expenses are very high. Monthly rent is also extremely high compared with that of rural areas. It's especially hard for low-wage earners to make ends meet in big cities. Moreover, the crime rate is high in urban areas and we have to be very careful to avoid being robbed at night. Even noise levels are high!

例えば、毎日の生活費がとても高いです。月の賃料も、地方のそれと比べるとかなり高いです。低所得の人にとっては、大都市で家計をやりくりするのは特に困難です。さらに、都市部では犯罪発生率が高いので、夜に泥棒に遭わないにように注意しなければいけません。騒音レベルも高いのです！

A
Assertion (Conclusion)
主張

To put it simply, big cities are becoming more and more industrialized and densely populated. Therefore, people living in big cities have busier, more hectic lives compared with those living in rural areas. Such a lifestyle makes one very stressed. Plus, everything in big cities is more expensive than elsewhere. Once again, I disagree with the idea that big cities are the best places to live.

(267 words)

簡単に言えば、大都市は、ますます工業化が進み、人口密度が高くなっています。そのため、大都市に住む人は、地方に住む人と比べて、より忙しく、よりせわしない生活をしています。そのような生活スタイルのせいで、人はストレスがたまってしまいます。さらに、大都市のすべてがその他の場所より高額です。繰り返しますが、大都市が住むのに最も良い場所だという考えには反対です。

Words and Phrases

For

□ can't be too careful	注意してもしすぎることはない
□ convenient facilities	便利な施設
□ Take education, for example.	教育を例にとってみよう。
□ private school	私立学校
□ prestigious	有名な
□ vocational	職業の
□ what is more	さらに
□ public transportation	公共交通機関
□ in urban areas	都市部では
□ as such	そのため
□ available	利用できる
□ within walking distance	徒歩圏内に
□ qualified	有能な；資格のある
□ opportunity	機会、チャンス
□ this being the case	そのため、そういう状況だから
□ a variety of ~	さまざまな~
□ suitable job	適切な仕事
□ trade and finance	貿易や金融
□ plus	さらに
□ to put it simply	簡単に言えば、つまり

Against

□ spacious	広々とした
□ stressful	ストレスがたまる
□ competitive	競争力が高い
□ commuting	通勤
□ generally speaking	一般的に言って
□ endure rush-hour traffic	ラッシュアワーを我慢する
□ on one's way to and from work	仕事への行き帰りで
□ pavement	舗装道路
□ extremely high	極端に高い
□ compared with	~と比べて
□ in rural areas	地方では
□ low-wage earner	低所得者
□ make ends meet	家計をやりくりする
□ crime rate	犯罪発生率
□ avoid being robbed	泥棒に遭うのを避ける
□ densely populated	人口密度の高い
□ hectic life	大忙しの生活
□ stressed	ストレスがたまっている

Tips | 論理的に展開するためのキーフレーズ

根拠を示す⑤

❶	There are numerous benefits to taking daily supplements.	サプリメントを毎日摂取することにはたくさんのメリットがあります。
❷	There are great advantages to owning a home.	家を所有することには大きなメリットがあります。
❸	There are some downsides associated with the use of antibiotics.	抗生物質を使うことで生じるリスクがあります。
❹	Is there any potential downside to online transactions?	オンライン取引には、潜在的なマイナス面があるのですか。
❺	There are some drawbacks you should be aware of before you live with your wife's family.	妻の家族と同居する前に承知しておくべきマイナス面がいくつかあります。
❻	What are the drawbacks of globalization for our company?	会社をグローバル化することのデメリットは何ですか。
❼	The deterioration of both relations has nothing but disadvantages for both Japan and the USA.	両国間の関係悪化は、日本とアメリカ合衆国両国にとって、マイナスでしかありません。

要約・結論・結果を示す②

❶	The unemployment rate is high, prices are high; in a nutshell, the economy is in trouble.	失業率が高く、物価が高いです。一言で言うと、経済が厳しい状況です。
❷	First, make a to-do list. Then, prioritize what you need to do. In a nutshell, a to-do list makes you become a good time manager.	やるべきことのリストを作りなさい。それから、やるべきことの優先順位をつけなさい。一言で言うと、やるべきことのリストを作ることで、時間の使い方がうまくなります。
❸	She is neither organized nor diligent. In short, she is hopeless.	彼女は計画的でも勤勉でもありません。要するに、彼女は見込みがありません。
❹	Riding a bicycle is good for your health. Bicycles are environmentally friendly. In summary, it's obvious that commuting by bicycle has plenty of advantages.	自転車に乗ることは健康に良いです。自転車は環境にやさしいです。要するに自転車通勤には、多くのメリットがあります。
❺	To wrap up, we provide the best service with strict management.	まとめると、私たちは、徹底した管理でよいサービスを提供しています。

Speech 28 Is it necessary to get married?

結婚は必要か？

背景知識とヒント

日本の未婚率は上昇中

日本人の生涯未婚率は、男性が 30% 近く、女性が 20% 近くに達しています。年を追うごとに、結婚しないことを選ぶ男性、女性が増えているようです。その理由は、「結婚しても生活を維持する給与が少ない」、「結婚により自分の自由が制限される」、「良い相手に巡り合えていない」 などさまざまです。

多様な生き方が尊重されている現代において、結婚はもはや必要不可欠なものではなくなっているようです。しかし、結婚を選択しないことによるデメリットも、当然存在します。日本の未婚率は、今後どうなるのでしょうか。

知っトク情報：頻出の関連トピック

Do arranged marriages have a place in modern society? / Do arranged marriages have a role to play in society today? / Japan's declining birthrate—a national crisis? / The cause of the decreasing birthrate in Japan.

コンセプトマップ

反対バージョンを参考にスピーチの土台となるコンセプトマップを作ってみましょう。

Assertion

I disagree with the idea of getting married.

Reason 1

difficult to find the right life partner

Reason 2

restrict one's freedom

Example 1

- nearly 200,000 couples divorce
- mentally and physically stressed and exhausted

Example 2

- can't enjoy one's hobbies
- financial burden

Assertion (Conclusion)

I disagree with the idea of getting married.

Speech | スピーチ

For | 賛成バージョン 28-❶

A
Assertion
主張

Nowadays, some people are hesitant to get married for a number of reasons. I don't understand why this is so. I agree with the idea of getting married. I have two points to make.

最近、いくつもの理由で結婚するのをためらう人がいます。なぜなのかわかりません。結婚するという考えに賛成です。2つのポイントがあります。

R1
Reason
理由

The first reason for supporting this opinion is that marriage makes us happy.

この理由を支持する第一の理由は、結婚は私たちを幸せにしてくれることです。

E1
Example
例

To be specific, we can receive increased emotional support through living with our loved one. It's often said that "A joy shared is double; a grief shared is halved." Through marriage, we can endure even the most difficult challenges, like someone's death or unemployment. Conversely, we can also double the joy of a child's birth or someone's promotion.

具体的に言えば、愛する人と一緒に住むことで、さらなる心の支えを得ることができます。「喜びは分かち合えば倍増し、悲しみは分かち合えば半減する」とよく言われます。結婚を通して、誰かの死や失業のような最も難しい試練に耐えることができます。逆に、子どもの誕生や昇進の喜びを倍にすることができます。

R2
Reason
理由

The second reason for supporting this opinion is financially related.

第二の理由は、お金が関係しています。

E2
Example
例

To be specific, with both spouses, husband and wife, working, we can double our income. In this way, we can enjoy a comfortable and affluent life. Plus, side by side, we can shoulder housework together. As a result, we are able to create time for further fulfillment in our lives.

具体的に言えば、両配偶者、夫婦両方で働いて収入を倍にできます。このようにして、快適でゆとりのある生活を享受することができます。しかも、協力して一緒に家事を担うことができます。結果として、人生を一層満足するための時間にできるのです。

A
Assertion (Conclusion)
主張

In a nutshell, I'm sure it's a good idea to halve sorrow and double both joy and income through marriage. We can share burdens and responsibilities. For these reasons, I agree with the idea of getting married.

(203 words)

要するに、結婚を通して、悲しみを半減し、喜びや収入を倍増させることは良い考えだと確信します。負担と責任を共有できます。これらの理由で、結婚するという考えに賛成です。

Against 反対バージョン 28-❷

083

A
Assertion
主張

It's often said that "love is blind". Literally speaking, especially during the dating period of a relationship, it's impossible to see a loved one as he or she really is. Furthermore, married people must compromise on at least something—large or small—every day. Therefore, I disagree with the idea of getting married. I have two points to make.

「恋は盲目である」とよく言われます。文字通りに言えば、交際している期間は特に、恋する人の本当の姿を見ることは不可能なのです。さらに、結婚した人は、毎日、大小何であれ、少なくとも何かに妥協しなければいけません。したがって、結婚するという考えに反対です。２つのポイントがあります。

R1
Reason
理由

First, it's difficult to find the right life partner.

第一に、人生の良きパートナーを見つけることは難しいからです。

E1
Example
例

To be specific, in Japan, these days, nearly 200,000 couples divorce every year. Divorce makes us both mentally and physically stressed and exhausted. It also hurts us financially. If we get married to the wrong person, we have to deal with disagreeable traits, habits, and finally, probable divorce. As a result, we are likely to experience emotional and financial distress.

具体的に言えば、最近、日本では、毎年 200,000 組に近い夫婦が離婚しています。離婚により、精神的にも肉体的にもストレスを受け、疲れ果てます。金銭的にも痛手を受けます。もし適切でない人と結婚したら、不愉快な性格、習慣に対応しなければいけないし、そして、最終的には、おそらく離婚しなければいけません。結果として、精神的、金銭的な苦しみを経験することになります。

R2
Reason
理由

Second, marriage and later parenthood can significantly restrict one's freedom.

第二に、結婚やその後の子育ては、人の自由を大きく制限する可能性があります。

E2
Example
例

To be specific, we can't pursue our hobbies with zeal, like playing a role-playing game (RPG) all night long. In a sense, we have to put up with our spouse's mood—good or bad—all the time. Plus, once we have children, we have to take care of them 24/7 until they become independent. Besides, children are also a great financial burden. Therefore, we can't spend our hard-earned money freely.

具体的に言えば、熱狂的に夜通しRPG ゲームをするような趣味を、追求できません。ある意味、良いことでも悪いことでも、いつも配偶者の気分に耐えなければならないのです。しかも、いったん子どもを授かったら、自立するまで毎日24時間、世話をしなければなりません。さらに子どもは、大きな家計の負担です。そのため、苦労して稼いだお金を自由に使えないのです。

A
Assertion (Conclusion)
主張

In a nutshell, there is no guarantee when choosing a person to marry. Marriage is like the lottery. We don't have to risk staking our life on the possibility of choosing the correct marriage partner. Remaining single, we can live happily. For these reasons, I disagree with the idea of getting married.

(260 words)

要するに、結婚する人を選ぶ時には、なんの保証もないのです。結婚は宝くじのようなものです。適切な結婚相手を選ぶ可能性に人生をかける必要はありません。独身でいても幸せに生きていけます。このような理由から、結婚するという考えに反対です。

Words and Phrases

For

□ be hesitant to	～するのをためらっている
□ for a number of reasons	いくつもの理由で、たくさんの理由で
□ to be specific	具体的に言えば、はっきり言えば
□ receive increased emotional support	さらなる心の支えを受ける
□ endure challenges	試練に耐える
□ unemployment	失業
□ conversely	逆に言うと
□ promotion	昇進、出世
□ financially related	お金が関係した
□ spouse	配偶者
□ double one's income	収入を倍にする
□ enjoy a comfortable and affluent life	快適でゆとりのある生活を享受する、楽しむ
□ side by side	協力して；並んで、一緒に
□ shoulder housework together	家事を一緒に担う
□ fulfillment	満足感
□ in a nutshell	要するに、一言で言えば
□ share burdens and responsibilities	負担と責任を共有する

Against

□ Love is blind.	恋は盲目である。
□ literally speaking	文字通り言えば
□ during the dating period of a relationship	交際している期間は
□ compromise on	～に関して妥協する
□ right life partner	人生の良きパートナー
□ divorce	離婚する
□ deal with disagreeable traits, habits	不愉快な性格や習慣に折り合いをつける
□ financial distress	金銭的苦しみ、財政難
□ parenthood	親であること
□ restrict one's freedom	自由を制限する
□ pursue one's hobbies	趣味を追求する
□ with zeal	熱狂的に
□ put up with	～を我慢する
□ 24/7	毎日24時間
□ financial burden	金銭的な苦痛
□ hard-earned money	苦労して稼いだお金
□ there is no guarantee	なんの保証もない
□ Marriage is like the lottery.	結婚は宝くじのようなものである。
□ stake one's life on	～に人生をかける

Tips | 論理的に展開するためのキーフレーズ

比較・対照を示す②

❶	Some regulations are loosening in some schools in Japan. Conversely, some Australian regulations are stricter than those in Japan.	日本の一部の学校では規則が緩和されつつあります。逆に、オーストラリアの規則は、日本より厳しいところもあります。
❷	Many countries still depend on limited energy sources like oil and gas. In contrast, some have started to use renewable solar energy.	多くの国は石油やガスのような限られたエネルギー源に、いまだに頼っています。対照的に、再生可能な太陽エネルギーを使い始めた国もあります。
❸	In my country, business conditions have been going smoothly recently. On the other hand, in France, the unemployment rate is high.	私の国では、最近、景気が順調です。一方、フランスでは、失業率が高いです。
❹	Now, about 40% of people support the ruling party. On the other hand, 50% of them support the opposition parties.	今、40%の人が与党を支持しています。一方、50%の人が野党を支持しています。
❺	You think you're right, whereas I assume that you are wrong.	あなたは自分が正しいと思っていますが、私はあなたが間違っていると思います。

反論を示す③

❶	I am strongly against the idea of legalizing casinos in Japan.	日本でカジノを合法化する考えに強く反対します。
❷	I totally disagree with whale hunting.	私は捕鯨に断固反対です。
❸	I don't approve of what you're suggesting right now.	今、提案していることに反対します。
❹	Some people are against this policy.	この政策に反対する人がいます。
❺	I am totally against your plan to cut the advertising budget.	広告予算をカットするという計画には、絶対反対です。

Speech 29

Should resale of concert tickets by scalpers be prohibited?

チケットの転売は禁止されるべきか？

背景知識とヒント

チケットの転売をめぐる意見の対立

チケット不正転売禁止法の施行により、チケットの高額転売が禁止され、本当にチケットを必要としている人に好意的に受け止められています。しかし、この法律では個人間での取引を完全に規制できない場面もあります。オンライン上のやり取りが一般的となった現在では、全ての問題が解決していません。

その一方で、「チケットの自由な売買は、資本主義社会の基本である」という意見もあります。チケットの高額転売は禁止されるべきなのでしょうか。

知っトク情報：頻出の関連トピック

Are monopolies in business ever acceptable? / Business ethics: Product quality vs. the profit motive. / Are large corporations solely interested in generating profits?

コンセプトマップ

反対バージョンを参考にスピーチの土台となるコンセプトマップを作ってみましょう。

Assertion

I disagree with prohibiting the resale of concert tickets by scalpers.

Reason 1

governed by the supply and demand

Reason 2

resale of tickets would be convenient

Example 1

- famous painting, rare
- very limited supply
- become priceless without stopping

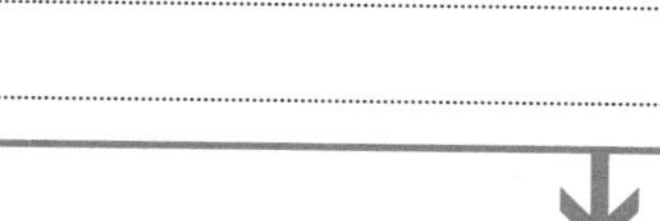

Example 2

- can't go to a concert for personal reasons

Assertion (Conclusion)

I disagree with prohibiting the resale of concert tickets by scalpers.

Speech | スピーチ

For | 賛成バージョン 29-❶

A
Assertion
主張

Nowadays, ticket scalpers buy large quantities of tickets in order to obtain huge profits. They often make profits more than 30 times the original ticket price. Therefore, I agree with prohibiting the resale of concert tickets by scalpers. I have two reasons to give.

今日、ダフ屋が巨額の利益を得るために、大量のチケットを買っています。彼らは往々にしてチケットの元の価格の30倍以上もの利益を手に入れます。そのため、ダフ屋によるコンサートチケットの転売を禁じることに賛成します。2つの理由があります。

R1
Reason
理由

First, we should not promote the increase of concert ticket prices. Concerts are precious and inspiring events where ordinary fans can experience their favorite musicians live. However, scalpers rob music fans of the chance to enjoy such live music.

第一に、コンサートチケットの値段をせり上げるべきではありません。コンサートは、普通のファンが、大好きなミュージシャンのライブを経験できる、貴重でパワーをもらえるイベントです。しかし、ダフ屋がそんなライブ音楽を楽しむチャンスを音楽ファンから奪うのです。

E1
Example
例

For example, music fans look forward to seeing and hearing great musicians directly at a particular concert venue. They often find that the concert tickets for popular and gifted musicians have already been bought up by scalpers by the time they get online to purchase them. Moreover, the tickets are being resold at prices higher than what they can afford. Such misconduct by scalpers should not be allowed.

例えば、音楽ファンは、特別なコンサート会場で素晴らしいミュージシャンを直接目にし、音楽を聴くのを楽しみにしています。彼らがオンラインでチケットを手に入れるまでに、人気があり才能もあるミュージシャンのコンサートチケットは、ダフ屋によってすでに買い占められていることに気づきます。しかも、チケットは、ファンが払うことのできない高値で売られているのです。ダフ屋のそんな違法行為は、許されるべきではありません。

R2 Reason 理由

Second, ticket prices should not be deceitfully changed, as musicians and their production companies purposely offer reasonably priced tickets for fans. However, the prices of resold tickets have nothing to do with the original prices' purpose.

第二に、チケットの値段は詐欺まがいに変えられるべきではありません。ミュージシャンやプロダクションは、意図的に手が届く値段のチケットをファンに提供しているのです。しかし、転売されるチケットの値段は元の値段の趣旨とは何も関係がありません。

E2 Example 例

For example, original tickets priced at 10,000 yen or less have been resold for more than 300,000 yen. Unfortunately, the ticket resale market has been rapidly expanding because of the spread of online transactions. The greater problem is that scalpers obtain an eye-popping profit from reselling tickets. Also, they rob fans of both their hard-earned money or their opportunity to see their favorite musicians in person.

例えば、元の値段が1万円以下でも、30万円以上で転売されているのです。不運にも、オンライン取引の普及のせいで、チケットの転売市場が拡大しているのです。大きな問題は、ダフ屋は、チケットを転売することで目が飛び出るほどの利益を得ることです。また彼らは、ファンが苦労して稼いだお金、もしくは大好きなミュージシャンと直接会う機会を奪っているのです。

A Assertion (Conclusion) 主張

In summary, the resale of concert tickets carries two disadvantages for fans. The first is that, due to increased ticket prices, ordinary fans who want to see concerts can't see them. The other is that the price of concert tickets is actually controlled by the scalpers. For these reasons, I agree with prohibiting the resale of concert tickets by scalpers.

(313 words)

結論として、コンサートチケットの転売は、ファンにとって2つのデメリットがあります。1つ目は、チケットの値段が高くなったため、コンサートを見たい普通のファンが見ることができないことです。もう1つは、チケットの値段が実際にはダフ屋によってコントロールされていることです。このような理由で、ダフ屋によるコンサートチケットの転売禁止に賛成です。

Against 反対バージョン 29-❷

086

A
Assertion
主張

According to recent news, online ticket scalping is on the rise. As a result, more than 100 musicians are calling for a halt to the resale of concert tickets. However, I disagree with prohibiting the resale of concert tickets by scalpers. I have two reasons to give.

最近のニュースによると、オンラインチケットのダフ屋が増えています。結果として、100人以上のミュージシャンがコンサートチケットの転売の中止を呼びかけています。しかし、ダフ屋によるコンサートチケットの転売を禁止することに反対です。2つの理由があります。

R1
Reason
理由

First, the sales market is governed by the laws of supply and demand.

第一に、販売市場は需要と供給の法則によって支配されています。

E1
Example
例

For example, a famous painting, being rare and thus in very limited supply, can be purchased at a record-high price. Or later, it will become priceless because it's in high demand. In this way, prices are determined by supply and demand. This rule applies to the sale of concert tickets as well. There is a great demand for the concert tickets of popular musicians. And so, it's only natural that the prices for these tickets should increase by a lot. Higher prices mean that such artists have succeeded in becoming very famous.

例えば、ある有名な絵は、最高の出きばえだけれども、数に限りがあるので、高値で購入されます。また後に、人気が出て、値段がつけられないほど高値になります。このように、値段は需要と供給によって決められます。このルールはコンサートチケットの売買にも適用されます。人気のあるミュージシャンのコンサートチケットには、大きな需要があります。そのため、値段がかなり上がるのは当然なのです。より高い値段は、アーティストが有名になって成功した証です。

R2
Reason
理由

Second, an online transaction system allowing the resale of tickets would be very convenient.

第二に、チケットの転売を認めるオンライン取引システムは大変便利です。

E2
Example
例

For example, there are always some fans with tickets who suddenly can't go to a particular concert for personal reasons. Somebody might say, "I can't make it to the next concert because of work." At that time, the online transaction system is an easy way to find someone who is still looking for tickets to the concert.

例えば、チケットを持っているファンの中には、個人的理由で突然コンサートに行けなくなる人が必ずいます。「次のコンサートは仕事で行けない」という人がいるかもしれません。そういう場合、オンライン取引システムは、コンサートのチケットをまだ探している人を見つける簡単な方法なのです。

A
Assertion (Conclusion)
主張

In summary, we live in a society with a free competitive market. Under the principles of such a market, we should not legally prohibit ticket resale systems. Therefore, I disagree with prohibiting the resale of concert tickets by scalpers.

(262 words)

結論として、私たちは自由競争の社会に住んでいます。そのような市場の原則の下では、法によってチケットの転売システムを禁止すべきではありません。そのため、ダフ屋によるコンサートチケットの転売を禁止することに反対です。

Words and Phrases

087

For

□ ticket scalper	ダフ屋、転売ヤー
□ large quantities of tickets	大量のチケット
□ make profits	利益を得る
□ original ticket price	チケットの元の価格
□ promote the increase of	～の増加を促す
□ precious and inspiring events	大切で元気づけてくれるイベント
□ ordinary fan	一般のファン
□ rob ～ of the chance	～からチャンスを奪う
□ look forward to ～ing	～することを楽しみにして待つ
□ concert venue	コンサート会場
□ gifted musician	才能のあるミュージシャン
□ purchase	～を購入する
□ misconduct	違法行為
□ deceitfully	詐欺的に
□ offer reasonably priced tickets	手が届く値段のチケットを提供する
□ original price	元の価格
□ spread of online transactions	オンライン取引の普及
□ obtain an eye-popping profit from	～から目が飛び出るほどの利益を得る
□ see ～ in person	～に直接会う

Against

□ be on the rise	増えている
□ call for a halt to	～の中止を呼びかける
□ be governed by the laws of supply and demand	需要と供給の法則によって支配されている
□ rare	最高の；珍しい
□ in limited supply	数に限りがある
□ at a record-high price	最高の価格で
□ in high demand	大きな需要がある、人気がある
□ become priceless	値段がつけられないほど高値になる
□ be determined by supply and demand	需要と供給によって決まる
□ this rule applies to	このルールは～に適用する
□ ～ as well	～もまた
□ there is a great demand for	～に対する大きな需要がある
□ online transaction system	オンライン取引システム
□ for personal reasons	個人的理由で
□ I can't make it.	都合がつかない。
□ society with a free competitive market	自由競争の社会
□ under the principles of	～の原則に従い、下で

Tips | 論理的に展開するためのキーフレーズ

強調を示す③

❶	What counts most is to keep fit and dedicate yourself to work.	最も重要なのは、健康を保ち、仕事に打ち込むことです。
❷	What matters is to describe the present situation in detail.	大切なことは、現在の状況を詳細に描写することです。
❸	What matters is that we fulfill our engagements with clients.	大切なことは、顧客との約束を果たすことです。
❹	The top priority is to share information with colleagues.	最優先すべきことは、同僚と情報を共有することです。
❺	My first priority is to have a job with high salary.	私が最優先すべきことは、高収入の仕事に就くことです。
❻	Most importantly, you must keep a record of all business transactions.	大切なことは、すべての仕事上の取引を記録に残さなければいけないことです。
❼	The crux of the matter is that people are afraid of change.	問題の核心は、人は変化を恐れるということです。

類似を示す

❶	These dishes are cooked in a similar way, but they taste very different.	これらの料理は似たような方法で調理されますが、味はずいぶん違います。
❷	In the same way, we have to be more careful dealing with confidential client information.	同じように、顧客の機密情報の取扱いに注意しなくてはいけません。
❸	By the same token, you are required to submit your regular report this month.	同じように、今月、定期レポートを提出しなければいけません。
❹	I don't love her, but by the same token, I don't want to hurt her.	彼女を愛してはいません。しかし、同様に彼女を傷つけたくないです。
❺	Likewise, we must develop good eating habits from childhood.	同じように、子どものころからよい食習慣を身につけなければなりません。

Are dating apps a worthwhile option?

出会い系サイトを試す価値はあるか？

背景知識とヒント

今やオンラインでの出会いは常識？

ある調査によれば、アメリカでは、結婚したカップルの３分の１以上が出会い系サイトで出会っているそうです。また、出会い系サイトで出会ったカップルは、オフラインで出会ったカップルと比べて、幸せの度合いが上回っているという結果も出ています。

このように、出会い系サイトは、アメリカなどではかなり一般的な出会いの方法になってきています。今や、インターネットも出会いの場の１つとして考えることのできる時代なのです。

知っトク情報：頻出の関連トピック

Is the Internet bringing the world's cultures closer together? / Will the Internet harm interpersonal communication? / Should more be done to protect people's privacy on the Internet?

コンセプトマップ

反対バージョンを参考にスピーチの土台となるコンセプトマップを作ってみましょう。

Assertion

I disagree that dating apps are worthwhile.

Reason 1

can be dangerous

Reason 2

difficult to know a person via the Internet

Example 1

- lost quite a lot of money
- fall victim to fraud
- remain anonymous

Example 2

- text messages
- still photos

Assertion (Conclusion)

I disagree that dating apps are worthwhile.

Speech | スピーチ

088

For | 賛成バージョン 30-❶

A Assertion 主張

Today many people use the Internet as a tool for finding a partner. Dating apps have opened a huge door for people who want to get married. This is also good for people who are busy, shy, in small towns or urban condominiums, and so on. The Internet brings various benefits. Therefore, I agree that dating apps are worthwhile. I have two points to make.

今日、多くの人はパートナーを探すためのツールとしてインターネットを使います。出会い系サイトは、結婚したいすべての人に大きな門戸を開いてくれました。これは、小さな町か都市部の分譲マンションなどに住んでいて、多忙で恥ずかしがり屋の人にも良いでしょう。インターネットはいろいろな恩恵をもたらします。そのため、出会い系サイトは価値があるということに賛成です。2つのポイントがあります。

R1 Reason 理由

First, the procedure is very simple.

第一に、手続きが大変簡単です。

E1 Example 例

For example, once you join a dating app, all you have to do is answer basic questions and create your profile including a photo. You can also pre-screen many profiles before you make contact with someone. Furthermore, you can check the potential partner's personal income, characteristics, and family background in order to make a decision about whether or not to date him or her.

例えば、いったん出会い系サイトのサービスに加入したら、基本的な質問に答え、写真を含むプロフィールを作りさえすればよいのです。誰かと連絡を取る前に、たくさんのプロフィールを事前に選別できます。さらに、交際するかどうかについて決めるために、パートナー候補の個人所得、性格、家庭環境を確認できます。

R2
Assertion
主張

Second, dating apps are cost-effective.

第二に、出会い系サイトは費用対効果が高いです。

E2
Reason
理由

For example, some offer free memberships online. Moreover, before actually meeting a potential partner, you are able to get to know them better and faster through online messages and chatting. Generally speaking, when dating someone, you spend a lot of money on gas, meals, and usually some form of entertainment, such as a movie or a musical. Then you decide whether or not you will become a couple. Dating apps, on the other hand, save time and money.

例えば、会員権を無料で提供しているところがあります。さらに、実際にパートナー候補と会う前に、オンラインのメッセージやチャットを通して、より良く早く、その人を理解できます。一般的に言って、誰かとデートするときには、車のガソリン代や食事代、そして、たいていは映画やミュージカルのような、なんらかの娯楽に、たくさんのお金を使います。そうして、カップルになるかどうかを決めます。一方、出会い系サイトは時間やお金を節約できます。

A
Assertion (Conclusion)
主張

In summary, dating apps are very convenient and save time and money. Dating apps are especially useful for busy, introverted, and isolated people. Therefore, I agree that dating apps are worthwhile due to these points.

(253 words)

要約すれば、出会い系サイトは、大変便利です。そして時間とお金を節約してくれます。出会い系サイトは、多忙で内向的で、人と交わらない人には特に役に立ちます。そのため、出会い系サイトは、これらの点で価値があるということに賛成します。

Against | 反対バージョン 30-❷

089

A
Assertion
主張

People tend to exaggerate personal facts and physical characteristics in online profiles. As a result, a number of profiles contain false information regarding age, face, yearly salary, and the like. You can't completely believe what is on the Internet. Therefore, I disagree that dating apps are worthwhile. I have two points to make.

人は、オンライン上のプロフィールでは、個人的な情報や身体的特徴を誇張する傾向にあります。結果として、たくさんのプロフィールに、年齢、顔、年収などに関して偽の情報が含まれています。インターネット上のことは完全に信じることはできません。そのため、出会い系サイトに価値があるということに反対です。2つのポイントがあります。

R1
Reason
理由

First, dating apps can be dangerous.

第一に、出会い系サイトは危険である可能性があります。

E1
Example
例

For example, there was a woman who lost quite a lot of money because of a boyfriend she met on a dating app. That was an actual fraud case. There is always the possibility of falling victim to fraud on a dating app like this. The ability for people to remain anonymous on the Internet often causes lots of problems.

例えば、出会い系サイトで会ったボーイフレンドのせいで、かなりの大金を失った女性がいました。それは、実際の詐欺事件です。このように、出会い系サイトでは、詐欺に引っかかる可能性が常にあります。インターネット上で匿名のままでいられることが、たくさんの問題を引き起こします。

R2
Assertion
主張

Second, it's difficult to really get to know a person and make sure that you are truly attracted to that person via the Internet.

第二に、インターネットを通してある人を本当に知り、その人に本当に惹きつけられたかどうか確かめることは難しいです。

E2
Reason
理由

For example, usually, a couple is first attracted to each other through facial expressions, gestures, tone of voice, and so on. You are neither easily attracted nor completely understood by each other through text messages and still photos alone.

例えば、普通カップルは、最初は、表情、ジェスチャー、声の調子などを通してお互いに惹かれます。テキストメッセージや静止画像だけで、簡単に惹かれたり、完全に理解したりすることはしません。

A
Assertion (Conclusion)
主張

In summary, the Internet is not ideal with respect to developing in-depth understanding of one another, actual attraction, and maintaining overall safety. Therefore, I disagree that dating apps are worthwhile considering these points.

(215 words)

要約すると、お互いの理解や実際の愛情を深めたり、全体的な安全を維持したりすることに関しては、インターネットは、理想的でありません。そのため、これらの点を考慮して、出会い系サイトは価値があるということに反対です。

Words and Phrases

090

For

□ as a tool for	～のための道具として
□ open a huge door for	～のために大きな門戸を開く
□ urban condominiums	都市部の分譲マンション
□ bring various benefits	さまざまな恩恵をもたらす
□ procedure	手続き
□ all you have to do is	～しさえすればよい
□ create profile	プロファイルを作成する
□ pre-screen	事前に選別する
□ personal income	個人所得
□ characteristics	性格
□ family background	家庭環境
□ cost-effective	費用対効果の高い
□ offer ~ free membership	会員権を～に無料で提供する
□ get to know	～を知るようになる
□ through online messages and chatting	オンラインメッセージやチャットを通して
□ generally speaking	一般的に言って
□ in summary	要約すれば
□ be useful for	～にとって役に立つ
□ introverted and isolated people	内向的で孤立した人

Against

□ tend to exaggerate	大げさに言う傾向がある
□ a number of profiles	たくさんのプロフィール
□ contain false information	偽の情報が含まれている
□ regarding age	年齢に関して
□ and the like	（具体例に続けて）など
□ actual fraud case	実際の詐欺事件
□ fall victim to fraud	詐欺に引っかかる
□ remain anonymous	匿名のままでいる
□ really get to know	～を本当に知る
□ make sure that	～であることを確認する
□ be attracted to	～に惹きつけられる
□ through facial expressions	表情を通して
□ tone of voice	声の調子
□ through text messages and still photos	テキストメッセージや静止画像を通して
□ ideal	理想的な
□ with respect to	～に関して
□ develop in-depth understanding of	徹底的に～の理解を深める
□ one another	お互いに
□ actual attraction	実際の魅力
□ maintain overall safety	全体的な安全を維持する

Tips | 論理的に展開するためのキーフレーズ

観点を示す④

❶	Statistically speaking, more typhoons approach Japan in September.	統計的に言えば、9月にはもっと多くの台風が日本に近づきます。
❷	Strictly speaking, your view is slightly different from mine.	厳密に言えば、あなたの意見は私のとは少し違います。
❸	Strictly speaking, this anecdote is not based on a true story.	厳密に言えば、この逸話は本当の話に基づいていません。
❹	Concretely speaking, we need to increase sales by 10% before the end of this year.	具体的に言えば、今年末前に、売り上げを10%上げる必要があります。
❺	Economically speaking, the consumption tax rate should be raised to 15%.	経済的に言って、消費税率は15%まで上げるべきです。

傾向を示す②

❶	Women tend to live longer than men do.	女性は男性より長生きする傾向にあります。
❷	Do you tend to agree with his analysis?	あなたは彼の分析に同意する傾向があるのですか。
❸	New cars are more likely to have safety features, such as for preventing crashes or detecting pedestrians.	新車は安全機能を搭載する傾向にあります。例えば、衝突防止や歩行者感知機能です。
❹	It is likely that hosting the Olympics will bring economic benefits.	オリンピックは経済効果をもたらす傾向にあります。
❺	He has a tendency to buy clothes on impulse. As a result, he really regrets his actions.	彼は服を衝動買いする傾向にあります。結果として、本当に行動を後悔しています。
❻	My colleague is prone to forget to save backup data to the hard drive.	同僚はハードドライブにバックアップデータを保存することを忘れがちです。

AREA式で英語2分間スピーキング

段階的実践トレーニング 完走チェック！

p.14～p.17のトレーニング方法を実践し、チェックをつけましょう。

STEP 1 テーマの背景知識を知る □□□□

STEP 2 自分の考えに関するキーワードをコンセプトマップにメモ □□□□

STEP 3 サンプルスピーチの音声を確認 □□□□

STEP 4 サンプルスピーチを読んで内容を理解 □□□□

STEP 5 音声を確認して音読 □□□□

STEP 6 オーバーラップリーディング □□□□

STEP 7 ディクテーション □□□□

STEP 8 シャドーイングに挑戦 □□□□

STEP 9 コンセプトマップを確認してスピーチを再構築 □□□□

STEP 10 毎日継続！ □□□□

Part 2

Dialogue

ダイアローグ

Should self-driving cars be allowed on the streets?

自動運転車を許可するべきか？

背景知識とヒント

自動車の自動運転化の技術開発が進み、すでに大手メーカーでは、ドライバー対応の条件付きの自動運転車の販売に至っています。将来的には、「運転手が必要のない」安全運転自動化を目指して、各社が競い合っています。自動運転車に対する反応は、「交通事故のリスクが減る」、「運転する体力的な負荷を減らしてくれる」、「自分で運転する楽しみが減る」などさまざまです。

091

TV Anchor: Under the amended Road Traffic Law, unmanned automated mobility services are now available in limited areas. However, there are some restrictions, such as a maximum speed of 12 km/h. This technology is still in the experimental stage. (37 words)

TV Anchor: 改正された道路交通法の下で、無人自動移動サービスが一部地域で利用可能になりました。しかし、最高速度が時速12キロメートルといった制限があります。この技術はまだ実験段階です。

Dialogue | ダイアローグ

Tim: Self-driving cars are more likely to become a reality in the near future. Would you like to ride in a self-driving car?

Meg: Definitely not. I don't want to die in an accident caused by poor maintenance of the car's Information Technology (IT) system. I mean I don't trust Artificial Intelligence (AI) completely.

Tim: What you are saying is totally wrong. The statistics show more than 80% of car accidents are caused by human error. People are prone to making errors when they are tired. The main causes of death in car accidents are distracted driving, speeding, and drunken driving.

Meg: I don't expect any AI to be perfect every time. After all, computers are programmed by humans. Besides, there are some drawbacks to self-driving cars.

Tim: What are they?

Meg: Well, when it comes to truck companies and taxi companies, self-driving cars will take away many driving jobs.

Tim: What you're saying is partially true, but the biggest benefit is free time while commuting by car. You can catch up on work, send a text message, take a rest, or play video games. Such cars are truly convenient for the elderly and the blind, too.

Tim: 近い将来、自動運転車は実現しそうだね。自動運転車に乗ってみたいかい？

Meg: 絶対いやよ。自動車の情報技術システムの整備不良が原因で起きる事故で死にたくないわ。つまり、私は人工知能を完全に信用していないの。

Tim: 君の言っていることは大間違いだよ。統計によると、自動車事故の80%が人的ミスによるものなんだ。人は疲れるとミスをしがちなんだよ。自動車事故死の主な原因は、不注意運転、スピード違反、それに飲酒運転なんだ。

Meg: 私は、どんなAIも常に完璧だとは期待していないの。結局、コンピュータは人間によってプログラムされているのだし。しかも、自動運転車にもいくつかマイナス点はあるわ。

Tim: 何があるんだい。

Meg: トラックやタクシーの会社に関して言えば、自動運転車は、多くの運転手の仕事を奪うでしょうね。

Tim: 君が言っていることは部分的に正しいけど、最大のプラス面は、自動車で通勤する間の自由時間だね。仕事を仕上げたり、メッセージを送ったり、休憩したり、テレビゲームをしたりできるしね。そんな自動車は高齢者や目の不自由な人にとっても、本当に便利だよ。

Furthermore, self-driving cars have lots of useful functions like auto-parking systems, automatic emergency brakes, rerouting around traffic jams, and so on. A self-driving car is an epoch-making innovation.

Meg: You have a point there. This time, the pros outweigh the cons.

(228 words)

さらに、自動運転車は自動駐車システムや緊急自動ブレーキ、交通渋滞の回避など、役に立つ多くの機能を備えているしね。自動運転車は画期的な革新だよ。

Meg: それもそうね。今回は、メリットがデメリットを上回っているわ。

Words and Phrases

□ a self-driving car	自動運転車
□ amended	（法律が）改正された
□ the Road Traffic Law	道路交通法
□ unmanned automated mobility service	無人自動移動サービス
□ maximum speed of 12 km/h	最高速度時速 12 キロメートル
□ in the experimental stage	実験段階の
□ be likely to	～しそうである
□ become a reality	実現する
□ poor maintenance of	～の整備不良
□ trust AI completely	人工知能を完全に信用する
□ the statistics show	統計によれば
□ be caused by human error	人的ミスによって引き起こされる
□ be prone to	～しがちである、傾向にある
□ distracted driving	不注意運転
□ speeding and drunken driving	スピード違反や飲酒運転
□ be programmed by	～によってプログラムされている
□ there are some drawbacks to	～にいくつかマイナス面がある
□ when it comes to	～に関して言えば
□ take away many jobs	多くの仕事を奪う
□ what you're saying is partially true, but	あなたが言っていることは部分的に正しいが
□ the biggest benefit is	最大のプラス面は～である
□ commute by car	車で通勤する
□ catch up on work	仕事を仕上げる
□ send a text message	メッセージを送る
□ take a rest	休憩する
□ be convenient for	～にとって都合がよい、便利である
□ the elderly and the blind	高齢者や目の不自由な人
□ useful function	役に立つ機能
□ auto-parking system	自動駐車システム
□ automatic emergency brakes	緊急自動ブレーキ

□ reroute around traffic jams	交通渋滞を避けて別のルートに変更する	□ You have a point there.	一理あるね。／それもそうだね。
□ epoch-making innovation	画期的革新	□ The pros outweigh the cons.	メリットがデメリットを上回る。

Tips | 論理的に展開するためのキーフレーズ

根拠を示す⑥

❶	I understand your point of view, but according to statistics, the rate of unemployment in Japan is on the decrease.	あなたの見解は理解しますが、統計によれば、日本の失業率は下がっています。
❷	Statistically speaking, there is no evidence to support this statement.	統計的に言えば、この発言を支持するための証拠は何もありません。
❸	Data shows that more Japanese are suffering from poverty than ever before.	データによれば、多くの日本人が以前よりも貧困に苦しんでいます。
❹	Polls indicate that more than half of all young people are not interested in politics.	世論調査によれば、すべての若者の半分以上が政治に興味がありません。
❺	Statistics show most Japanese are against fighting in the war.	統計的に言えば、大多数の日本人は戦争で戦うことに反対です。
❻	Statistics show the world population will exceed nine billion by 2050.	統計によれば、世界人口は 2050 年までに 90 億を超えるでしょう。
❼	According to a survey, nearly 10% of all women have had cosmetic surgery.	ある調査によれば、すべての女性の10%近くが美容整形手術をしています。
❽	According to a report released on Monday, these species are close to extinction.	月曜日に発表された報告によれば、これらの種は絶滅に近いです。

Should Japan continue space exploration?

日本は宇宙探査を続けるべきか？

背景知識とヒント

第２次世界大戦後の冷戦時に、アメリカ合衆国とソビエト連邦との間で、宇宙開発をめぐり、宇宙開発競争が始まりました。そして月面着陸、宇宙遊泳、人工衛星開発などを経て、いくつか副産物が生まれました。GPS システムはその１つで、日常生活を便利にしてくれています。

TV Anchor: There have been some conspicuous achievements in Japan's space exploration such as the return of an unmanned asteroid probe, Japanese astronauts' active role at the International Space Station, and so on. (31 words)

TV Anchor: 日本の宇宙探査は、いくつものめざましい業績を上げています。例えば、無人の小惑星探査機の帰還や、国際宇宙ステーションにおける日本人宇宙飛行士の積極的な役割などです。

Dialogue | ダイアローグ

Meg: Japan is making a great contribution toward the development of the International Space Station. It's amazing.

Tim: I know of Japan's tremendous achievements in space exploration. I understand the significance of it. But in Japan, we have urgent problems to be solved. For example, poverty, the lack of nursery schools for children, and so on are pressing issues. The money used for space exploration comes from taxpayers. Tax money should be used on social services and welfare.

Meg: You're missing the point. I believe space exploration is indispensable for improving scientific research and encouraging innovation. In a sense, it paves the way to advanced innovations such as GPS systems, Teflon-coated fiberglass and so on, which have become essential to modern life. Space exploration has created a large number of spin-offs like these.

Tim: Well, I see your point, but what about the dangers? Many tragic accidents have already happened. Japanese astronauts haven't been involved yet, though. Plus, traveling into space and visiting other planets are very hazardous to our health.

Meg: Don't you feel excited when you think of finding something amazing in space? It gives us plenty of dreams and hopes for the future. I hope we will find another planet where humans can live.

Meg: 日本は、国際宇宙ステーションの発展に向けて大きな貢献をしているわね。素晴らしいことよ。

Tim: 僕も日本の宇宙探査の素晴らしい業績は知っているよ。その重要性も理解している。でも、日本では、解決すべき緊急の問題があるよね。例えば、貧困、子どもの保育園の不足など差し迫った課題だよ。宇宙探査に使われるお金は、納税者が負担しているんだ。税金は社会サービスや福祉に使われるべきだよ。

Meg: あなたは、論点がわかっていないわ。宇宙探査は科学研究を向上させ、革新を促すのに不可欠だと思っているわ。ある意味、高度な技術革新への道を開いているのよ。例えば、GPS システムやテフロン加工のグラスファイバーとか、現代の生活には不可欠になっているわよね。宇宙探査は、これらの多くの副産物を生み出しているのよ。

Tim: 言いたいことはわかるけどね、危険性はどうなの？　多くの悲しい事故がすでに起きているよね。日本人の宇宙飛行士は、まだ巻き込まれていないけれどね。しかも、宇宙への旅行や他の惑星を訪れることって健康に悪いよ。

Meg: 宇宙で何か素晴らしいものを見つけるって考えたらワクワクしてこない？　宇宙探査は、未来へのたくさんの夢と希望を与えてくれるわ。人間が住むことのできるもう１つの惑星が見つかることを願うわ。

Tim: It's unrealistic. Space exploration requires an enormous amount of resources. I don't believe it's worth the time, effort and money. I'm not saying that we should stop space exploration forever. What I'm saying is we should suspend pouring money into space exploration for the time being and put a higher priority on more immediate problems before us.

Meg: Let's just agree to disagree, today.

(261 words)

Tim: 非現実的だよ。宇宙探査には、非常に多くの資源が必要なんだ。時間と労力とお金を費やすだけの価値があるとは思えないよ。宇宙探査を永久にやめるべきだと言っているわけじゃないんだ。僕が言いたいのは、当分の間、宇宙探査へお金をつぎ込むのを一時中断して、当面の課題を重要視すべきだということなんだ。

Meg: 今日は、見解の相違があるということにしましょうね。

Words and Phrases

094

□ conspicuous achievement	めざましい業績
□ return of an unmanned asteroid probe	無人の小惑星探査機の帰還
□ astronaut	宇宙飛行士
□ the International Space Station	国際宇宙ステーション
□ make a great contribution toward the development of	～の発展に向けて大きく貢献する
□ tremendous achievement	素晴らしい業績
□ space exploration	宇宙探査
□ significance	重要性
□ have an urgent problem	緊急の問題がある
□ poverty	貧困
□ lack of nursery schools	保育園の不足
□ pressing issue	差し迫った課題
□ taxpayer	納税者
□ social services and welfare	社会サービスや福祉
□ You're missing the point.	あなたは論点がわかっていない。
□ be indispensable for	～にとって不可欠である
□ scientific research	科学研究
□ encourage innovation	革新を促す
□ pave the way to	～への道を開く
□ advanced innovations	進歩的な革新
□ GPS system	GPS システム
□ teflon-coated fiberglass	テフロン加工のグラスファイバー
□ become essential to	～にとって必須になる
□ a large number of spin-offs	多くの副産物
□ I see your point, but	あなたの言おうとすることはわかるが
□ be hazardous to	～に有害である

□ an enormous amount of resources	非常に多くの資源
□ It's worth the time, effort and money.	時間と労力とお金を費やすだけの価値がある。
□ suspend pouring money into	～へお金をつぎ込むのを一時的に中断する
□ for the time being	しばらくの間、当分の間
□ put a high priority on	～を重要視する、優先する
□ immediate problem	当面の問題
□ Let's just agree to disagree.	見解の相違があるということにしましょう。

Tips | 論理的に展開するためのキーフレーズ

提案を示す

❶	I understand what you mean, but what about abolishing the retirement age policy?	言いたいことはわかりますが、定年制度政策を廃止するのはどうでしょうか。
❷	I like your idea, but what about targeting women in their 40's?	あなたの考えは気に入りましたが40代の女性をターゲットにするのはどうでしょうか。
❸	That's nice, but what about starting a crowdfunding campaign for disabled people?	それはいいですが、障害者へのクラウドファンディングを始めるのはどうでしょうか。
❹	That sounds nice, but how about this Italian restaurant for tonight?	それは素晴らしいですが、今晩はイタリアンはいかがでしょうか。
❺	I see your point, but how about traveling to Australia in winter?	あなたの言いたいことはわかりますが、冬にオーストラリアへ旅行に行くのはいかがでしょうか。
❻	I like your idea, but how about investing in the stock market?	あなたの考えは気に入りましたが、株式市場に投資するのはどうでしょうか。
❼	I understand your point, but what do you say to implementing a flexible-time policy?	あなたの言いたいことはわかりますが、フレックスタイム制を始めるのはどうでしょうか。
❽	I like your opinion, but what do you say to hiring a housekeeper?	あなたの考えは気に入りましたが、家事代行を雇うのはどうでしょうか。

Should we invest in the stock market?

株式に投資すべきか？

背景知識とヒント

資産運用とは、自分の余裕資金を活用して投資、運用することです。インターネットの発達により、自宅にいてもインターネット証券会社で資産運用のための口座の開設が可能になりました。株式投資とは、企業が資金調達のために発行する株式を売買することです。一個人でも、株式を保有することで、会社の所有者の一員になれます。株式投資にはメリットもデメリットもありますので、注意が必要です。

 095

TV Anchor: In the U.S.A., more than 50% of personal financial assets are invested in stocks or mutual funds, while, in Japan, only about 15% of them are invested in this way. How can we increase the percentage of stock-market investors in Japan? (42 words)

TV Anchor: アメリカでは、個人の金融資産の50%以上が株式か投資信託に投資されています。一方日本では、この方法で投資されているのは約15%のみです。どうしたら、日本における株式市場の投資家の割合を増やせるのでしょうか。

Dialogue | ダイアローグ

Meg: How do you manage your money?

Tim: I regularly deposit a portion of my monthly salary into a savings account. I make it a priority to protect my assets. How about you?

Meg: I make it a rule to invest my money. I invest 20% of my monthly wages in the stock market. It has a high earning potential. I'm dreaming of becoming a billionaire. I'm sure it's a good way to increase my assets.

Tim: I have a different opinion. Investing in the stock market is like gambling. Any returns on the initial investment can't be guaranteed. The profitability of the investment totally relies on the performance and growth of the company. You could lose all of the initial investment, right?

Meg: What you're saying is a little extreme. It's not gambling like buying lottery tickets. Millions of people buy lottery tickets, and they lose most of their investment. Investing in the stock market is not like that. Of course, returns are not guaranteed at all. As history proves, however, over the long run, the stock market usually experiences positive returns.

Tim: I didn't know that. Don't you think the timing of when to buy or sell stocks is hard to predict?

Meg: どのようにお金を運用しているの？

Tim: 毎月の給料の一部を定期的に預金口座へ預けているよ。自分の資産を守るのを最優先しているのさ。君はどうなの？

Meg: 私は、お金を投資することにしているの。毎月の給料のおよそ20%を株式市場に投資しているわ。高い利益が期待できるの。億万長者になりたいしね。資産を増やす良い方法だと確信しているの。

Tim: 僕は違う考えだな。株式市場に投資するのって、ギャンブルみたいなものじゃないか。初期投資の利益は保証されていないよね。投資の収益性は完全に会社の業績と成長頼みだからね。初期投資のすべてを失う可能性だってあるでしょ？

Meg: あなたが言っていることは少し極端ね。株式は、宝くじのようなギャンブルじゃないわ。たくさんの人が宝くじを買って、投資のほとんどを失うわね。株式市場への投資は、そんなんじゃないのよ。もちろん、利益はまったく保証されていないわ。でも、歴史が証明しているように、長い目で見れば、株式市場はたいていはプラスの利益が上がっているのよ。

Tim: それは知らなかったな。株式を買ったり売ったりするタイミングを予想するのが難しくないかい？

Meg: You're totally right. Therefore, I always make efforts to analyze the stock market and buy the right stock. We need to be sensitive to economic trends. The bigger the risk of losing money, the higher the returns on investments and pleasure in investing.

Tim: I kind of understand what you mean, but I still can't support you on this matter.

(205 words)

Meg: そのとおりよ。だから、株式市場を分析して、正しい株式を買う努力をしているのよ。経済の動向に敏感である必要があるの。お金を失うリスクが大きければ大きいほど、投資の利益と投資の喜びが大きくなるわ。

Tim: 言いたいことはある程度わかるけど、この件に関しては、まだ君に賛成できないな。

Words and Phrases

096

□ personal financial assets	個人の金融資産
□ be invested in stocks or mutual funds	株式か投資信託に投資される
□ stock-market investor	株式市場の投資家
□ manage money	お金を管理する、運用する
□ deposit ~ into a savings account	預金口座へ~を預ける
□ a portion of monthly wages	月給の一部
□ make it a priority to	~することを最優先する
□ protect one's assets	自分の資産を守る
□ make it a rule to	~することにしている
□ high earning potential	高い予想利益
□ become a billionaire	億万長者になる
□ I have a different opinion.	私は考えが違う。
□ guarantee return	利益を保証する
□ initial investment	初期投資
□ profitability	収益性
□ rely on the performance	業績に頼る
□ What you're saying is a little extreme.	あなたが言っていることは少し極端だ。
□ buy lottery tickets	宝くじを買う
□ over the long run	長期的に見れば
□ experience positive returns	プラスの利益が上がる
□ predict	~を予測する
□ You're totally right.	まったく君の言うとおりだ。
□ analyze	~を分析する
□ be sensitive to economic trends	経済の動向に敏感である
□ I still can't support you on this matter.	この件に関してはまだあなたを支持できない。

Tips | 論理的に展開するためのキーフレーズ

反論を示す④

❶ You're wrong on that part.	あなたはその点で間違っています。
❷ What you said is wrong.	あなたが言ったことは間違いです。
❸ You are totally wrong.	全面的に間違っています。
❹ You've got it all wrong.	まるっきり勘違いしています。
❺ All that is wrong.	それはおかしいです。
❻ You have me all wrong.	ひどい誤解です。
❼ Don't get me wrong.	私を誤解しないでください。
❽ That's not true.	それは違います。

Should consumer loan advertising on TV be allowed?

消費者ローンのテレビコマーシャルを許すべきか？

背景知識とヒント

消費者金融からお金を借りるにはまず、必要書類を揃えて申し込みをします。書類審査が無事に通れば、契約をしてお金を借りることができます。しかし、消費者金融の無人契約機が登場してから、この一連の流れを無人契約機だけで完結することができるようになりました。しかも、100万円単位で借りることも可能です。世界でもあまり例がない日本の無人契約機は、本当に必要なのでしょうか。

097

TV Anchor: According to current statistics, the number of people who take out consumer loans is over 10 million. Of these, 1.2 million people are registered with three or more consumer loan companies. Furthermore, the amount borrowed per person greatly exceeds 1 million yen.

(42 words)

TV Anchor: 現行統計によると、消費者ローンを契約している人の数は1,000万人を超えています。そのうち、120万人が3社以上の消費者ローン会社に登録しています。さらに1人あたりの借入額は100万円を大幅に超えています。

Dialogue | ダイアローグ

Meg: I thought the number of debt-related problems had decreased after implementing revised laws to lower the maximum interest rate of consumer loan companies.

Meg: 消費者金融会社の上限金利を下げる改正法が施行されたあとに、借金が関係する問題の数は減ったと思ってたわ。

Tim: Yes, the situation is actually improving. However, there are still some serious issues.

Tim: うん。状況は、実際に改善しているんだ。しかし、いくつかまだ重要な問題があるんだ。

Meg: For example?

Meg: 例えば？

Tim: Well, first of all, it's quite easy to get a loan. All you have to do is to find an automated loan dispensing machine. These are in every corner of Japan. There you can be issued a card after a quick credit check via voice guidance. You could borrow millions of yen if you have a healthy credit rating. Besides, you would feel less embarrassed accessing a small, unmanned machine than a manned counter. This is unfortunately the first step on the road to debt hell.

Tim: まず第一に、ものすごく簡単にローンが借りられるんだ。無人契約機を見つけさえすればいいんだから。無人契約機は日本の至る所にあるんだ。音声ガイダンスの簡単な信用調査のあとに、カードが発行されるんだ。健全な信用格付けがあれば、数百万円借りられることもあるんだ。しかも、人がいるカウンターと違い、小さな無人契約機に行くのに気まずい思いをすることはほとんどないしね。不幸にも、これが借金地獄への第一歩だけどね。

Meg: Wow! It's very easy and convenient to get a loan. I don't see anything wrong with this system. Could you elaborate on it? If you repay the money you borrowed by the deadline, that causes no problem, right?

Meg: まあ！　お金を借りるのが、そんなに簡単で便利なの？　そのシステムのどこが悪いかわからないわ。もっと詳しく話してよ。借りたお金を期限までに返済すれば、何も問題ないわけでしょう？

Tim: You're correct. However, please keep in mind that people borrow money for a reason. The top reason for heavy debtors to borrow money is an income decrease or having a low income. How do you think these people can possibly repay the borrowed money by the deadline?

Tim: そうだよ。でもね、人は理由があってお金を借りるってことを忘れないで。多重債務者がお金を借りる一番の理由は、収入減か低収入なんだ。そんな人が、期限までに借りたお金を返せるわけがないと思わない？

What's worse, consumer loan companies create a lot of advertising using famous actors or singers to improve their companies' negative images. A desperate consumer is easily fooled!

さらに悪いことに、消費者金融会社はマイナスイメージを払拭するために、有名な俳優や歌手を使ってたくさん広告を出しているんだ。必死な消費者は、簡単にだまされてしまう。

Meg: That's why they use well-known TV personalities! I hadn't realized that before. What should we do to solve this issue?

Meg: そういうわけで、有名なテレビタレントを起用しているのね！それには気づかなかったわ。この問題を解決するために何をすべきなのかしら。

Tim: What counts most is to get rid of the automated loan dispensing machines granting easy loans and ban televised consumer loan advertisements, especially those featuring famous TV personalities. What's more, it's essential to launch a nationwide consumer education program.

(292 words)

Tim: 最も大切なことは、簡単なローンを認める無人契約機を撤去することと、消費者金融の広告、特に有名なテレビタレントを起用することを禁止することだね。さらに、消費者教育プログラムを全国規模で始めることが不可欠だね。

Words and Phrases

□ consumer loans	消費者金融	□ be in every corner of	～の至る所にある
□ according to current statistics	現行統計によると	□ issue a card	カードを発行する
□ take out a loan	お金を借りる	□ after a quick credit check	素早い信用調査の後で
□ be registered with	～に登録される	□ via voice guidance	音声ガイダンスで
□ greatly exceed 1 million yen	100万円を大幅に超える	□ have a healthy credit rating	健全な信用格付けがある
□ decrease	減る	□ besides	さらに
□ implement revised laws	改正法を施行する	□ feel embarrassed	恥ずかしいと思う、気まずいと思う
□ lower the maximum interest rate of	～の上限金利を下げる	□ unmanned machine	無人機
□ consumer loan companies	消費者金融会社	□ manned counter	有人のカウンター
□ automated loan dispensing machine	無人契約機	□ the first step on the road to debt hell	借金地獄へつながる第一歩

□ Could you elaborate on it?	それについてもっと詳しく話していただけませんか。
□ repay the money	返済する
□ keep in mind that	～を覚えておく
□ for a reason	わけがあって
□ the top reason for heavy debtors to	多重債務者が～する一番の理由
□ by the deadline	締め切りまでに
□ improve negative images	マイナスイメージを払拭する
□ desperate consumer	必死な消費者
□ be easily fooled	簡単にだまされる
□ well-known TV personalities	よく知られたテレビタレント
□ what counts most is to get rid of	最も重要なことは～を取り除くことである
□ grant	～を認める
□ feature famous TV personalities	有名なテレビタレントを起用する
□ be essential to	～することは不可欠である
□ launch a nationwide consumer education program	全国規模の消費者教育プログラムを始める

Tips | 論理的に展開するためのキーフレーズ

確認を示す①

❶ Could you elaborate on what you said?	あなたがおっしゃったことを具体的に詳しく説明してもらえませんか。
❷ Can you elaborate on your statement?	あなたの意見を具体的に説明してもらえますか。
❸ Could you give me more information about your project?	あなたのプロジェクトについてもっと情報をいただけませんか。
❹ Please explain further concerning your opinion.	あなたの意見についてもっと説明をしてください。
❺ Will you describe the matter in great detail?	その件について、もっと詳しく説明してくれませんか。
❻ Could you explain it in more detail?	それについて、もっと詳しく説明してくれませんか。
❼ We need a detailed reason.	もっと詳しい理由が必要です。
❽ Could you clarify this point, please?	この論点を明確にしてもらえますか。

Are online clothing rental shops worthwhile?

オンラインの洋服レンタルは価値がある？

背景知識とヒント

最近では、さまざまなモノをレンタルできます。現代は、買う時代ではなくて、モノをレンタルする時代かもしれません。例えば、「介護に必要なベッドや車いす」、「冬の旅先でのスキー板やスキーウエア」、「擬似デートを楽しむためにレンタルできる恋人」などです。カーシェアもその１つです。次はどんなレンタルが流行るのでしょうか。

TV Anchor: Nowadays, we're seeing a rise in rental services, particularly clothing rental, similar to renting electrical goods and camping equipment. Clothing rentals with fixed-price subscriptions are becoming especially common. The fashion industry is surely entering a new era. (37 words)

TV Anchor: 最近、電化製品やキャンプ用品のレンタルと同様に、レンタルサービス、特に衣料品のレンタルが増加しています。定額制の衣類レンタルが特に一般的になっています。ファッション業界は確実に新しい時代に入っています。

Dialogue | ダイアローグ

Tim: The number of users of clothing rental shops is on the rise. Do you think online clothing rental shops are a good idea?

Tim: 衣料レンタル店の利用者数が増えている。衣料品レンタルのネットショップは良い考えだと思う？

Meg: Yes, I'm all for them. Actually, I'm a member of such an online shop. All you have to do to become a member is apply for the type of membership you want and pay approximately five thousand yen or more per month according to your choice. You will receive three sets of clothes and you can return them after use without washing them. This system is fabulous and a good deal for those who have a hectic schedule every day and have no time for shopping.

Meg: そうね。大賛成よ。実際に、私もそんなネットショップの会員なの。メンバーになるには、希望するタイプの会員に申し込んで、その選んだタイプに応じて1か月5,000円かそれ以上払えばいいだけなの。3種類の洋服を受け取り、使用後は洗濯しないで返却できるわ。このシステムは、毎日過密なスケジュールを抱えていて、買い物をする時間のない人には素晴らしくお得ね。

Tim: How do those shops select clothes for you? I would rather try a lot of different clothes on before I decide what to buy in a shop.

Tim: 店は、どのように君に合う服を選ぶの？　僕は、店で何を買うか決める前には、たくさんの種類の服を試着したいけどね。

Meg: Stylists select clothes for you according to your taste. They might find you a new style of clothes and actually help you to develop your sense of style.

Meg: スタイリストが好みに応じて服を選んでくれるわ。新しいタイプの服を選んでくれるかもしれないし、実際にファッションセンスを磨いてくれるわ。

Tim: Your point is well taken, but don't the clothes on the screen look quite different when you receive them and try them on?

Tim: 言いたいことはわかるけどさ。画面で見る服って、受け取って試着した時とは違って見えるよね。

Meg: I understand your concerns. That's why we rent clothes from rental shops. If we don't like the selections, we can replace them with other items. Usually, the shop doesn't charge you any return shipping fees.

Meg: 心配はごもっともよ。だからレンタルショップから服を借りるのよ。選んだ服が気に入らなければ、他の服と交換できるの。通常は、店は返品費用を請求しないの。

Tim: Rental shops deal in second-hand clothes, and so they sometimes smell strange or have stains on them, right?

Meg: Yes. But if I don't want clothes with an odor, I can replace those, too. What's more, I can go on to buy any piece of clothing if I like it.

Tim: I don't think I can go along with your idea. However, this system seems to meet the needs of the times because it's a time-saving and cost-effective way to shop.

(302 words)

Tim: レンタルショップって、古着を扱うから、服に変な臭いがしたり、しみがついていたりしてるでしょ?

Meg: そうね。でも、もし変な臭いがする服が欲しくなければ、交換できるわ。それに、服が気に入ったら買うこともできるの。

Tim: 君の考えにはついていけないよ。でもこのシステムは時代のニーズに応えているね。買い物する時間の節約になり、費用対効果が高いからね。

Words and Phrases

□ clothing rental	衣料品レンタル
□ see a rise in	～の上昇を目撃する
□ with fixed-price subscriptions	定額制の契約で
□ enter a new era	新たな時代に入る
□ be on the rise	増えている
□ Yes, I'm all for them.	大賛成です。
□ all you have to do to become a member is ～	メンバーになるのにしなければいけないことは～だけである
□ apply for	～に申し込む
□ according to one's choice	～の選択に応じて
□ fabulous and a good deal	素晴らしく、そしてお得だ
□ have a hectic schedule	予定が詰まっている、過密なスケジュールを抱えている
□ have no time for shopping	買い物をする時間がない
□ I would rather try ～ on	～を試着してみたい
□ stylist	スタイリスト
□ according to one's tastes	～の好みに応じて
□ develop one's sense of style	～のファッションセンスを磨く
□ your point is well taken, but	おっしゃることはわかりますが
□ I understand your concerns.	あなたの心配はわかります。
□ that's why	そういうわけで～
□ replace ～ with …	～を…と交換する
□ item	商品
□ charge ～ any return shipping fees	～に返品費用を請求する
□ deal in second-hand clothes	古着を扱う
□ smell strange	変なにおいがする

□ have a stain on	～にしみがついている
□ clothes with an odor	臭いのする洋服
□ what's more	さらに
□ go on to	引き続き～する
□ I can go along with your idea.	あなたの考えに同意します。
□ meet the needs of the times	時代のニーズに応える
□ time-saving and cost-effective	時間の節約になり、費用対効果が高い

Tips | 論理的に展開するためのキーフレーズ

同意を示す②

❶ I'm all for your suggestion.	提案に大賛成です。
❷ You're absolutely right.	おっしゃるとおりです。
❸ You got that right.	同感です。
❹ That's absolutely true.	それはまったく正しいです。
❺ You've said it.	まったくそのとおりです。
❻ That's just what I was thinking.	それはまさに私が考えていたことです。
❼ That's exactly what I think.	まさに同感です。

Should people be imposed fines for not voting in elections?

選挙に投票しない人に罰金を科すべきか？

背景知識とヒント

世界各国の議会選挙の投票率ランキングで、日本は139位でした。投票率の高い国、例えば、3位のシンガポール、8位のオーストラリアなどでは、投票しないと罰金が科されます。また、18位のスウェーデンでは、12歳から模擬投票を実施したり、選挙前には、候補者が学校で演説したりする方法を講じています。

101

TV Anchor: The current administration's approval rating has slipped below 25% in Japan. Because of issues such as factional fights inside the party as well as the scandal involving a Member of the Diet, the citizens have concerns regarding the Prime Minister's leadership. If these issues continue, there's a risk that interest in politics will diminish among citizens. (56 words)

TV Anchor: 日本では、現在の政権の支持率が25%以下に下がっています。党内の派閥闘争や国会議員のスキャンダルなどの問題があり、国民は首相のリーダーシップに関して懸念を抱いています。これらの問題が続くと、国民の政治への関心が低下するリスクがあります。

Dialogue | ダイアローグ

Tim: Voter turnout in Japanese elections is low, isn't it? I wonder why people don't go out to vote.

Meg: I believe it's because people have a strong sense of distrust towards politics. For example, political funds are generally meant to be utilized for public purposes. However, some lawmakers misuse them for personal gain.

Tim: That's a problem indeed. Lawmakers should prioritize the country's interests over their own.

Meg: Yeah, you are right. To what extent are American people interested in politics?

Tim: I think that they are highly interested in politics. Even within families, they discuss which candidates' policies are better and who is more suitable to lead the country long before the presidential primaries. Most U.S. citizens want someone with strong leadership and a long-term vision for the country.

Meg: That's impressive.

Tim: That's why voter turnout in the United States is always over 60%, and in high turnout years, it can exceed 80%.

Meg: That's unimaginable in today's Japanese elections. I wonder if there's a solution.

Tim: 日本の選挙の投票率は低いね。なんで人々が投票に行かないのか不思議だよ。

Meg: 政治への強い不信感があるからだと思う。例えば、政治資金って一般的に公共の目的に利用されるものでしょ。でも、一部の議員は個人的な利益のために間違った使い方をしているのよ。

Tim: 確かにそれは問題だね。議員は自分の利益より自国の利益を優先するべきだよ。

Meg: ええ、そのとおりよ。アメリカの人たちはどの程度政治に興味があるの？

Tim: すごく政治に興味があると思うよ。家族の間でも、大統領予備選挙の前から、どの候補者の政策がいいか、誰が国をリードするのに適しているかを議論するんだ。ほとんどのアメリカ人は、強いリーダーシップと国の長期的なビジョンを持つ人物を求めているね。

Meg: それは心に刺さるわ。

Tim: だから、アメリカの選挙の投票率はいつも60%以上だし、投票率の高い年には80%を超えることもあるんだ。

Meg: 今の日本の選挙では想像できないわ。解決策はないのかしら。

Tim: What if we impose fines for not voting in elections? Some countries have increased voter turnout by imposing fines.	**Tim:** 選挙で投票しないことに罰金を科すのはどう？　罰金制度を導入することで投票率を上げた国もあるよ。
Meg: Hmm, that's a bit extreme, isn't it? For citizens, voting is a right, not an obligation. Even with fines, I doubt it would increase public interest in politics.	**Meg:** うーん、それは少し極端じゃない？　国民にとって、投票は権利であって義務ではないもの。罰金があっても、国民の政治への関心が高まるとは思えないわ。
Tim: Well then, politicians need to clean up their act, eliminate factional politics, slush fund scandals, and so on. And then, it's important for lawmakers to take into account what's necessary for the citizens from their perspective. Though it might take time, it could be the best solution. (248 words)	**Tim:** それなら、政治家は自らの行動を改善し、派閥政治や不正資金のスキャンダルを排除する必要があるね。そして、国民の視点から国民に必要なことを考慮することが重要だ。時間はかかるかもしれないけど、それが最良の解決策かもしれないよ。

Words and Phrases

102

□ current administration's approval rating	現政権の支持率	□ politics	政治
□ slip below ～%	～%を切る	□ political fund	政治資金
□ factional fights inside the party	党内派閥争い	□ utilize	～を使う
□ scandal	スキャンダル	□ for public purposes	公共の目的で
□ Member of the Diet	国会議員（日本などの）	□ lawmaker	国会議員
□ have concerns regarding	～について心配する	□ misuse	～を誤用する、乱用する
□ the Prime Minister's leadership	総理大臣の指導力	□ for personal gain	私利私欲のために
□ risk	危険性	□ prioritize ～ over …	…よりも～を優先する
□ diminish	小さくなる；～を小さくする	□ interest	利益
□ voter turnout	投票率	□ to what extent	どの程度まで
□ have a strong sense of distrust towards ～	～に対する強い不信感がある	□ be suitable to ～	～するのに適している
		□ lead the country	国を率いる

□ presidential primaries	大統領予備選挙
□ long-term vision	長期的な視野
□ That's impressive.	それは素晴らしい。
□ exceed	～を超える
□ unimaginable	想像できない
□ solution	解決策
□ impose fines for	～に罰金を科する
□ That's a bit extreme, isn't it?	それは少し極端ではありませんか。
□ obligation	義務
□ clean up one's act	～の行いを正す
□ eliminate factional politics	派閥争いをなくす
□ slush fund scandal	不正資金のスキャンダル
□ take into account	～を考慮に入れる
□ from one's perspective	～の視点から

Tips | 論理的に展開するためのキーフレーズ

意見を示す④

❶ I think your statement is extreme.	あなたの発言は極端です。
❷ Don't you think you may be exaggerating a bit?	あなたは少し極端だと思いませんか。
❸ You're going too far with that matter.	その件については、言いすぎだと思います。
❹ I may be exaggerating a bit.	すこし誇張したかもしれません。
❺ What you're saying is a little extreme.	あなたの発言は少し極端です。
❻ Aren't you being a little harsh?	ちょっと言いすぎじゃないですか。
❼ Your case is a bit on the extreme side.	あなたの例はちょっと極端です。
❽ You're way out of line.	あなたは言いすぎですね。

Should smartphone-related common sense and manners be taught in schools?

スマートフォンのマナーを学校で教えるべきか？

背景知識とヒント

スマートフォンは、道を検索したり、写真を撮影したり、天気予報を確認したりと本当に便利な道具です。しかしスマートフォンを操作しながらの歩行や運転で、大きな事故が増えています。駅のホームの転落事故や、交通事故などです。使い方を一歩間違えれば、大きな落とし穴があるのです。

103

TV Anchor: It's obvious that smartphones are an indispensable device for people. However, in some ways, they are also putting people in danger. Smartphone-related accidents have become an issue. Actually, an 18-year-old driver who was texting behind the wheel got arrested for killing an elementary school student on the way to school. (50 words)

TV Anchor: 人々にとってスマートフォンが不可欠な道具であることは明らかです。しかしいくつかの点で、スマートフォンは人を危険にさらしています。スマートフォンが関係する事故が問題視されてきました。実際に、自動車の運転中にメールを打っていた18歳の運転手が、登校中の小学生を死亡させたとして逮捕されました。

Dialogue | ダイアローグ

Tim: What do you think of this news?

Meg: That's terrible. The driver probably didn't have a chance to learn how to use a smartphone properly at school, and so he caused an accident just after graduating from high school.

Tim: What do you mean by that?

Meg: Well, it's time to teach smartphone-related common sense and manners to students at schools. We should accept all the benefits smartphones have. For example, they give us a convenient means of sending text messages, reading email, playing games, and editing documents while on the go. Besides those applications, smartphones come with an infinite variety of other apps, such as health and fitness, photo modification, and so on. The list is endless.

Tim: You mean, we need to allow students to bring their smartphones to school and teach them how to use them properly?

Meg: That's right.

Tim: No way. If we allow them to do that, they will not be able to concentrate on their studies at all. As you well know, smartphones enable students to take pictures, watch videos, and send and receive email. In a sense, bringing smartphones to schools is like bringing toys to schools. They can't help but distract students.

Tim: このニュースをどう思う？

Meg: ひどいわね。おそらく、運転手は、学校でスマートフォンの適切な使い方を学ぶチャンスがなかったのね。それで高校卒業直後に事故を起こしたのね。

Tim: それってどういう意味？

Meg: そうね、学校で、スマートフォンの常識とマナーを生徒に教える時期なのよ。スマートフォンのすべてのメリットを受け入れるべきだわ。例えば、スマートフォンは、外出中にもメッセージを送ったり、メールを読んだり、ゲームをしたり、文書を編集したりする便利な道具よね。それに、スマートフォンのアプリは、際限なく多種多様なものがあるわ。例えば、健康とフィットネス、写真修正などね。数えたらきりがないわ。

Tim: つまり、スマートフォンを学校に持ってこさせて、正しい使い方を教える必要があるってことかい？

Meg: そのとおりよ。

Tim: とんでもない。それを許可したら、学業にまったく集中できなくなるよ。君もよく知ってるよね。生徒たちはスマートフォンで写真を撮ったり、動画を見たり、メールを送ったり受け取ったりするんだよ。ある意味、スマートフォンを学校に持ってくることは、おもちゃを学校に持ってくることだよ。生徒の気を散らすことにしかならないよ。

Meg: I understand what you mean. But, if they don't learn to use smartphones correctly and safely at school, where and how will they learn such things? As an aspect of the school curriculum, we should teach them these things.

Tim: I'm sure you're wasting your time. It's too difficult to teach everything about smartphone-related common sense and manners. Right now, we are worried about causing smartphone-related accidents while behind the wheel. But the answer to that question is simple. Sooner or later, new functions will be invented. For example, smartphones will then freeze when they detect the movement of the vehicle itself. Besides, we can't just depend on schools to solve every social problem.

(309 words)

Meg: あなたの言いたいことはわかるわ。でも生徒は、学校で正しく安全に使う方法を身につけなければ、どこでどうやってそれを身につけられるのよ。教育課程の一部として、生徒に教えるべきよ。

Tim: 時間の無駄だよね。スマートフォンに関する常識とマナーをすべて教えることは難しいよ。今、運転中にスマートフォンが関連して起こる事故について心配しているよね。でも、その答えは簡単だよ。遅かれ早かれ、新しい機能が発明されるよ。例えば、車の動きを感知したら、スマートフォンがフリーズするんだ。それに、すべての社会問題を解決するのに学校だけに頼ることはできないよ。

Words and Phrases

104

□ it's obvious that	～なのは明らかである	□ common sense and manner	常識と礼儀
□ indispensable device for	～にとって不可欠な道具	□ a convenient means of	～の便利な方法
□ put ～ in danger	～を危険にさらす	□ send a text message	メッセージを送る
□ smartphone-related accident	スマートフォンが関連する事故	□ edit a document	文書を編集する
□ text	(携帯電話で) メールを打つ	□ while on the go	外出中に
□ behind the wheel	車を運転して	□ application	アプリ
□ get arrested for	～で逮捕される	□ an infinite variety of	際限なく多種多様な
□ on the way to school	学校へ行く途中で	□ photo modification	写真修正
□ graduate from	～を卒業する	□ The list is endless.	数えたらきりがない。

□ use ~ properly	～を適切に使う	□ an aspect of	～の一面
□ concentrate on	～に集中する	□ school curriculum	教育課程
□ can't help but	～せざるを得ない	□ freeze	動きを止める
□ distract	～の気を散らす	□ detect the movement of	～の動きを感知する
□ correctly and safely	正しく安全に	□ depend on	～に頼る

Tips | 論理的に展開するためのキーフレーズ

確認を示す②

1	What are you implying?	何が言いたいのですか。
2	What do you intend to do?	何をするつもりですか。
3	What do you mean by that?	それはどういう意味ですか。
4	What do you have in mind?	何を考えているのですか。
5	What you want to say is we should tailor services to customers' needs, right?	あなたが言いたいことは、顧客のニーズに応えるサービスをすべきだということですよね。
6	What you mean is we need to clarify the object of this project, right?	あなたが言いたいことは、このプロジェクトの目的を明確にする必要があるということですよね。
7	What you're trying to say is we should be more environmentally friendly, right?	あなたが言いたいことは、環境にもっとやさしくすべきだということですよね。

Dialogue 08 Should cosmetic surgery be more socially acceptable?

美容整形手術は社会的にもっと受け入れられるべきなのか？

背景知識とヒント

美容整形手術は、医療機関で医師が行うレーザー療法による脱毛やしみ取り、コラーゲンやヒアルロン酸注入療法、脂肪吸引、二重まぶた手術などの美容を目的とした医療サービスです。若々しい印象をキープでき、自分で施す化粧とは比較にならないメリットがあることは確かです。一方、シリコンを用いた手術で起こる異物反応の可能性や、2～3年に1度のメンテナンスなどのデメリットも理解する必要があります。美容整形手術に対する抵抗感は薄らいでいるようですが、メリットとデメリットはしっかり念頭に置く必要がありそうです。

105

TV Anchor: South Korea is famous for its reputation in cosmetic surgery. Therefore, many people visit Korea from abroad, including Japanese, for cosmetic procedures. It's quite common for students to have surgery before their graduation.

(33 words)

TV Anchor: 韓国は美容整形手術で有名です。そのため、日本人を含め多くの人々が美容整形手術を受けに海外から韓国を訪れます。学生が卒業前に手術を受けるのもよくあることです。

Dialogue | ダイアローグ

Tim: Do you support the idea of cosmetic surgery?

Meg: I don't want to answer such a question. I'm content with my appearance. This is who I am. I like myself just the way I am. How about you?

Tim: Me? I don't seek perfection, but I'm not completely satisfied with my appearance.

Meg: Do you mean you want to have some changes made to your face or body?

Tim: To be honest, yes. For instance, I want to get rid of my crow's feet, freckles, moles, and so on. That way, I would appear even more youthful and energetic. Besides, cosmetic surgery not only changes one's appearance but also improves one's confidence. I believe making minor changes is acceptable. Isn't it like changing clothes every day?

Meg: I disagree. We inherit certain traits from our ancestors. Our bodies are an integral part of our identity. We should love our current appearance. Besides, nobody can stop aging.

Tim: I know, but don't you understand why people undergo cosmetic surgery? Cosmetic surgery may be costly, but if it boosts one's confidence, isn't it a worthwhile investment? It's a lifelong change, after all.

Tim: 美容整形手術を支持する？

Meg: そんな質問には答えたくないわ。私は自分の外見に満足しているの。これが私よ。ありのままの自分が好きなの。あなたはどうなの？

Tim: 僕？　僕は完璧を求めないけど、自分の見た目に完全には満足してないな。

Meg: 顔とか体をどこか変えたいってこと？

Tim: 正直に言うと、そうだね。例えば、目じりのしわ、しみ、ホクロなんかを取りたい。そうすれば、もっと若々しく、エネルギッシュに見えるんじゃないかな。それに、美容整形手術は外見を変えるだけじゃなくて、自信にもつながるよ。マイナーチェンジは許容範囲だと思う。毎日服を着替えるようなものじゃない？

Meg: そうは思わないわ。私たちは祖先から特定の特徴を受け継いでいるのよ。私たちの身体は、私たちのアイデンティティの不可欠な一部だわ。私たちは今の自分の姿を愛するべきよ。それに、年齢を重ねることは誰にも止められないんだから。

Tim: そうだけど、なぜ人が美容整形手術を受けるのかわからない？　美容整形手術は高額かもしれないけれど、それで自信がつくなら、価値のある投資じゃない？　結局、一生ものの変化なんだから。

Meg: Keep in mind, after the surgery, your face is changed permanently. Also, don't forget that there's also the risk of failure. Cosmetic surgery is not free from problems and unwanted side effects.

(216 words)

Meg: 手術をしたら、自分の顔が永久に変わってしまうってことを覚えておいて。美容整形手術には失敗のリスクもあることを忘れないでね。美容整形手術に問題や望まない副作用がないわけじゃないんだから。

Words and Phrases

106

□ cosmetic surgery	美容整形手術
□ be famous for	～で有名である
□ reputation	評判
□ cosmetic procedure	美容目的の処置
□ graduation	卒業
□ be content with	～で満足している
□ appearance	外見、容姿
□ seek perfection	完璧を求める
□ be satisfied with	～で満足する
□ to be honest	正直に言うと
□ get rid of	～を取り除く
□ crow's feet	目じりのしわ
□ freckles	そばかす、しみ（複数形で用いられることが多い）
□ mole	ホクロ
□ improves one's confidence	～の自信を高める
□ make minor changes	小さな変更を行う
□ acceptable	容認できる
□ inherit certain traits from	～から遺伝的特徴を受け継ぐ
□ ancestor	祖先
□ integral	不可欠な
□ identity	アイデンティティ、独自性
□ current appearance	現在の容姿
□ undergo cosmetic surgery	美容整形手術をする
□ boost one's confidence	～の自信を高める
□ worthwhile investment	価値ある投資
□ keep in mind (that)	～ということを覚えておく
□ permanently	永久に
□ risk of failure	失敗のリスク
□ be free from	～がない、～から免れる
□ unwanted side effect	望ましくない副作用

Tips | 論理的に展開するためのキーフレーズ

確認を示す③

❶	Do you mean you don't know about this issue?	この問題を知らないということですか。
❷	What exactly do you mean?	一体何が言いたいのですか。
❸	Is that what you're trying to say?	それがあなたが言おうとしていることですか。
❹	Are you absolutely sure of that?	絶対にそれを確信していますか。
❺	What in the world is that all about?	一体全体それはどういうことですか。
❻	What on earth do you mean?	一体全体どういう意味ですか。
❼	What has that got to do with you?	あなたとどういう関係があるというのですか。
❽	That's not exactly what I'm talking about.	私が言っているのはそういうことではありません。

Dialogue 09

Should the policy of a mandatory retirement age be abolished?

定年制を廃止すべきか？

背景知識とヒント

日本企業の多くが、60 歳の定年制度を設けています。しかし、健康寿命が延びたことや年金支給年齢が延びたこともあり、最近 60 歳以上でも働くことができる企業が徐々に増えているようです。労働人口が減る中、知識や技能を十分に備えている 60 代の労働力は、企業を支える貴重な人材として有力視されています。定年制の廃止に関して、どのように考えますか。

107

TV Anchor: According to a study, about 72% of companies have a mandatory retirement age of 60 and about 21% of them have it set at 65. More companies are trying to increase the mandatory retirement age. However, there are arguments for and against this movement. (44 words)

TV Anchor: ある研究によれば、およそ 72%の会社が 60 歳を、およそ 21%が 65 歳を定年としています。多くの会社が定年年齢を上げようとしています。しかし、この動きには賛否両論の議論があります。

Dialogue | ダイアローグ

Meg: Do you agree with abolishing the mandatory retirement age policy?

Meg: 定年制度を廃止することに賛成する？

Tim: No, I don't. It's because the elderly may have a negative impact on Japanese society. For example, the older they become, the more their productivity declines.

Tim: しないよ。高齢者が日本社会にマイナスの影響を与えるかもしれないからね。例えば、年をとればとるほど、ますます生産性が落ちるからね。

Meg: What you're saying is true, but you're missing something important. Nowadays, the average life span of Japanese people has dramatically increased. Statistically speaking, Japanese people can expect to live into their 80s. This means they have more than 20 years to live after retirement, and they have to make ends meet with low pensions. Furthermore, it's often said that once they quit working, they are more susceptible to disease. Therefore, I believe the elderly need to work even after age 60 to stay healthy and active.

Meg: あなたの言っていることは正しいけど、何か大事な部分を見落としているわね。最近は、日本人の平均寿命が劇的に伸びたわ。統計的に言えば、日本人は80代まで生きることになるわ。これは、退職後に20年以上あって、少ない年金で家計をやりくりしなければならないってことよ。さらに、いったん仕事をやめたら、人は病気にかかりやすくなるわ。だから、60歳以降も健康で活動的でいるためには、高齢者には働くことが必要だと思うの。

Tim: It's you who is missing the big picture. You are only worried about the future of the elderly. What matters is not only their future but also the future of Japanese society.

Tim: 全体像を見失っているのは君のほうだよ。高齢者の未来を心配しているだけだね。大切なのは高齢者の未来だけでなくて、日本社会の未来なのさ。

Meg: I see your point, but the elderly have irreplaceable practical experience and inside knowledge of their work and industries. Such experience is needed for companies to maintain a competitive edge. What I mean is that they can play important roles as instructors and trainers for new and younger employees.

Meg: 言いたいことはわかるわ。でも、高齢者はかけがえのない実践的経験があり、仕事や産業界の内部事情に詳しいわ。そんな経験が、会社が競争力を維持するために必要なのよ。つまり高齢者は、新人や若い従業員の指導者として、重要な役割を果たすことができるのよ。

Tim: I see what you mean. But if we start to rehire the elderly after retirement, it may become more difficult for college graduates to get jobs.

Meg: You have a good point there, but I'm suggesting that the elderly should be rehired not as full-timers but as part-timers.

Tim: I like your idea. In that way, we will see the positive impact that the elderly can have on Japanese society. Right?

(272 words)

Tim: 君の意図はわかったよ。でも、もし退職後の高齢者を再雇用し始めたら、大学の卒業生が就職するのが難しくなるかもしれないよ。

Meg: 良いところをついているわね。でも高齢者を常勤者としてではなく、パートとして再雇用することを提案しているの。

Tim: 君の考えが気に入ったよ。そのようにして、高齢者が日本社会に与えるプラスの影響を受けられるんだね。そうだろう？

Words and Phrases

108

□ have a mandatory retirement age	定年制度がある
□ There are arguments for and against this movement.	この動きに賛否両論の議論がある。
□ abolish a policy	制度を廃止する
□ have a negative impact on	～にマイナスの影響を与える
□ productivity declines	生産性が下がる
□ average life span	平均寿命
□ dramatically increase	劇的に増加する
□ statistically speaking	統計的に言えば
□ after retirement	退職後
□ make ends meet	家計をやりくりする
□ low pension	少ない年金
□ quit working	働くことをやめる
□ be susceptible to disease	病気にかかりやすい
□ It's you who is missing the big picture.	全体像を見失っているのはあなたである。
□ be worried about	～について心配している
□ what matters is	大切なのは～である
□ I see your point, but	言いたいことはわかるが、～
□ have irreplaceable practical experience	かけがえのない実践的経験がある
□ maintain a competitive edge	競争力を維持する
□ play an important role as	～として重要な役割を果たす
□ instructor	指導者
□ trainer	指導者
□ rehire	～を再雇用する
□ college graduate	大学の卒業生
□ full-timer	常勤者
□ part-timer	パートタイマー
□ positive impact	プラスの影響

Tips | 論理的に展開するためのキーフレーズ

反論を示す⑤

❶ You're missing the big picture.	全体像を見失っていますね。
❷ Your opinion lacks something.	あなたの意見は何か欠けています。
❸ You're ignoring something important.	何か重要なことを見落としています。
❹ You're not looking at the bigger issue.	大きな問題に目を向けていません。
❺ If that's what you think, you're terribly mistaken.	それがあなたの考えていることなら、とんでもない間違いです。
❻ If you look at only pieces of something, you miss something important.	何かの一部だけを見ていると、何か重要なことを見落としてしまいます。
❼ You can't see the forest for the trees.	木を見て森を見ていません。
❽ Be careful not to miss something critical.	何か重要なことを見落とさないように、注意してください。

Should new diesel and gas cars be banned in Japan?

ディーゼル車とガソリン車の新車を日本で禁止すべきか？

背景知識とヒント

イギリス、EU が、2035 年までに国内でのガソリン車とディーゼル車の販売を禁止すると発表しました。しかし、2023 年に EU はこの方針を変更し、再生可能エネルギー由来の合成燃料を使うエンジン車の新車販売は可能としました。ガソリン車とディーゼル車の販売禁止は、環境保護のためには嬉しいニュースですが、本当に実現可能なのでしょうか。

TV Anchor: England and the EU made a similar pledge, which is to ban new diesel and gas cars by 2035. This is the latest step to curb carbon emissions and fight climate change. Also, it will have the added benefit of promoting electric cars. (41 words)

TV Anchor: イギリスと EU は同じような誓いを立てました。2035 年までに新たなディーゼル車とガソリン車を禁止することです。これは炭素排出量を制限し、気候変動と戦うための最新の方法です。また、電気自動車を普及させるという付加価値もあります。

Dialogue | ダイアローグ

Tim: I agree with this idea, but are there any special reasons why those countries made such a decision so suddenly?

Meg: It's because they wanted it to be part of the renewed commitment to the Paris Accord. In reality, in England, an estimated four thousand people at most are expected to die as a result of pollution caused by cars every year. In a sense, they had no choice but to make this pledge.

Tim: That's terrible. But I don't consider it totally bad news. There are some advantages; for example, electric cars are 100% eco-friendly because they do not emit toxic gases like nitrogen oxide or carbon dioxide. Plus, electric cars don't require gas. Compared with gas, electricity is much cheaper. Therefore, electric cars are family budget-friendly.

Meg: It would be ideal for us to ban all new diesel and gas cars. But that's a big if for the time being. The list goes on and on. First, the price of electric cars is very expensive without subsidies from the government. It's obvious that no government can afford to subsidize most new car purchases.

Tim: What's next?

Tim: この考えに賛成だけど、それらの国がこれほど急にそんな決意をするのは、何か特別の理由があるのかな？

Meg: それをパリ協定への新たな決意の1つにしたいからよ。現実的に、イギリスでは、車による汚染の結果として、毎年およそ4千人の人が亡くなると予想されているのよ。ある意味、彼らにはこの誓いを立てる以外に選択肢はないのね。

Tim: それはひどいね。でも、それを悪いニュースだとは思わないよ。メリットもいくつかある。例えば、電気自動車は、窒素酸化物や二酸化炭素のような有害ガスを排出しないので、100%環境にやさしい。しかも、電気自動車はガソリンを必要としないしね。ガソリンと比べると、電気はかなり安いからね。そのため、電気自動車は家計にやさしいんだ。

Meg: すべての新しいディーゼル車とガソリン車を禁止することは理想的だわ。でも、当面、それはまず考えられないことよ。例を挙げればきりがないわ。第一に、電気自動車の価格は政府からの補助金なしでは、非常に高価ね。どの政府も、ほぼすべての新車購入に補助金を出す余裕がないのは明らかだわ。

Tim: 次は何なの？

Meg: Second, at the moment, electric cars with a short driving range can run only 200 to 300 km per charge and therefore need to be recharged again soon. Plus, it takes much longer for electric cars to fully charge, but it only takes a few minutes to fill the tank of gas cars. There are still fewer battery-charging stations than gas stations. Therefore, we can't use electric cars for long journeys. So, I don't agree with you on this matter.

Tim: I understand what you mean. Ideally, electric cars should be adopted, but in reality, it's rather impractical right now.

(283 words)

Meg: 第二に、走行距離の短い電気自動車だと、1回の充電で200kmから300kmしか走らないの。だからすぐに再充電する必要があるわ。しかも、充電ステーションで電気自動車が完全に充電するのに、かなり長い時間がかかるわ。でも、ガソリン自動車は数分で満タンになるの。ガソリンスタンドより充電ステーションの数が少ないしね。そのため、電気自動車を長距離移動には使えないわ。だから、この件については賛成しないわ。

Tim: 君の言いたいことはわかった。理想的には、電気自動車が選ばれるべきだけど、それは現実的には、現時点では実現困難だね。

Words and Phrases

110

□ make a similar pledge	似た誓いを立てる
□ ban new diesel and gas cars	新しいディーゼル車とガソリン車を禁止する
□ this is the latest step to	これが～する最新の方法である
□ curb emissions	（排気ガスの）排出を制限する
□ fight climate change	気候変動と戦う
□ added benefit	付加価値
□ promote electric cars	電気自動車を普及させる
□ renewed commitment to the Paris Accord	パリ協定への新たな決意
□ estimated four thousand people	およそ4千人
□ as a result of pollution caused by	～によって引き起こされた汚染の結果

□ in a sense	ある意味
□ have no choice but to	～する以外に選択肢がない、手がない
□ there are some advantages	いくつかのメリットがある
□ eco-friendly	環境にやさしい
□ emit toxic gases like	～ のような有毒ガスを発生する、出す
□ nitrogen oxide	窒素酸化物
□ carbon dioxide	二酸化炭素
□ plus	さらに
□ require gas	ガソリンを必要とする
□ compared with	～と比べて

□ therefore	そのため	□ recharge	～を再充電する
□ family budget-friendly	家計にやさしい	□ fully charge	完全に充電する
□ That's a big if for the time being.	当面、それはまず考えられないことだ。	□ gas cars	ガソリン自動車
□ without subsidies from the government	政府からの補助金なしで	□ battery-charging station	充電ステーション
□ it's obvious that	～は明らかである	□ for long journeys	長距離の移動には
□ can afford to	～する余裕がある	□ adopt	～を採用する、～を選ぶ
□ subsidize new car purchases	新車購入に補助金を出す	□ impractical	実現困難な
□ short driving range	短い走行距離		

Tips | 論理的に展開するためのキーフレーズ

理由を示す③

❶ Are there any special reasons why we have so much food waste?	食品廃棄物がこれだけ多いのには、何か特別な理由がありますか。
❷ Are there any special reasons why you overlooked such a mistake?	あなたがそのような間違いを見過ごしたのは、特別な理由が何かありますか。
❸ Are there any good reasons to smoke?	喫煙するのに、何か正当な理由がありますか。
❹ Are there any good reasons to work overtime for such a long time?	そんなに長い間、残業をする正当な理由が何かありますか。
❺ Do you know why I'm satisfied with the result?	私がその結果に満足している理由を知っていますか。
❻ Do you know why I took a detour today?	今日、私が遠回りをした理由を知っていますか。
❼ Do you have a valid reason to convince us?	私たちを納得させるだけの、正当な理由がありますか。

Dialogue 11

Is college worthwhile?

大学に進学する価値があるのか？

背景知識とヒント

大学への進学率がおよそ50%を超え、高校生の半分以上が進学していることになります。一方、少子化の影響で、2018年以降18歳人口が減り続け、定員割れを起こす大学の数も増えてきました。大学への進学率が高くなる一方で、入りやすい大学の数は増えています。そんな中、単に大学に進学するだけでなく、何の目的で大学に進学するのかを明確にすることが必要です。

111

TV Anchor: According to the statistics on high school graduates, 61% enrolled in college, 14% got jobs, 20% entered vocational schools and 5% have yet to decide their futures. (27 words)

TV Anchor: 高校卒業生に関する統計によると、61%が大学に進学し、14%が就職し、20%が専門学校に進学し、5%は進路が未定です。

Dialogue | ダイアローグ

Meg: So, many students want to go to college. What do you think about this?

Tim: Needless to say, students want to further their education in the major and minor subjects of their choice.

Meg: I don't think so. Some take it for granted that they will enroll in college. Actually, many of them are more absorbed in doing part-time jobs in their free time. Some don't even save enough time to study. In order to enroll in college, a certain amount of money and time are required. Is such enrollment truly worthwhile?

Tim: I see your point, but there's more to learn and do at college than just studying your major. Students acquire practical skills, which come in handy later during their careers. For example, they learn time management, problem-solving, prioritization, critical thinking, communication, and people skills.

Meg: They don't have to go to college to acquire such skills, then. They can simply acquire them while working.

Tim: Well, that's true. But I guess the main reason is that, on average, people with bachelor's degrees can expect to make more money than those without. Particularly those who become lawyers, accountants, and doctors tend to get paid quite well. They earn two or three times as much as average salaried workers.

Meg: 非常に多くの生徒が大学に進学するわね。これについてどう思の？

Tim: 言うまでもなく、生徒は自分が選ぶ専攻科目や副専攻科目をさらに学びたいんだろう。

Meg: 私はそう思わないわ。大学に進学することが当然だと思っている生徒もいるわ。実際に多くの学生が、自由時間にはアルバイトに熱中しているもの。勉強するための十分な時間を確保していない学生もいるわ。大学に進学するためには、一定のお金と時間が必要でしょう。そんな入学に本当に価値があるの？

Tim: 言いたいことはわかる。でも、自分の専門分野を勉強する以上に、大学では学ぶことがあるんだ。学生たちは実践的なスキルを身につける。それが後のキャリアに役立つんだ。例えば、時間管理、問題解決、優先順位、クリティカルシンキング、コミュニケーションと社交術だね。

Meg: 生徒はそんな技術を得るために大学に進学する必要がないわ。働いている間に単純に身につくことなんだから。

Tim: まあ、そうだね。でも、僕が思うのは、平均的に、学士号を持つ人は持たない人より多くのお金を稼ぐことが期待できるんだ。特に弁護士、会計士、医者になる人は高給をとるよね。彼らは普通のサラリーマンより2倍から3倍多く稼げるよ。

Meg: That may be true, but it doesn't necessarily hold true for everyone.

Tim: Well, I believe the point is that, at college, they also get the chance to meet people with different backgrounds and discover new sides of themselves to become multi-talented people.

Meg: I kind of understand you now.

(254 words)

Meg: そうかもしれないけど、それは、すべての人に必ず当てはまるわけではないわ。

Tim: そうだね。重要なのは、大学では、異なるバックグラウンドを持つ人と会うチャンスを得て、そして多彩な才能を身につけるために、自分自身の新しい一面を見るチャンスが得られることだと思う。

Meg: なんとなくわかるわ。

Words and Phrases

112

□ according to the statistics on	～に関する統計によると	□ study a major	専門分野を勉強する
□ enroll in college	大学に入る	□ acquire practical skills	実践的な技術を身につける
□ enter vocational schools	専門学校に入学する	□ come in handy	役に立つ
□ have yet to decide one's future	進路がまだ決定していない	□ during one's career	キャリアを積む間に
□ needless to say	言うまでもなく	□ time management	時間管理
□ further one's education	さらに進学する	□ problem-solving	問題解決
□ major and minor subject	専攻科目と副専攻科目	□ prioritization	優先順位付け
□ take it for granted that	～を当然のことと思う	□ critical thinking	クリティカルシンキング、批判的思考
□ be absorbed in ～ing	～に熱中する	□ people skills	社会性、人との接し方
□ part-time job	パートタイムの仕事	□ the main reason is that	主な理由は～である
□ save enough time to	～するために十分な時間を確保する	□ on average	平均で；概して
□ enrollment	入学	□ people with bachelor's degrees	学士号を持つ人
□ I see your point, but	言いたいことはわかりますが	□ lawyer	弁護士

□ accountant	会計士
□ get paid quite well	高給をとる
□ earn two or three times as much as	～の 2、3 倍多く稼ぐ
□ average salaried workers	普通のサラリーマン
□ not necessarily	必ずしも～ない
□ hold true for	～に当てはまる
□ the point is that	要点（大切なこと）は～である
□ become multi-talented people	多才な人になる
□ I kind of understand you now.	多少わかる。

Tips | 論理的に展開するためのキーフレーズ

質問を示す①

1	I have a simple question about your proposal.	あなたの提案について簡単な質問があります。
2	I have a few questions concerning your idea.	あなたのアイディアについていくつか質問があります。
3	May I ask a question regarding your opinion?	あなたの意見について質問をしてもよろしいですか。
4	I'd like to ask you a question about your proposal.	あなたの提案について質問をしたいのですが。
5	Would you summarize your point?	あなたの意見を要約してもらえませんか。
6	May I ask a tangential question?	本件と直接関係がない質問をしてもよろしいですか。
7	May I ask a quick follow-up question about your project?	あなたのプロジェクトについて補足質問をしてもよいですか。
8	May I ask a question regarding your statement?	あなたの発言について質問をしてもよろしいですか。

Dialogue 12 Should more debates be held in English classes?

授業でもっと英語のディベートを行うべきか？

背景知識とヒント

文部科学省は、「グローバル化に対応した英語教育改革実施計画」に則して、新たな英語教育の抜本的な改革を進めてきました。その中でも、高等学校では、発表、討論、交渉等の高度な言語活動を行うことを目指しています。高度な言語活動とは、どのようにして行われるのでしょうか。

 113

TV Anchor: English education in Japan has been radically changed. According to MEXT, high school students are now required to learn to debate through reasoning and acquiring useful expressions. (27 words)

TV Anchor: 日本の英語教育が根本的に変革されています。文部科学省によると、現在、高校生は論理的思考や役に立つ表現を身につけることで、ディベートできるように求められています。

Dialogue | ダイアローグ

Meg: That's a big burden on high school English teachers. Most of them have never experienced debating in English. How will they be able to manage teaching the know-hows of debate in class?

Meg: 高校の英語の先生には大きな負担ね。ほとんどの先生が英語でディベートした経験がないだろうし。どうやって授業でディベートのノウハウを教えられるのかしら。

Tim: You're missing something important. This policy has a positive side for students. Teachers exist for students, not the other way around. If there are positive sides for students, teachers have to make efforts to carry out the policy.

Tim: 何か重要なことを見落としているよ。この政策は生徒にプラス面があるんだよ。先生は、生徒のために存在していて、その逆ではないんだ。生徒にプラス面があるなら、先生は、その政策を実行する努力をしなければいけないんだ。

Meg: That may be true, but even if students learn how to debate in English, I'm sure they will have little chance to personally incorporate it into their daily lives. They just come to learn to argue for the sake of arguing.

Meg: そうかもしれないわね。でも、たとえ生徒が英語でディベートの仕方を学んでも、日常生活でそれを個人的に使うチャンスはほとんどないわよ。ただ、議論のための議論をするようになるのよ。

Tim: I don't think so. Debating has many benefits. I'd like to tell you some based on my personal experiences. First, students need to read a lot of material in English before the debate. Then, they learn to research better. Second, during the debate, they need to think critically in order to rebut the others' statements. Third, they need to work as a team and learn to enhance teamwork. Fourth, they are required to act cool under pressure.

Tim: そうじゃないよ。ディベートには多くのメリットがあるんだ。自分の経験に基づいて話すよ。第一に、生徒はディベートの前には、多くの資料を英語で読む必要がある。そうしてよりよい調べ方を学ぶ。第二に、ディベートの最中、他の人の意見に反論するために、批判的に考える必要がある。第三に、チームとして動く必要があり、チームワークの高め方を学ぶ。第四に、追い詰められても冷静に対応する必要がある。

Meg: Ideally speaking, what you're saying is true. But not all of the students are good at speaking English.

Meg: 理想的に言えば、あなたの意見は正しいわ。でも、生徒すべてが英語を話すことが得意なわけじゃないのよ。

Tim: Let me add even more benefits to those mentioned. Fifth, students can improve their speaking skills by debating. Also, they learn to think outside of the box. The list goes on and on.

Meg: Well, your opinion is convincing .

Tim: I understand your concerns about teachers and students. However, Japanese English teachers are excellent. I do believe they will be able to overcome such difficulties in the near future.

(273 words)

Tim: さらにメリットを追加しよう。第五に、生徒はディベートすることで話す技術を向上させることができる。また、独創的に考えることを学ぶ。例を挙げればきりがないよ。

Meg: そうね、あなたの意見は説得力があるわね。

Tim: 先生と生徒に対する懸念は理解できるよ。でも、日本の英語の先生は優秀だよ。近い将来、そんな困難を乗り越えることができると強く信じているのさ。

Words and Phrases

□ radically change	根本的に変わる	□ even if	たとえ~であっても
□ according to MEXT	文部科学省によれば	□ incorporate ~ into …	~を…へ組み込む
□ MEXT (Ministry of Education, Culture, Sports, Science and Technology)	文部科学省	□ argue for the sake of arguing	議論のための議論をする
		□ based on one's personal experiences	個人的経験に基づくと
□ debate through reasoning	論理的思考を通して議論する	□ research	調査する、研究する
□ big burden on	~にとって大きな負担	□ think critically	批判的に考える
□ teaching the know-hows of debate	ディベートのノウハウを教えること	□ rebut one's statement	意見に反論する
□ You're missing something important.	何か大切なことを見逃している。	□ enhance teamwork	チームワークを高める
□ have a positive side for	~にとってプラスな面がある	□ act cool under pressure	追い詰められても冷静に対応する
□ not the other way around	その逆ではない	□ ideally speaking	理想的に言って
□ carry out the policy	その政策を実行する	□ not all	すべてが~だというわけではない
□ that may be true, but	それは真実かもしれないが~	□ think outside of the box	既成概念にとらわれずに考える

□ The list goes on and on.	例を挙げればきりがない。	□ I understand your concerns about	～についての心配は理解します
□ Your opinion is convincing.	あなたの意見は、説得力がある。	□ overcome difficulties	困難を乗り越える

Tips | 論理的に展開するためのキーフレーズ

意見を示す⑤

❶	Your opinion is convincing.	あなたの意見には説得力があります。
❷	We need convincing evidence to prove his innocence.	彼の無実を証明するために有力な証拠が必要です。
❸	You made a convincing statement.	説得力ある発言ですね。
❹	Your speech is persuasive.	あなたのスピーチは説得力があります。
❺	Your claim is difficult to refute.	あなたの主張は、反論しがたいです。
❻	It's very convincing.	それは、大変説得力があります。
❼	You have a strong opinion about it.	それについてはっきりした意見をお持ちですね。

Dialogue

13

Should we prolong life for the elderly and terminally ill?

延命治療をすべきか?

背景知識とヒント

人は、皆いつかは死を迎えます。しかし、脳梗塞などで突然意識不明になってしまい、回復を見込めない患者もいます。医療が発達したおかげで日本人の平均寿命は80歳を超え、社会の高齢化も進んでいます。このような状況で、延命治療についての意思を本人に確認することができない場合、残された家族は難しい対応を迫られます。延命治療にはどう対応すべきなのでしょうか。

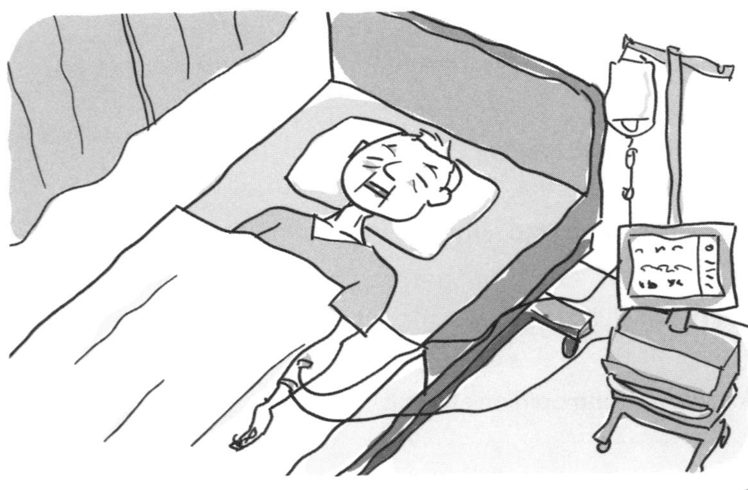

115

TV Anchor: Japan is recognized as the country with the longest life expectancy. However, one problem is that some people are using a feeding tube inserted directly into the stomach to prolong their lives. It's becoming more and more difficult to decide whether to start life-sustaining treatments or not. (47 words)

TV Anchor: 日本は最も寿命の長い国とみなされています。しかし、1つの問題は、延命するために胃に栄養を直接入れるチューブをつけた人がいることです。延命治療を始めるべきか否か、決めるのが難しくなってきています。

Dialogue | ダイアローグ

Meg: Have you heard of such life-sustaining treatments?

Meg: 延命治療って聞いたことがある？

Tim: Yes, I have heard of them before. These days, elderly people are making efforts to extend their life-span with a well-balanced diet and moderate exercise. At the same time, some elderly people are bedridden and are forced to receive life-sustaining treatments.

Tim: うん。聞いたことがあるよ。最近、高齢者はバランスの取れた食事と適切な運動で寿命を延ばす努力をしているね。同時に、寝たきりになって延命治療を受けざるを得ない高齢者もいるよね。

Meg: There must be pros and cons for such drastic actions, but I'm opposed to it. If the illness is terminal and there is no chance of recovery, it's wrong to prolong one's life with those life-sustaining treatments. Such patients will never be as healthy as they used to be.

Meg: そんな極端な対応には、賛否両論があるに違いないけど、私は反対だわ。もし病気が末期で回復の見込みがまったくないなら、延命治療で人の命を延ばすことはよくないわ。そんな患者は、以前のように健康には戻れないのだから。

Tim: If that's what you think, you're terribly mistaken. It's unethical not to prolong the lives of patients. I'm 100% sure all of the people involved would disagree with your opinion. Nowadays, thanks to medical advances, nobody can disregard the possibility of discovering a new drug, or treatment.

Tim: もし、それが君の考えていることなら、とんでもない間違いだよ。患者の命を延命しないのは倫理に反するよ。関係者全員、君の意見に絶対反対するよ。最近は医学の発達のおかげで、新しい薬、治療を発見する可能性を誰も否定できないんだから。

Meg: You may be right, but what I mean is preventing or ending patients' suffering is more important than keeping them alive with a poor quality of life.

Meg: そうかもしれないけど、人としての生活が難しい状態のまま生き続けてもらうより、患者の苦しみを防いだり終わらせたりするほうが大切なのよ。

Tim: I don't think we have the right to force terminally ill patients to die without their consent.

Tim: 末期患者を、彼らの同意なしに死なせる権利は、僕たちにはないと思うよ。

Meg: Bedridden patients often suffer from dementia. They can't decide what to do on their own. What would you do then? They will have to stay in bed all day long till they die. I don't want to see them with such a poor quality of life.

(232 words)

Meg: 寝たきりの患者は認知症を患っていることが多いわ。彼らはどうすべきか、自分では決められないのよ。あなたならどうする？　彼らは死ぬまでベッドに寝ていなくてはならないわ。そんなふうに人としての生活が難しい状態でいる人を見たくないわ。

Words and Phrases

116

□ be recognized as	～としてみなされている	□ I'm opposed to it.	それには反対である。
□ life expectancy	平均寿命	□ terminal	末期的な；絶望的な
□ one problem is that	1つの問題は～である	□ there is no chance of recovery	回復の見込みがまったくない
□ feeding tube	栄養チューブ	□ it's unethical not to	～しないことは倫理に反する
□ insert ～ into the stomach	～を胃内に挿入する	□ thanks to recent medical advances	最近の医療の発達のおかげで
□ prolong one's life	～を延命する	□ disregard	～を無視する
□ life-sustaining treatment	延命治療	□ prevent	～を防ぐ
□ extend one's life-span	寿命を延ばす	□ end patients' suffering	患者の苦しみを終わらせる
□ with a well-balanced diet and moderate exercise	バランスの取れた食事と適当な運動で	□ with a poor quality of life	（人としての）生活の質が低い状態で
□ bedridden	寝たきりの	□ without one's consent	～の同意なしに
□ There must be pros and cons for such drastic actions.	そんな極端な対応には賛否両論あるに違いない。	□ suffer from dementia	認知症にかかる

Tips | 論理的に展開するためのキーフレーズ

反論を示す⑥

❶	I can't support you on this matter.	この件に関しては、あなたを支持できません。
❷	I can't support your idea.	あなたの考えを支持できません。
❸	I can't support that.	それを支持できません。
❹	I'm not in favor of your opinion.	あなたの意見に賛成しません。
❺	I'm not in favor of investing in the stock market.	株式市場に投資することに賛成しません。
❻	I find it difficult to support your opinion.	あなたの意見を支持するのは難しいと思います。
❼	I'm 100% sure such devices have negative effect on teenagers.	そのような機器は 10 代に悪い影響を与えると強く確信しています。
❽	It's wrong to think that Japan is superior to other countries.	日本が他の国より優れていると考えるのは間違いです。

Dialogue 14 Should animal testing be carried out?

動物実験を実施すべきか？

背景知識とヒント

世界の 40 を超える国で、化粧品のための動物実験が法的に禁止されており、中には動物実験をした成分を含んだ化粧品の販売・輸入を禁止している国や地域もあります。尊い動物の命を犠牲にするため、動物実験に反対する立場も理解できます。しかし、動物実験を重ねた結果、人間の健康に役立つ薬品類が生成されてきたのも事実です。

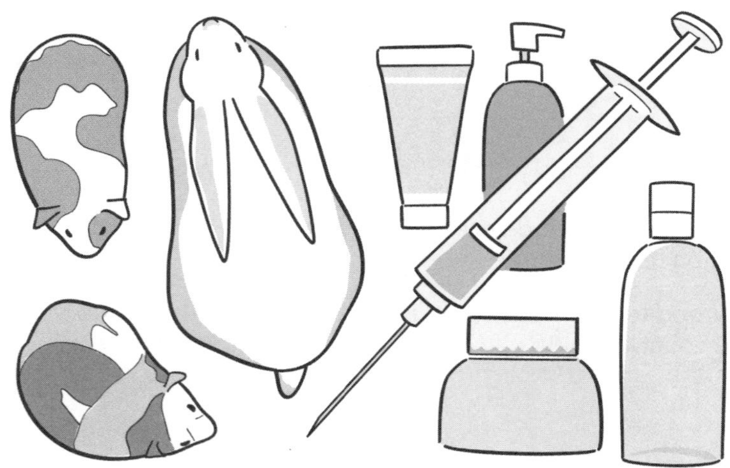

 117

TV Anchor: More than 3 million animals are being kept for animal testing in Japan. They are to be used in safety tests for cosmetics, food, and drugs. However, testing cosmetics on animals is prohibited in more than 40 countries around the world. (41 words)

TV Anchor: 日本では、300 万頭以上の動物が動物実験のために飼育されています。化粧品や食物、薬品の安全性検査で使われるのです。しかし、動物で化粧品の検査をすることは、世界の 40 か国以上で禁止されています。

Dialogue | ダイアローグ

Meg: This means we are still using thousands of animals as test subjects in animal testing. Do you agree with animal testing?

Tim: Yes, at present, we have no choice left but to use them in experiments. These animals are used for the benefit of human health. For example, before new vaccines and new cosmetics are introduced to the public, thousands of animal tests need to be conducted to make sure that those products are safe. Can you think of any alternative testing methods besides animal testing?

Meg: Yes, how about doing computer simulations? We must have a lot of data based on previous animal testing. It must be possible to analyze and use that data to determine whether new products are safe or not.

Tim: Your point is well taken, but I doubt your idea would really work. There are still a lot of incurable diseases, such as AIDS and cancer. We don't have sufficient data on such diseases yet. We still need to conduct a lot of animal testing in order to find new approaches to treating these diseases.

Meg: I see what you mean, but it's still worthwhile to make efforts to decrease the number of animals used in experiments.

Meg: これは、今も動物実験の実験対象として、私たちが依然としてたくさんの動物を使っているということでしょう。動物実験に賛成するの？

Tim: そうだね。現在のところ、実験では、動物を使う以外に方法がないよ。動物は、人間の健康のために使われているのさ。例えば、新しいワクチンや化粧品が一般に販売される前には、製品が安全であることを確かめるために、たくさんの動物実験が行われる必要があるんだ。動物実験以外に代わりの実験方法を何か思いつくかい？

Meg: そうね。コンピュータ・シミュレーションはどうかしら。これまでの動物実験に基づくたくさんのデータがあるに違いないもの。新しい製品が安全かどうかを決めるために、そのデータを分析して使うことは可能に違いないわ。

Tim: 君の言っていることはよくわかるよ。でも、その考えが本当にうまくいくかどうか疑わしいね。不治の病がまだたくさんあるからね、エイズとかガンとか。そういう病気に関する十分なデータはまだないんだ。これらの病気を治療するための新しいアプローチを見つけるため、たくさんの動物実験を行う必要があるのさ。

Meg: 言いたいことはわかるけど、実験で使われる動物の数を減らす努力をすることは価値があるわ。

Tim: On that point, I absolutely agree with you. For example, cosmetics are not directly related to human health. However, thousands of animals are killed in experiments for cosmetics every year. That's why there is a movement against buying animal-tested cosmetics.

(239 words)

Tim: その点においては、100%賛成だね。例えば、化粧品は人間の健康に直接関係がないよね。しかし、毎年たくさんの動物が化粧品のための実験で殺されているんだ。そういうわけで、製造過程で動物実験が行われている化粧品を買うことに反対する運動があるのさ。

Words and Phrases

118

☐ be kept for animal testing	動物実験のために飼育される
☐ use ~ in safety tests	安全性テストで~を使う
☐ cosmetics	化粧品
☐ however	しかしながら
☐ prohibit	~することを禁止する
☐ use ~ as test subjects	~を被験体として使う
☐ at present	現在のところ
☐ have no choice left but to	~する以外に他に方法がない
☐ use ~ in experiments	実験で~を使う
☐ for the benefit of human health	人間の健康のために
☐ vaccine	ワクチン
☐ be introduced to the public	一般に販売される
☐ conduct	~を行う
☐ make sure	~を確認する
☐ alternative testing method	代替の試験方法

☐ data based on previous animal testing	先行する動物実験に基づくデータ
☐ analyze	~を分析する
☐ determine whether ~ or not	~かどうか決める
☐ incurable disease	不治の病
☐ AIDS (Acquired Immune Deficiency Syndrome)	エイズ；後天性免疫不全症候群
☐ have sufficient data on	~に関する十分なデータがある
☐ find a new approach to	~への新しいアプローチを見つける
☐ treat a disease	病気を治療する
☐ I see what you mean, but	おっしゃることはわかりますが
☐ it's still worthwhile to	~するのはまだ価値がある
☐ make efforts	努力する
☐ decrease the number of	~の数を減らす
☐ I absolutely agree with you.	100%あなたに同意します。
☐ be directly related to	~と直接関係している
☐ animal-tested cosmetics	製造過程で動物実験が行われている化粧品

Tips | 論理的に展開するためのキーフレーズ

同意を示す③

❶ I understand your point.	あなたの考えはわかります。
❷ I get what you're saying.	おっしゃることはわかります。
❸ I understand exactly what you're talking about.	おっしゃっていることはよくわかります。
❹ I understand what you mean.	おっしゃることはわかります。
❺ I catch your drift.	おっしゃることはわかります。
❻ That kind of makes sense.	それも一理ありますね。
❼ You make a good point.	説得力がありますね。
❽ I see your point regarding the design.	デザインに関しては、理解できます。
❾ I understand your concern.	心配はごもっともです。

Dialogue 15

Should speed-eating contests be held?

早食い競争の是非

背景知識とヒント

早食い競争では、さまざまなものが食されます。「スイカ」、「ホットドッグ」、「もずく」、「ピザ」、「おにぎり」、「えだ豆」などです。開催地の特産品を用いて地域興しに役立てることもあります。一方、おにぎり早食い競争で死亡事故が出るなど、早食い競争に伴う事故の件数も増えています。参加希望者は、安全管理に十分配慮することが大切です。

119

TV Anchor: Speed-eating contests are very popular events in Japan. The number of eating contest-related accidents is increasing nowadays. Actually, the other day, a man choked in a speed-eating contest and then fell unconscious. Three days later, he died in the hospital without ever regaining consciousness. (44 words)

TV Anchor: 早食い競争は、日本で大変人気のある行事です。最近、早食い競争が関係する事故の数が増えています。実際に、1人の男性が早食い競争中に喉をつまらせ、意識不明になりました。3日後、彼は一度も意識を取り戻すことなく亡くなりました。

Dialogue | ダイアローグ

Meg: Did you know about that? I was surprised to find out that a man died from choking in a contest. Are you for speed-eating contests?

Tim: As far as I'm concerned, TV programs on speed-eating contests are enjoyable because it's interesting to watch contestants compete to see how fast they can eat foods such as hot dogs, hamburgers, oysters, and even corn-on-the- cob.

Meg: What's the point of eating so much food in a limited time?

Tim: The eating contestants regard such contests as competitive sports like boxing and wrestling. That's why they have training regimens. They practice eating a lot before the events. Then, they fast for several days. As a result of making such efforts, they will possibly win the contest and receive the prize money.

Meg: What do you think of the health damage they suffer because of speed-eating contests? As a matter of fact, speed-eating contestants risk damaging their stomachs or choking to death during an event. Moreover, in a world full of starvation, it's not ethical to waste so much food.

Meg: そのことを知ってた？　男性が競争で窒息死したなんて驚いたわ。あなたは早食い競争に賛成？

Tim: 僕に関して言えば、早食い競争のテレビ番組は楽しいね。というのも、出場者がホットドッグ、ハンバーガー、カキやトウモロコシを食べるスピードを競うのを見るのは面白いからね。

Meg: そんなに多くの食べ物を限られた時間で食べることに、何の意味があるの？

Tim: 早食いの出場者は、そんな競争をボクシングやレスリングのような競技スポーツとみなしているのさ。それで、彼らはトレーニング法を持っている。イベントの前にたくさん食べる練習をするんだ。それから、数日間断食をするのさ。そんな努力の結果として、場合によっては賞金を受け取るんだ。

Meg: 早食い競争から受ける健康被害についてはどう思う？　実際に、出場者は胃の調子を害したり、競技中に窒息死したりするリスクがあるのよ。さらに、飢餓であふれている世界で、そんなに大量の食べ物を無駄にするのは倫理に反しているわ。

Tim: I can think of advantages for organizations hosting speed-eating contests such as promoting local economies and specialties. However, I have to admit that you win this time.

(199 words)

Tim: 早食い競争には主催者団体にとってのメリットもあるよ。例えば、地域経済や名産品を振興するのさ。しかし、今回は君の勝ちを認めざるを得ないね。

Words and Phrases

120

□ speed-eating contest	早食い競争
□ eating contest-related accident	早食い競争が関係する事故
□ the other day	先日
□ fall unconscious	意識不明になる
□ regain consciousness	意識を取り戻す
□ be surprised to	～して驚く
□ die from choking	窒息死する
□ as far as I'm concerned	私に関して言えば
□ contestant	出場者、競技者
□ compete	競争する
□ oyster	カキ
□ corn-on-the-cob	トウモロコシ
□ What's the point of ～ing?	～の意味は何ですか。
□ in a limited time	限られた時間で
□ regard ～ as …	～を…とみなす
□ competitive sport	競技スポーツ
□ that's why	そのようなわけで～なのである
□ have a training regimen	トレーニング法がある
□ fast for	～の間断食する
□ as a result of	～の結果として
□ receive the prize money	賞金を受け取る
□ health damage	健康被害
□ as a matter of fact	実を言えば
□ damage one's stomach	胃の調子を害する
□ choke to death	窒息死する
□ in a world full of starvation	飢餓であふれている世界で
□ it's not ethical to waste	～を浪費することは倫理に反している
□ advantages for organizations	組織にとってのメリット
□ promote local economies and specialties	地域経済や名産品を振興する

Tips | 論理的に展開するためのキーフレーズ

質問を示す②

❶ What do you think about my suggestion?	私の提案についてはどう思いますか。
❷ Do you have a question regarding my proposal?	私の提案について質問がありますか。
❸ What do you think about abolishing the death penalty?	死刑を廃止することについてどう思いますか。
❹ What about hiring someone to manage your schedule?	あなたのスケジュール管理をしてくれる人を雇うのはどうですか。
❺ Which do you support?	どちらを支持しますか。
❻ Which do you prefer, the city or the countryside?	都会と田舎と、どちらが好きですか。
❼ Which is more important, user-friendly products or environmentally friendly ones?	ユーザーにやさしい製品と環境にやさしい製品とでは、どちらが重要ですか。
❽ Are there any ways to solve this issue?	この問題を解決する方法が何かありますか。

Are dating-ban contracts for pop idols reasonable?

アイドルの恋愛禁止条項は、許される？

背景知識とヒント

アイドルはデビューする前に、芸能プロダクションと芸能活動について契約を交わします。この中に恋愛禁止条項があり、アイドルは異性との交際が禁止され、発覚すると契約解除となり、損害賠償請求の対象になりえる旨が規定されていることがあります。実際に、恋愛関係が明るみになり、一定期間活動禁止にされたアイドルもいます。この契約は、アイドルの人権侵害に当たるのでしょうか。

121

TV Anchor: The Tokyo District Court issued two rulings concerning lawsuits filed by talent agencies. The rulings concern cases in which agencies sought damages from pop idols who broke their dating-ban contracts. One required the pop idol to pay damages to her agency and the other did not.

(46 words)

TV Anchor: 東京地方裁判所は、タレント事務所によって起こされた訴訟に２つの判決を下しました。恋愛禁止条項を破ったアイドルによって事務所が被った損害賠償に関する判決です。一方は所属事務所に損害賠償を払うよう、アイドルに求め、もう一方は求めませんでした。

Dialogue | ダイアローグ

Meg: What do you think of this news? I mean, are you for dating-ban contracts?

Tim: Well, I understand the feelings of male fans because I used to be a big fan of a pop idol group when I was a teen. I felt betrayed when one of them suddenly got married. The job of idols is to sell the idea of fantasies possibly coming true and fans expect an image of purity from them.

Meg: I don't think pop idols should agree to such contracts. The most important thing in life is love. Love is a natural thing; a dating-ban contract is quite unnatural.

Tim: I disagree with you. Plus, your opinion is vague. Could you be more specific?

Meg: I mean, going on dates is an important part of growing up. I strongly believe falling in love is the most exciting experience a human being can have.

Tim: I don't understand what you mean. The fact is that the pop idols in question signed dating-ban contracts with their talent agencies. This clearly allows the agencies to sue for damages if they are found to be dating. Nothing more, nothing less.

Meg: このニュースについてどう思う？　つまり、恋愛禁止条項について賛成？

Tim: そうだね、男性ファンの気持ちは理解できるね。というのも僕が10 代の頃、あるアイドルグループの大ファンだったからね。1 人が突然結婚した時には、裏切られた気持ちがしたよ。アイドルの仕事は「空想が現実になるかも」っていう夢を売ることで、ファンはアイドルに純粋なイメージを期待しているからね。

Meg: アイドルはそんな条項に同意すべきでないと思うわ。人生で最も大切なことって愛でしょう。愛は自然なことで、恋愛禁止条項はかなり不自然なのよ。

Tim: 君の意見には反対だな。それに、君の意見はあいまいだよ。もっと具体的に話してくれないか。

Meg: つまり、デートに出かけることは成長の重要な一部なのよ。愛することは、人間にとって最もワクワクする経験だと強く思うわ。

Tim: 君の言いたいことが理解できないよ。問題のアイドルたちがタレント事務所との恋愛禁止条項にサインしたのは事実だよね。もしデートしていることがわかれば、事務所が損害賠償を請求できるのは明らかだよ。それ以上でも、それ以下でもないんだよ。

Meg: Idols are human beings just like us. We should permit them the freedom to pursue their happiness. What's wrong with them pursuing their happiness?

Tim: A rule is a rule. There is no leniency with breaking a contract. Revealing love affairs harms their image and the sales of their merchandise. If they want to date, they should quit being pop idols.

(246 words)

Meg: アイドルだって私たちのように人間なの。幸せを追求する自由を認めるべきだわ。幸せを追求して何が悪いの？

Tim: 規則は規則なんだよ。契約を破ることに情状酌量はないのさ。恋愛関係が明らかになると、イメージを傷つけたり、商品の売り上げに響いたりするのだからね。もしデートしたいなら、アイドルを辞めるべきなんだよ。

Words and Phrases

122

□ Tokyo District Court	東京地方裁判所
□ issue a ruling	判決を下す、裁定を下す
□ concerning lawsuits filed by talent agencies	タレント事務所によって起こされた訴訟に関して
□ seek	～を求める
□ break a dating-ban contract	デート禁止条項を破る
□ pay damages to	～に損害賠償を払う
□ used to be a big fan of	以前は～の大ファンだった
□ feel betrayed	裏切られたと感じる
□ expect an image of purity	純粋なイメージを期待する
□ Your opinion is vague.	あなたの意見はあいまいである。
□ Could you be more specific?	もっと具体的に話してくれませんか。
□ fall in love	恋する
□ the pop idol in question	問題になっているアイドル
□ sign a dating-ban contract	デート禁止条項にサインをする
□ Nothing more, nothing less.	それ以上でもそれ以下でもない。
□ permit ~ the freedom to pursue ...	～に…を追求する自由を許す
□ What's wrong with ~?	～のどこが悪いのですか。
□ A rule is a rule.	規則は規則である。
□ There is no leniency with breaking a contract.	契約を破ることに情状酌量はない。
□ reveal love affairs	恋愛関係を暴露する
□ harm one's image	イメージを傷つける
□ sales of merchandise	商品の売り上げ

Tips | 論理的に展開するためのキーフレーズ

確認を示す④

❶	What you're saying is too abstract. Give me some examples.	あなたの言っていることは抽象的すぎます。例をいくつか示してください。
❷	That's a broad statement. Could you be more specific?	それは大まかな発言ですね。もっと詳しく話していただけますか。
❸	Your opinion is vague. Give me some examples.	あなたの意見はあいまいですね。いくつか例をください。
❹	Your idea is illogical. Could you expand a bit on what you've just said?	あなたの考えは非理論的です。言ったことをもう少し詳しく話していただけますか。
❺	Those findings seem to contradict each other. Could you be more specific?	それらの結論は互いに矛盾しているようです。もっと具体的に話していただけますか。
❻	Your opinion is too abstract. Could you give a concrete example?	あなたの意見は抽象的すぎです。具体例を示していただけますか。
❼	Could you be more specific about your proposal, please?	あなたの提案をもっと具体的に話していただけますか。

Dialogue
17

Apartments or detached houses?

マンションか、一戸建てか

背景知識とヒント

いつかは一戸建てに住みたいと思いながら、マンションに住んでいる人がいます。いつかは駅近くの高層マンションに住みたいと思いながら、一戸建てに住んでいる人がいます。「虫が苦手だから庭は不要なので、一戸建てには住みたくない」、「一戸建ては、冬は寒いので住みたくない」、「マンションは狭いから、広い一戸建てに住みたい」、「木造の一戸建ては、耐震補強に限界がある」など、さまざまな意見があります。

 123

TV Anchor: According to a recent survey, nearly half of the population live in apartments within big cities. Particularly, in densely populated areas, more and more people prefer living in apartments to living in detached houses. (34 words)

TV Anchor: 最近の調査によると、大都市の人口のおよそ半分近くが、マンションに住んでいます。特に、人口が密集している地域では、一戸建てよりもマンションに住むことを好む人が増えています。

Dialogue | ダイアローグ

Meg: I prefer living in an apartment to living in a detached house.

Tim: Really? What makes you feel that way?

Meg: First of all, living in apartments is time-saving and safe. Before going out, all you have to do is to lock the door. It's a snap. Furthermore, buildings are equipped with code-activated doors and sophisticated surveillance cameras at the entrance nowadays. Therefore, we don't have to worry about being burgled too much.

Tim: It may be true, but I don't quite agree with your opinion. Did you know that more than 10 percent of apartments get broken into? It's because the people living there rely too heavily on the security system and therefore have less awareness of anti-crime measures. This lax attitude makes it easy for thieves to break into apartments.

Meg: Do you have any convincing data to prove it?

Tim: No, but I prefer living in a detached house. Detached houses have many benefits. They give us a lot of space and privacy. For instance, houses are usually more spacious and have lots of room for furniture, household appliances, and so on. We can also have gardens and easily keep pets. Most importantly, children can have enough space to play.

Meg: 私は、一戸建てに住むよりもマンションに住みたいわ。

Tim: 本当に？　どうしてそう思うの？

Meg: まず第一に、マンション住まいは時間が節約できて、安全ね。外出する前には、ドアのカギを締めさえすればいいのよ。簡単よ。それに、特に最近は、入口には暗証番号で開くドアや高感度の防犯カメラが装備されているわ。だから、泥棒についてそれほど心配する必要もないの。

Tim: それは事実かもしれないけど、君の意見には賛成しかねるね。10パーセントを超えるマンションが泥棒に入られているのを知ってた？　マンション住まいの人は、セキュリティーシステムに頼りすぎて、防犯意識が低くなっているからなのさ。この甘い態度のせいで、泥棒を簡単にマンションに侵入させてしまうんだ。

Meg: それを証明するだけの、説得力あるデータはあるのかしら？

Tim: ないよ。でも僕は一戸建てに住みたいよ。一戸建てには多くのメリットがあるしね。広いスペースやプライバシーがある。例えば、たいてい広くて、家具や家電なんかを置くスペースがたくさんあるよ。庭も持てるしペットも飼いやすい。最も重要なのは、子どもが遊ぶのに十分なスペースがあること。

Meg: I understand your point. However, without official statistical data, your opinion lacks persuasiveness. I believe separate houses are pricier than apartments, especially in urban areas. Moreover, an apartment's floor has no raised thresholds and is, therefore, barrier-free. The older you get, the harder it is to walk over bumps. Therefore, I believe living in apartments is suitable for elderly people.

Tim: I don't think you get my point. I prefer living in a detached house because I value my privacy and would like my own space. We each have our preferences and opinions about the type of housing we want. Let's face it. You can't force your ideas on me.

(305 words)

Meg: 言いたいことはわかるわ。でも、公式な統計データなしでは、あなたの意見は説得力に欠けるわね。独立した家屋はマンションより値段が高いわ。特に都市部ではね。しかも、マンションには、敷居の段差がないから、バリアフリーよ。年をとればとるほど、段差をまたぐのがきつくなるわ。だから、年配の人にはマンション住まいが適していると確信しているわ。

Tim: 僕の意図を理解していないよね。プライバシーが大切で、自分のスペースが欲しいから一戸建てに住みたいんだ。住みたい家のタイプに関しては、好みや意見が違うんだ。現実を直視しようよ。君の考えを押しつけないでくれよ。

Words and Phrases

124

□ nearly half the population	人口の半分
□ particulary, in densely populated areas	特に人口の密集地では
□ detached house	一戸建て住宅
□ prefer ~ to …	… よりも~を好む
□ first of all	まず第一に
□ time-saving and safe	時間の節約ができ、安全な
□ It's a snap.	それは簡単だ。
□ be equipped with code-activated doors	暗証番号で起動するドアを備え付けている
□ sophisticated surveillance camera	高性能の監視カメラ
□ worry about being burgled	泥棒を心配する
□ get broken into	泥棒に侵入される
□ it's because	それは~だからである
□ rely on the security system	防犯装置に頼る
□ have less awareness of anti-crime measures	防犯対策の意識が低い
□ lax attitude	甘い態度、手ぬるい態度
□ convincing data	説得力のあるデータ
□ have many benefits	多くのメリットがある
□ spacious	広々とした
□ furniture, household appliances	家具、家電
□ most importantly	最も重要なことだが

□ without official statistical data	公式な統計データなしに
□ Your opinion lacks persuasiveness.	あなたの意見は説得力に欠けます。
□ separate house	独立した家屋
□ pricey	値段の高い
□ have no raised thresholds	高い段差がない
□ barrier-free	バリアフリーの
□ walk over bumps	段差をまたぐ
□ be suitable for	～に適している
□ I don't think you get my point.	私の意図が伝わっていないと思います。
□ have one's preferences and opinions about	～に関して好みや意見がある
□ Let's face it.	現実を見据えよう。
□ You can't force your ideas on me.	自分の考えを私に押しつけないでください。

Tips | 論理的に展開するためのキーフレーズ

反論を示す⑦

❶ You misunderstand something.	何か誤解していますね。
❷ You misunderstand me.	それは誤解ですよ。
❸ This is a big misunderstanding between us.	これは、私たち 2 人の間の大きな誤解ですよ。
❹ I don't think you get my point.	私の意図が伝わっているとは思いません。
❺ I have a different perspective on this from you.	これに関しては、あなたと違う意見です。
❻ You and I got our wires crossed.	あなたと私はお互いに誤解していますよ。
❼ We seem to misunderstand each other.	お互いに誤解しているようですね。

Dialogue 18

A cat person or a dog person?

猫好きか、犬好きか

背景知識とヒント

ペットとして飼われている猫や犬の数が、人間の子どもの数を超え、この傾向は続いています。猫や犬を飼う理由は、さまざまあります。猫派は、「寝顔にとても癒やされる」、「少食だから、食費がかからない」、「ワンワン吠えないから」などの理由です。犬派は、「人間になつくから」、「一緒に散歩すると健康的になれるから」、「賢いから」などの理由です。なお、飼い方が問題視される場合もあります。ペット飼う際には、動物を理解し、健康や安全に気を配り、最後まで責任を持って飼うことが必要です。

125

TV Anchor: According to a survey, the percentage of cat people is around 24%; on the other hand, that of dog people is around 37%. It seems that more people like dogs than cats. (32 words)

TV Anchor: ある調査によると、猫派の割合はおよそ24%です。一方、犬派の割合はおよそ37%です。猫よりも犬を好む人が多いようです。

Dialogue | ダイアローグ

Meg: I am a cat person. Which type of person are you, a dog person or a cat person?

Tim: I am definitely a typical dog person. I like dogs because they are tremendously helpful in many ways. For instance, there are service dogs, therapy dogs, rescue dogs, watchdogs, guide dogs, drug-detecting dogs, hound dogs…. The list goes on and on.

Meg: Your point is well-taken. Cats are helpful, too. They have played an important role in getting rid of mice. From ancient times, cats have been getting rid of mice that feed on crops. In doing so, they also prevent flea infestations and plague.

Tim: I see what you mean, but nowadays, we have modern ways to get rid of mice, such as mouse traps and mouse poison. These ways are much more effective than cats. We don't have to rely on cats anymore. Could you name a few more examples of ways that cats are helpful?

Meg: Well, let me see…. My cat Sunshine protected my home by chasing a stray dog out of our garden. He was amazing!

Tim: He must be an exception! There are a lot of good stories about faithful dogs. A well-known story of a faithful dog is "Chuken Hachiko." He returned daily to the station for his owner's return for nearly 10 years. Do you have good stories about faithful cats?

Meg: 私は猫派よ。あなたはどっちなの？　犬派、それとも猫派？

Tim: 僕は断然、典型的な犬派だよ。犬は、多くの点ですごく役に立つから好きなんだ。例えば、介助犬、セラピー犬、救助犬、番犬、盲導犬、麻薬探知犬、猟犬だろう。例を挙げればきりがないよ。

Meg: 言っていることはわかるわ。猫も役に立つわよ。ネズミを駆除するのに大活躍してきたわ。昔から猫は、穀物を餌とするネズミを駆除してきたの。そうすることで、ノミのまん延や伝染病を防いできたのよ。

Tim: それもそうだね。でも、最近は、ネズミを駆除するのに現代的な方法があるよね。例えば、ネズミ捕りや殺鼠剤（さっそざい）だね。これらの方法が、猫よりもずっと効果的だよね。猫にこれ以上頼る必要がないよ。猫が役に立つ例をいくつか挙げてもらえるかい？

Meg: ええと、そうね…。うちの猫のサンシャインは、野良犬を庭から追い払って、家を守ったわ。彼はすごいのよ。

Tim: 彼は、例外に違いないよ！　忠犬についての良い話がたくさんあるよ。有名な忠犬の話は、「忠犬ハチ公」だよね。彼は、10 年近くも毎日駅に戻り、主人の帰りを待っていたんだ。忠猫についての良い話はあるかい？

Meg: It's not about faithful cats, but there are cats called beckoning cats. Cats are thought to attract people and fortune into their owners' houses. That's why we place a statue of a beckoning cat as a lucky charm in the entrance hall of a restaurant or shop.

Tim: I see. Let me add a few words to conclude. There are lots of expressions like cat monster but no dog monster. Why is that?

Meg: What about dog demons then?

Tim: Well, we are having an endless discussion. Let's stop here.

(311 words)

Meg: 忠猫の話についてではないけど、招き猫という猫がいるわ。猫は人や幸運を家に引き寄せるのよ。それで、幸運を呼ぶものとして、レストランや店の入口に招き猫の置き物を置くのよ。

Tim: なるほど。最後に一言言わせてくれ。化け猫のような表現がたくさんあるけど、化け犬はないよね。どうしてだろう。

Meg: それじゃあ、犬の悪魔はどうなの?

Tim: 終わりのない議論をしているね。ここで終わりにしよう。

Words and Phrases

126

□ around	およそ	□ hound dog	猟犬
□ on the other hand	一方で	□ The list goes on and on.	例を挙げればきりがない。
□ I am definitely a typical dog person.	間違いなく典型的な犬派です。	□ Your point is well-taken.	言っていることはよくわかります。
□ be tremendously helpful	とても役に立つ	□ play an important role in	～において重要な役割を果たす
□ for instance	例えば	□ get rid of mice	ネズミを駆除する
□ service dog	介助犬	□ from ancient times	昔から
□ therapy dog	セラピー犬	□ feed on crops	穀物を餌とする、常食とする
□ rescue dog	救助犬	□ prevent flea infestations	ノミのまん延を防ぐ
□ watchdog	番犬	□ plague	伝染病
□ guide dog	盲導犬	□ I see what you mean, but	おっしゃることはわかりますが
□ drug-detecting dog	麻薬探知犬	□ mouse traps and mouse poison	ネズミ捕りと殺鼠剤

□ rely on	～に頼る	□ a statue of a beckoning cat	招き猫の置き物
□ could you name a few more examples of	～の例をもう少し挙げていただけますか	□ lucky charm	幸運を呼ぶもの
□ protect	～を守る	□ cat monster	化け猫
□ chase a stray dog	野良犬を追い払う	□ but no dog monster	化け犬はいない
□ exception	例外	□ dog demon	犬の悪魔
□ well-known story of a faithful dog	忠犬の有名な話	□ have an endless discussion	終わりのない議論をする

Tips | 論理的に展開するためのキーフレーズ

例を示す②

❶	There are plenty of similar examples in other languages.	他の言語にたくさんの似たような表現があります。
❷	There are numerous examples that support the theory.	その理論を裏付けるたくさんの例があります。
❸	There is no other example in any scientific field.	どの科学分野にも他に例を見ません。
❹	There are exceptions to every rule.	どんな規則にも例外はあります。
❺	Let me offer another example of joint collaboration.	協同研究のもう１つの例を提示しましょう。
❻	This project is a shining example of international cooperation.	このプロジェクトは国際協力の１つの模範例です。
❼	This is a prime example of why you should not judge a book by its cover.	これは、外見で物事を判断してはいけないという最も良い例です。

Dialogue 19

Should we use a housekeeping service?

家事代行サービスを使うべきか？

背景知識とヒント

家事代行サービスが注目を浴びています。その背景には夫婦の共稼ぎが一般的になったことがあります。週末の貴重な時間を、掃除、洗濯、料理だけで終わらせたくない夫婦には、必要なサービスと言えそうです。働き方改革を推進すると言われていますが、家事の在り方改革についても検討する時期なのかもしれません。

127

TV Anchor: According to a survey, only 5% of households in Japan use a housekeeping service. As the number of working women increases, will they be more willing to use such a service? (31 words)

TV Anchor: ある調査によると、日本で家事代行サービスを使っている家庭はわずか5%だということです。働く女性の数が増えるにつれて、女性たちは、そのようなサービスを積極的に使うようになるのでしょうか。

Dialogue | ダイアローグ

Tim: Do you agree with the idea of hiring a housekeeper?

Meg: Yes, I fully agree with it. I have a couple of reasons for it. First, we can spend plenty of time with our family and children, and be ready for work the next day. Second, a housekeeper can do the household chores like cooking and laundry as well as cleaning and tidying up. It surely reduces the burden on working women. Cleaning is exhausting and time-consuming.

Tim: I get your point. However, it's a huge waste of money. If we clean our house on our own, it costs nothing. Plus, we might feel uncomfortable letting a housekeeper into our home.

Meg: As for the cost, hiring a housekeeper is equal to buying time. It's not a waste of money. As for the latter point, we have to trust in their pride as experts. After all, they are professionals in their field. Besides, I'm sure their references are already carefully checked.

Tim: What matters most to me is privacy. We need a certain degree of privacy. We have to allow housekeepers to touch our things. Our valuable possessions like bags, clothes, and so on would be accessible to them. Do you feel comfortable with that?

Tim: 家事代行を雇うという考えに賛成かい？

Meg: ええ、大賛成よ。それには、いくつか理由があるわ。第一に、家族と子どもに多くの時間を使えるし、翌日の仕事の準備もできるわ。第二に、家事代行は掃除や後片付けだけでなく、料理や洗濯のような家事もしてくれる。間違いなく働く女性の負担を減らすわ。掃除はとても疲れるし、時間がかかるもの。

Tim: 言いたいことはわかるよ。でも、ものすごくお金の無駄だよ。自分で家を掃除すれば、お金はかからないよ。それに、家事代行を家に入れるのは嫌な感じがするかもね。

Meg: 費用については、家事代行を雇うことは、時間を買うことと同じよ。お金の無駄遣いじゃないわ。後者については、専門家のプライドを信用しなくちゃ。結局、その道のプロなのだから。しかも、彼らの身元はすでに十分に保証されているのよ。

Tim: 僕にとって最も大切なのはプライバシーだよ。ある程度のプライバシーは必要だからね。家事代行に、私物に触れさせなければならないよ。バッグとか衣服とか、僕らにとって価値のある持ち物にも近づける。それは平気なの？

Meg: Well, that's the most pressing concern. Why don't we try using a service once or twice while we are at home? We'll decide what to do after that. The decision is still ours, whether we hire a housekeeper or not.

(241 words)

Meg: そうね、それが最も大きな心配事ね。私たちが家にいる時に、そのサービスを1回か2回使ってみたらどうかしら。そのあとで、決めれば良いのよ。家事代行を雇うかどうか、決定権はまだ私たちにあるのよ。

Words and Phrases

128

□ household	家庭、一世帯
□ housekeeping service	家事代行サービス
□ increase	増える
□ be willing to	進んで~する
□ hire	~を雇う
□ I fully agree with it.	それに全く同感である。
□ I have a couple of reasons for it.	それに関していくつかの理由がある。
□ plenty of time	多くの時間
□ be ready for work	仕事の準備ができている
□ household chores	家事
□ laundry	洗濯
□ tidying up	後片付け
□ reduce the burden on	~の負担を減らす
□ exhausting and time-consuming	とても疲れて、時間のかかる
□ a huge waste of money	大金の無駄遣い
□ on one's own	一人で、自分で
□ plus	さらに
□ feel uncomfortable	不快に感じる
□ let ~ into …	~を…へ入れる
□ as for	~に関して言えば
□ be equal to	~に等しい
□ the latter	後者
□ trust in one's pride as an expert	専門家としてのプライドを信用する
□ professionals in one's field	~の分野での専門家
□ besides	さらに
□ check a reference	身元を確認する
□ what matters most to me is	私にとって最も大切なことは~である
□ a certain degree of	ある程度の
□ valuable possessions	価値のある持ち物、(個人的な)宝物
□ be accessible to	~に接近しやすい
□ That's the most pressing concern.	それが最も差し迫った関心事である。
□ The decision is still ours.	決定権はまだ私たちにある。
□ whether ~ or not	~するかどうか

Tips | 論理的に展開するためのキーフレーズ

同意を示す④

❶ I agree with you.	同意します。
❷ I share the same view.	同感です。
❸ I feel the same way.	同感です。
❹ I am with you.	同感です。
❺ I couldn't agree more.	まったく同感です。
❻ I'm all in favor of living in a rural area.	田舎に住むことに賛成です。
❼ I fully agree with you.	まったく同感です。
❽ That's exactly what I think.	まったく同感です。

Dialogue 20

Is traveling overseas alone of value?

一人旅は楽しい？

背景知識とヒント

旅行は何歳になっても、楽しいものです。また一人旅であれ、団体旅行であれ、旅の楽しみ方はさまざまです。目的は、「仕事を頑張った自分へご褒美をあげたい」、「自分を見つめなおして１人になりたい」、「美味しいものを食べたい」、「歴史ある建造物が見たい」など、人それぞれ違ってもよいのです。

129

TV Anchor: A major travel agency surveyed about 4,000 people concerning traveling overseas. The survey showed more than 60% of respondents checked the box for "I prefer traveling alone." The survey also showed that more men prefer traveling alone than do women, and more elderly people prefer traveling alone than do young people.

(51 words)

TV Anchor: 大手の旅行代理店が、4,000人を対象に海外旅行に関する調査をしました。その調査によると、回答者の60%以上が「一人旅を好む」と回答しました。また、女性よりも男性のほうが、若者より高齢者のほうが、一人旅を好むようです。

Dialogue | ダイアローグ

Tim: Quite a lot of people prefer traveling alone. It's kind of a surprise to me. What do you think about the result of this survey?

Meg: Well, in fact, I prefer traveling overseas alone to traveling with friends. I want to enjoy my freedom while traveling abroad. I'm always dreaming of meeting someone good-looking and sophisticated. If I travel with friends, I may miss such an unexpected encounter.

Tim: I think I understand what you mean, but I prefer traveling with friends. I need someone to help me, especially when I encounter unexpected problems, such as feeling sick, getting lost in an unfamiliar area, being pickpocketed and so forth. Plus, it's miserable to eat at a restaurant alone, especially in a foreign country.

Meg: I don't think so. The most enjoyable moment is having the meal I want. I can do that if I'm by myself. I'm picky about what I eat. So, when it comes to choosing restaurants, I'm not willing to compromise. I want to choose the cuisine that appeals most to me.

Tim: I think your statement is extreme. It's fantastic to have a laugh and a chat with someone you know over dinner while traveling. As for choosing food, we can talk and decide what to eat together.

Tim: かなり多くの人が一人旅を好むんだね。少し驚きだよ。この調査結果をどう思う？

Meg: そうね、実際に私も友達と行くより、１人で海外に行くほうが好きだけどね。旅行中は自由を満喫したいのよ。ハンサムで洗練された人と会うことを夢見ているの。友達と一緒だと、予期せぬ出会いを逃すかもしれないでしょう。

Tim: それも理解できるけど、僕は友達との旅行が好きだな。誰かの助けが必要だよ、特に、予想外の問題に遭遇したらね。例えば、病気になったり、知らない場所で道に迷ったり、スリにあったり。しかも、レストランで１人で食べるのは、みじめじゃないのかな。特に外国ではね。

Meg: 私はそう思わないわ。最も楽しい瞬間は、好きなものを食べるときでしょう。１人でならできるわ。私は食べ物の好みがうるさいのよ。レストラン選びに関しては妥協はしたくないわ。私の好きなものを味わいたいのよ。

Tim: 君の意見は極端だよね。旅行中に夕食をとりながら、仲間と笑ったりおしゃべりしたりするのはすてきだよ。食べ物を選ぶのだって、一緒に相談して何を食べるか決めればいいよ。

Meg: I guess it's not a bad idea to travel overseas with friends and it might be fun to enjoy each other's company. However, I don't want to spend more than a week traveling abroad with someone I know. I experienced trauma on such a trip and have bad memories even now. During that trip, even though we were friends, they were too stubborn and selfish. I could barely tolerate their behavior. I don't want to have a similar experience ever again.

(289 words)

Meg: 友達と海外旅行するのは悪くないし、お互いが一緒にいることも楽しいかもしれない。でも知り合いと海外旅行で1週間以上も過ごしたくないわ。そんな旅行でトラウマがあって、今でも苦い思い出があるのよ。友達だったけど、旅行中、彼らは頑固でわがままだったの。その振る舞いには我慢するのがやっとだったわ。二度と同じような経験はしたくないの。

Words and Phrases

130

□ major travel agency	大手の旅行代理店	□ be willing to	進んで～する
□ concerning	～に関して	□ compromise	妥協する
□ respondent	回答者	□ cuisine	食事
□ check the box for	～のボックスにチェックを入れる	□ appeal to	～にアピールする
□ enjoy one's freedom	自由を楽しむ	□ I think your statement is extreme.	あなたの意見は極端だと思う。
□ good-looking and sophisticated	見た目がよく洗練された	□ it's fantastic to	～するのは素晴らしい
□ miss an unexpected encounter	予期せぬ出会いを逃す	□ have a chat with	～とおしゃべりする
□ encounter unexpected problems	予想外の問題に遭遇する	□ enjoy one's company	～と一緒にいることを楽しむ
□ pickpocket	～をすり取る	□ experience trauma	トラウマを体験する
□ it's miserable to	～するのはみじめである	□ stubborn and selfish	頑固で利己的な
□ by oneself	1人で	□ tolerate one's behavior	～の振る舞いに我慢する
□ be picky about	～の好みがうるさい	□ similar experience	同じような経験
□ when it comes to ~ing	～に関して言えば	□ not ~ ever again	二度と～ない

Tips | 論理的に展開するためのキーフレーズ

観点を示す⑤

❶	As for myself, I was able to adapt to the American way of life.	私に関して言えば、アメリカの生活様式に適応することができました。
❷	I should feel guilty for saying such a thing as it is wrong in my book.	私の考えではそれは間違いなので、そんなふうに言ったことに罪悪感を覚えます。
❸	In this regard, your statement is not objective but subjective.	この点に関して、あなたの意見は客観的でなくて主観的です。
❹	In that respect, we should not blame him for this failure.	その点に関して、私たちは彼の失敗を責めるべきではありません。
❺	In my view, it's important to monitor customer responses and identify market trends.	私の意見では、顧客の反応を観察し、市場動向を把握することが大切です。
❻	As far as I'm concerned, this project doesn't matter.	私に関する限り、このプロジェクトは重要ではありません。
❼	Personally, I prefer American English to British.	個人的に、アメリカ英語がイギリス英語より好きです。
❽	In my opinion, it's important to use a club savings account.	私の意見では、定額積立預金を使うことが大切です。

AREA 式で英語 2 分間スピーキング

段階的実践トレーニング 完走チェック！

p.14 ～ p.17 のトレーニング方法を実践し、チェックをつけましょう。

STEP 1 テーマの背景知識を知る □□□□

STEP 2 自分の考えに関するキーワードをコンセプトマップにメモ □□□□

STEP 3 ダイアローグの音声を確認 □□□□

STEP 4 ダイアローグを読んで内容を理解 □□□□

STEP 5 音声を確認して音読 □□□□

STEP 6 オーバーラップリーディング □□□□

STEP 7 ディクテーション □□□□

STEP 8 シャドーイングに挑戦 □□□□

STEP 9 コンセプトマップを確認してス自分のスピーチを構築 □□□□

STEP 10 毎日継続！ □□□□

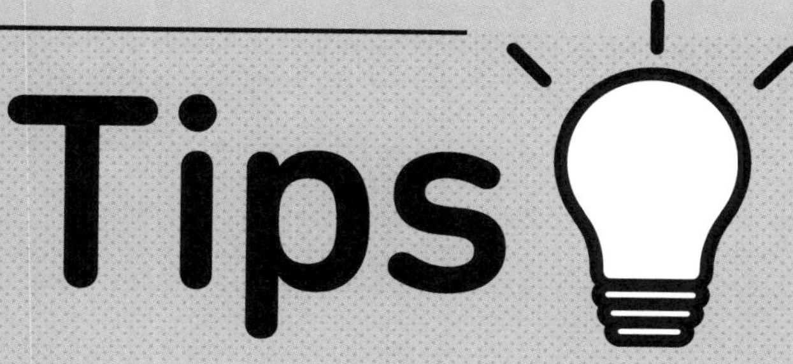

論理的に展開するためのキーフレーズ一覧

言い換えを示す①、②
意見を示す①～⑤
因果関係を示す①、②
確信を示す
確認を示す①～④
可能・能力を示す
観点を示す①～⑤
強調を示す①～③
禁止を示す
繰り返しを示す①、②
傾向を示す①、②
結論・結果を示す

原因を示す
効果を示す
ことわざ・根拠を示す
根拠を示す①～⑥
事実を示す
質問を示す①、②
譲歩・逆接を示す①～③
代替を示す①、②
追加を示す①～③
提案を示す
程度を示す
同意を示す①～④

反論を示す①～⑦
比較・対照を示す①、②
必要性を示す
部分否定を示す
問題を示す①～④
要約・結論・結果を示す①、②
理由を示す①～③
類似を示す
例を示す①、②
連結語①、②

言い換えを示す

❶ Speech 03 ……… 043

- □ Your performance in the speech didn't reach the required level. In other words, you failed.
- □ We minimized the size of the company. In other words, 30% of workers were fired.
- □ The tax system revision affects people with an annual income exceeding 10 million yen; in other words, the rich.
- □ Smoking makes your blood thick and sticky. To put it another way, you should stop smoking.
- □ This book is very difficult. To put it differently, it's too early for you to read this.

❷ Speech 18 ……… 163

- □ The population of Japan is declining; that is to say, there is a possibility that the Japanese economy will slow down.
- □ I am so busy I don't have any free time, I mean, I want to cut my workload.
- □ This gymnasium is so hot and humid that we can't move anymore. To put it simply, we need to cancel all the activities today.
- □ If other stores change their prices, we will adjust our prices promptly. More simply put, prices and availability can change in the blink of an eye.
- □ Personal data is confidential. More simply put, personal data including name, address, telephone number, and email address will only be used to contact you.

意見を示す

❶ Speech 01 ……… 027

- □ What I want to say is that it's a big challenge for us to solve.
- □ My point is that business model innovation is crucial for any business.
- □ The point I'm trying to make here is that we should reach a compromise ASAP.
- □ What I mean is that it's important to squeeze a high profit from every sale.
- □ The bottom line is that drunk driving is illegal and dangerous.

❷ Speech 04 ……… 051

- □ There are both pros and cons to being vegetarian.
- □ There are both merits and demerits to promoting a smoking ban.
- □ Your proposals have both advantages and disadvantages.
- □ Your strength can compensate for my weakness and vice versa.
- □ There are arguments for and against online dating.

❸ Speech 06 ……… 067

- □ Yoga is effective in alleviating sleep problems.
- □ Making university tuition free benefits the public.
- □ Drug testing can be helpful in determining the cause of car accidents.
- □ Bicycles are not good for a long distance commute.
- □ Early rising can be beneficial for you because it improves your performance.
- □ Big data can be useful for deciding the next strategy.

❹ Dialogue 06 ……… 285

- □ I think your statement is extreme.
- □ Don't you think you may be exaggerating a bit?
- □ You're going too far with that matter.
- □ I may be exaggerating a bit.
- □ What you're saying is a little extreme.
- □ Aren't you being a little harsh?
- □ Your case is a bit on the extreme side.
- □ You're way out of line.

❺ Dialogue 12 ……… 309

- □ Your opinion is convincing.
- □ We need convincing evidence to prove his innocence.
- □ You made a convincing statement.
- □ Your speech is persuasive.
- □ Your claim is difficult to refute.
- □ It's very convincing.
- □ You have a strong opinion about it.

因果関係を示す

❶ Speech 04 ……… 051

- □ Overworking can lead to stress and more serious health problems.
- □ Drinking sugary beverages too much can lead to obesity.
- □ Overworking can lead to high blood pressure and insomnia.
- □ Drinking alcohol could trigger high blood pressure or worsen diabetes.
- □ Installing security cameras might bring about a decrease in the overall crime rate.
- □ Taking action on small problems can bring about larger outcomes.

- ☐ What factors could bring about a change in climate?

❷ Speech 09 091

- ☐ Pollens can cause allergies.
- ☐ I don't really know what could cause such a problem.
- ☐ Elderly drivers could cause a lot of fatal accidents.
- ☐ Food poisoning is caused by bacteria.
- ☐ Hundreds of car accidents are caused by drivers talking on smartphones.
- ☐ Hundreds of car accidents are caused by drivers talking on smartphones.

確信を示す

Speech 23 203

- ☐ I'm 100% sure it's important to feature new products in advance.
- ☐ I'm absolutely certain my colleagues will support my opinion in this situation.
- ☐ I'm confident my boss would support the decision as a right move.
- ☐ I'm fully confident that I can manage both work and study at the same time.
- ☐ I'm not convinced that you got all the necessary information on your PhD studies.

確認を示す

❶ Dialogue 04 277

- ☐ Could you elaborate on what you said?
- ☐ Can you elaborate on your statement?
- ☐ Could you give me more information about your project?
- ☐ Please explain further concerning your opinion.
- ☐ Will you describe the matter in great detail?
- ☐ Could you explain it in more detail?
- ☐ We need a detailed reason.
- ☐ Could you clarify this point, please?

❷ Dialogue 07 289

- ☐ What are you implying?
- ☐ What do you intend to do?
- ☐ What do you mean by that?
- ☐ What do you have in mind?
- ☐ What you want to say is we should tailor services to customers' needs, right?
- ☐ What you mean is we need to clarify the object of this project, right?
- ☐ What you're trying to say is we should be more environmentally friendly, right?

❸ Dialogue 08 293

- ☐ Do you mean you don't know about this issue?
- ☐ What exactly do you mean?
- ☐ Is that what you're trying to say?
- ☐ Are you absolutely sure of that?
- ☐ What in the world is that all about?
- ☐ What on earth do you mean?
- ☐ What has that got to do with you?
- ☐ That's not exactly what I'm talking about.

❹ Dialogue 16 325

- ☐ What you're saying is too abstract. Give me some examples.
- ☐ That's a broad statement. Could you be more specific?
- ☐ Your opinion is vague. Give me some examples.
- ☐ Your idea is illogical. Could you expand a bit on what you've just said?
- ☐ Those findings seem to contradict each other. Could you be more specific?
- ☐ Your opinion is too abstract. Could you give a concrete example?
- ☐ Could you be more specific about your proposal, please?

可能・能力を示す

Speech 05 059

- ☐ Politicians should be capable of making decisions and implementing policies to overcome crises.
- ☐ You are able to tackle and handle various problems.
- ☐ This conflict can be solved only by negotiations not by military force.
- ☐ I believe it is possible to prove their guilt with this evidence.
- ☐ He is competent enough to cope with various troubles.

観点を示す

❶ Speech 15 139

- ☐ When it comes to money, he can't be trusted.
- ☐ I've had good and bad memories when it comes to studying abroad.
- ☐ Our company is excellent in terms of product quality, reliability, and customer satisfaction.
- ☐ As to business in our office, we have various perspectives.
- ☐ With respect to your work, I can't help you at all.

❷ Speech 17 155

- ☐ From a scientific point of view, it's important to review all the evidence we've acquired.

☐ From the point of view of consumers, inexpensive quality products are still lacking.
☐ From a broader point of view, it's a must to improve global security.
☐ From another point of view, can you see this is all a trick?
☐ From an artistic point of view, what is so great about Edward Munch?

☐ As for adults, it's important to apply sunscreen lotion to exposed areas of skin.
☐ Concerning this topic, we should discuss how to handle this in more detail at the next meeting.
☐ With respect to your proposal, we are sorry to say that we can't agree to it.
☐ Regarding cooking, he doesn't stick to procedure if tastes are good.
☐ Speaking of spring, what's the weather like here?

☐ Statistically speaking, more typhoons approach Japan in September.
☐ Strictly speaking, your view is slightly different from mine.
☐ Strictly speaking, this anecdote is not based on a true story.
☐ Concretely speaking, we need to increase sales by 10% before the end of this year.
☐ Economically speaking, the consumption tax rate should be raised to 15%.

☐ As for myself, I was able to adapt to the American way of life.
☐ I should feel guilty for saying such a thing as it is wrong in my book.
☐ In this regard, your statement is not objective but subjective.
☐ In that respect, we should not blame him for this failure.
☐ In my view, it's important to monitor customer responses and identify market trends.
☐ As far as I'm concerned, this project doesn't matter.
☐ Personally, I prefer American English to British.
☐ In my opinion, it's important to use a club savings account.

強調を示す

☐ Without a doubt, it's one of the most effective ways to assess the quality of the data.
☐ There is no doubt that the top priority is to offer quality goods.
☐ There is no question that we should protect confidential documents.
☐ Undoubtedly, this situation has to be changed.
☐ What I'd like to stress is the importance of publicizing new products.

☐ Such damages are quite common, in particular, in car accidents.
☐ If there is something in particular you are looking for, please let us know.
☐ As a matter of fact, it's not easy to get detailed information about that.
☐ Definitely, it's difficult to evaluate the risk of investing in the stock market.
☐ Certainly, net sales are increasing every year.
☐ It's obvious that security cameras are a must to protect your property.
☐ Apparently, the number of foreign tourist is higher than usual.

☐ What counts most is to keep fit and dedicate yourself to work.
☐ What matters is to describe the present situation in detail.
☐ What matters is that we fulfill our engagements with clients.
☐ The top priority is to share information with colleagues.
☐ My first priority is to have a job with high salary.
☐ Most importantly, you must keep a record of all business transactions.
☐ The crux of the matter is that people are afraid of change.

禁止を示す

☐ False and misleading advertisements are prohibited.
☐ Smoking in public places must be strictly prohibited by law.
☐ The use of smartphones is not allowed during the meeting.
☐ Cellular phone use should be banned in public places.
☐ Bad-mannered driving should be punished severely.

繰り返しを示す

❶ Speech 02 035

- ☐ As I have described previously, it's risky to enter into a new business market.
- ☐ As I stated before, our company will be taken over by an investment company.
- ☐ As I explained earlier, a particular gesture can cause misunderstandings in communication.
- ☐ As I explained earlier, I cannot agree to price revisions.
- ☐ As I repeated before, I am not in favor of a consumption tax rise.
- ☐ As I mentioned earlier, new customer development is the priority.

❷ Speech 03 043

- ☐ To reiterate, this research is outdated.
- ☐ To reiterate, voting in elections is not compulsory in Japan.
- ☐ I want to reiterate that it's critical to cut down on advertising costs.
- ☐ Once again, what we really need is to boost our company's profits.
- ☐ I just don't want to repeat what I have said.

傾向を示す

❶ Speech 24 211

- ☐ We are prone to make mistakes when we are tired.
- ☐ We are apt to criticize something new and different.
- ☐ It is likely that everyone will choose new gadgets.
- ☐ It is likely that hosting the Olympics will bring economic benefits.
- ☐ The elderly are more likely to choose talking robots.

❷ Speech 30 259

- ☐ Women tend to live longer than men do.
- ☐ Do you tend to agree with his analysis?
- ☐ New cars are more likely to have safety features, such as for preventing crashes or detecting pedestrians.
- ☐ It is likely that hosting the Olympics will bring economic benefits.
- ☐ He has a tendency to buy clothes on impulse. As a result, he really regrets his actions.
- ☐ My colleague is prone to forget to save backup data to the hard drive.

結論・結果を示す

Speech 15 139

- ☐ This apartment is bigger and therefore more comfortable than mine.
- ☐ We are not that rich. Therefore, we cannot afford to buy a fancy sports car.
- ☐ College students are too busy with their part-time jobs. After all, they can't secure enough time for studying.
- ☐ He lost both his parents in a car accident. For that reason, he has no one to depend on.
- ☐ Consequently, it was difficult to pinpoint the cause of the explosion.

原因を示す

Speech 19 171

- ☐ Due to legalizing casinos, new businesses and more jobs will be created.
- ☐ Due to flight delays, many passengers may miss their connection to their next destination.
- ☐ I made a terrible mistake because of a lack of experience.
- ☐ It was on account of traffic congestion that I missed my flight to New York.
- ☐ Owing to overeating, people are at high risk of becoming obese.

効果を示す

Speech 13 123

- ☐ The revised rule could have a deterrent effect on teenagers.
- ☐ Researchers found no evidence of a deterrent effect of surveillance cameras on crimes.
- ☐ Video surveillance is helpful in deterring street crimes.
- ☐ Capital punishment is a strong deterrent to violent crimes.
- ☐ Strategically placed cameras can be deterrents against criminal activities.
- ☐ Do such decisions have a restraining effect on the development of nuclear weapons?

ことわざ・根拠を示す

Speech 26 227

- ☐ There is a famous saying, "When in Rome, do as the Romans do."
- ☐ It is often said that love does not consist of looking at each other but looking in the same direction.

☐ As the proverb goes, "Boys be ambitious."
☐ He once quoted, "No pain, no gain."
☐ As the proverb goes, "You see trees but not a mountain."
☐ Hunger is the best sauce.
☐ Nothing ventured, nothing gained.
☐ Money can't buy everything.

根拠を示す

❶ Speech 07 075

☐ The first upside of becoming a freelancer is flexibility on the job.
☐ The first advantage of commuting by bicycle is that it is good for your health.
☐ On the positive side, people can remain anonymous on the Internet.
☐ Is there any potential benefit to outsourcing IT operations?
☐ What are the disadvantages of relocating the headquarters?

❷ Speech 10 099

☐ We have no more evidence.
☐ We have no more evidence for the existence of extraterrestrials.
☐ There is no scientific evidence to support this theory.
☐ There is still no clear scientific explanation available about the accident.
☐ Do you have any evidence to back up anything you say?
☐ Do you have enough data to fully support your claim?
☐ Do you have any proof to support your case?
☐ There is no correlation between happiness and amount of money.

❸ Speech 11 107

☐ According to an alarming report, it's difficult to stop drug smugglers from entering Japan.
☐ Survey results show many people support living in high-rise condominiums.
☐ This indicates that the weather this year could cause serious damage to crops.
☐ This graph tells us that domestic sales this summer are in decline.
☐ Past studies suggest moderate exercise and proper diet lower mortality.

❹ Speech 12 115

☐ We can use video from a security camera as evidence.
☐ Fingerprints are used as evidence against him.
☐ Based on scientific evidence and data, I'm going to present you three ways to be happy.
☐ Is this medical procedure supported by scientific evidence?
☐ Is there any evidence to prove that conclusion?
☐ Do you have any proof to support your statement?
☐ Is the data sufficient to support your proposal?

❺ Speech 27 235

☐ There are numerous benefits to taking daily supplements.
☐ There are great advantages to owning a home.
☐ There are some downsides associated with the use of antibiotics.
☐ Is there any potential downside to online transactions?
☐ There are some drawbacks you should be aware of before you live with your wife's family.
☐ What are the drawbacks of globalization for our company?
☐ The deterioration of both relations has nothing but disadvantages for both Japan and the USA.

❻ Dialogue 01 265

☐ I understand your point of view, but according to statistics, the rate of unemployment in Japan is on the decrease.
☐ Statistically speaking, there is no evidence to support this statement.
☐ Data shows that more Japanese are suffering from poverty than ever before.
☐ Polls indicate that more than half of all young people are not interested in politics.
☐ Statistics show most Japanese are against fighting in the war.
☐ Statistics show the world population will exceed nine billion by 2050.
☐ According to a survey, nearly 10% of all women have had cosmetic surgery.
☐ According to a report released on Monday, these species are close to extinction.

事実を示す

Speech 09 091

☐ The fact is that one out of three business people are overweight.
☐ The fact is that analyzing customer feedback is worthwhile.
☐ The truth is that negotiating with any client is worth trying.

☐ The truth is that such unreliable information is posted online anonymously.
☐ The reality is that it's important to meet customer demands.
☐ The reality is that we tend to ignore small problems until they have transformed into crises.

質問を示す

☐ I have a simple question about your proposal.
☐ I have a few questions concerning your idea.
☐ May I ask a question regarding your opinion?
☐ I'd like to ask you a question about your proposal.
☐ Would you summarize your point?
☐ May I ask a tangential question?
☐ May I ask a quick follow-up question about your project?
☐ May I ask a question regarding your statement?

☐ What do you think about my suggestion?
☐ Do you have a question regarding my proposal?
☐ What do you think about abolishing the death penalty?
☐ What about hiring someone to manage your schedule?
☐ Which do you support?
☐ Which do you prefer, the city or the countryside?
☐ Which is more important, user-friendly products or environmentally friendly ones?
☐ Are there any ways to solve this issue?

譲歩・逆接を示す

☐ He is lazy, nonetheless, I love him.
☐ Although some people agree with this plan, I personally disagree with it.
☐ Although it is important to set goals with your students, it is equally important to review their progress toward those goals regularly.
☐ Three-star restaurants charge overly high prices, yet, customers keep visiting constantly.
☐ About two-thirds of the residents voted in favor of the plan. However, the rest of them abstained from voting.

☐ In spite of these problems, there is progress in many areas.
☐ Despite many problems, there is a possibility of success.
☐ Despite your efforts, we were unable to meet your expectations.
☐ Regardless of age or sex, anyone can apply for the job.
☐ Even though she can't cite ample evidence for her claim, she insists she's innocent.

☐ It may be true, but the problem is more profound than that.
☐ It may be right, but the drug is effective for some people.
☐ You have a good point, but I don't agree with your opinion.
☐ You are partially right, but it doesn't hold true for all customers.
☐ Indeed smartphones have made our lives easier, but excessive use of them can lead to addiction.
☐ What you said may be true, but it doesn't apply to every single person.

代替を示す

☐ Do you have an alternative solution to this problem?
☐ Do you agree with a substitute proposal?
☐ Why do you need a backup plan?
☐ The ruling party doesn't have a good counterplan to replace it.
☐ It's better to consider an alternative approach.

☐ Prepaid cards may take the place of cash.
☐ Robots may take the place of current staff.
☐ Cats cannot substitute for dogs.
☐ Security cameras can replace guards.
☐ Human beings will be replaced by artificial intelligence robots.

追加を示す

☐ Furthermore, we tailor our products to specific markets.
☐ Also, we have developed an efficient inventory control system.
☐ Plus, we have established ourselves as a leading company of smartphone applications.
☐ On top of that, we are devising a procedure to monitor all the costs and processes of a new project.

□ Beyond that, some people get addicted to gambling and stop working.

❷ Speech 18 163

□ I lost my wallet in London. On top of that, I got lost there.

□ In big cities, there are lots of things to do like going to a concert and a musical. Besides, there are lots of chances to work.

□ In big cities, trains are crowded. Moreover, there is less nature there.

□ Casinos create places for businesses like hotels and shopping malls. In addition, casinos attract lots of tourists from all over the world.

❸ Speech 25 219

□ She is not a good singer. What's worse, she can't dance well.

□ The new American teacher is good at teaching, and to put the icing on the cake, she is charming.

□ The rooms are available even during peak seasons, what's more, prices are unbelievingly low.

□ A travel company went bankrupt. Not only that, some executives at the company disappeared.

□ I got stuck in a traffic accident. To make matters worse, I missed an important meeting.

提案を示す

Dialogue 02 269

□ I understand what you mean, but what about abolishing the retirement age policy?

□ I like your idea, but what about targeting women in their 40's?

□ That's nice, but what about starting a crowdfunding campaign for disabled people?

□ That sounds nice, but how about this Italian restaurant for tonight?

□ I see your point, but how about traveling to Australia in winter?

□ I like your idea, but how about investing in the stock market?

□ I understand your point, but what do you say to implementing a flexible-time policy?

□ I like your opinion, but what do you say to hiring a housekeeper?

程度を示す

Speech 14 131

□ In general, customers' questions and complaints are of great value to us.

□ Generally, we have wrong impressions about some countries owing to false information on the Internet.

□ On the whole, we have a shortage of funds to start a new business.

□ Overall, the project is progressing better than originally expected.

□ As a rule, it's important to monitor economic trends before making the next move.

同意を示す

❶ Speech 08 083

□ I agree with the idea of meeting people through social media.

□ I am strongly in favor of robots replacing people.

□ I support the idea of owning pets.

□ I completely agree with the idea of abolishing nuclear power plants.

□ I second the proposal of a compulsory voting system.

❷ Dialogue 05 281

□ I'm all for your suggestion.

□ You're absolutely right.

□ You got that right.

□ That's absolutely true.

□ You've said it.

□ That's just what I was thinking.

□ That's exactly what I think.

❸ Dialogue 14 317

□ I understand your point.

□ I get what you're saying.

□ I understand exactly what you're talking about.

□ I understand what you mean.

□ I catch your drift.

□ That kind of makes sense.

□ You make a good point.

□ I see your point regarding the design.

□ I understand your concern.

❹ Dialogue 19 337

□ I agree with you.

□ I share the same view.

□ I feel the same way.

□ I am with you.

□ I couldn't agree more.

□ I'm all in favor of living in a rural area.

□ I fully agree with you.

□ That's exactly what I think.

反論を示す

❶ Speech 05 ………… 059

- ☐ You are mistaken about that.
- ☐ You are terribly mistaken.
- ☐ What you said is not true.
- ☐ I'm opposed to the death penalty.
- ☐ I'm totally against living together before marriage.
- ☐ That's not the way I see it.

❷ Speech 14 ………… 131

- ☐ I disagree with your idea of renting new facilities.
- ☐ I can't agree with any restrictions on social media.
- ☐ I can't accept your opinion on this matter.
- ☐ I can't back you up on this issue.
- ☐ I have a different opinion on this subject.
- ☐ I can't go along with your idea concerning employee benefits.

❸ Speech 28 ………… 243

- ☐ I am strongly against the idea of legalizing casinos in Japan.
- ☐ I totally disagree with whale hunting.
- ☐ I don't approve of what you're suggesting right now.
- ☐ Some people are against this policy.
- ☐ I am totally against your plan to cut the advertising budget.

❹ Dialogue 03 ………… 273

- ☐ You're wrong on that part.
- ☐ What you said is wrong.
- ☐ You are totally wrong.
- ☐ You've got it all wrong.
- ☐ All that is wrong.
- ☐ You have me all wrong.
- ☐ Don't get me wrong.
- ☐ That's not true.

❺ Dialogue 09 ………… 297

- ☐ You're missing the big picture.
- ☐ Your opinion lacks something.
- ☐ You're ignoring something important.
- ☐ You're not looking at the bigger issue.
- ☐ If that's what you think, you're terribly mistaken.
- ☐ If you look at only pieces of something, you miss something important.
- ☐ You can't see the forest for the trees.
- ☐ Be careful not to miss something critical.

❻ Dialogue 13 ………… 313

- ☐ I can't support you on this matter.
- ☐ I can't support your idea.
- ☐ I can't support that.
- ☐ I'm not in favor of your opinion.
- ☐ I'm not in favor of investing in the stock market.
- ☐ I find it difficult to support your opinion.
- ☐ I'm 100% sure such devices have negative effect on teenagers.
- ☐ It's wrong to think that Japan is superior to other countries.

❼ Dialogue 17 ………… 329

- ☐ You misunderstand something.
- ☐ You misunderstand me.
- ☐ This is a big misunderstanding between us.
- ☐ I don't think you get my point.
- ☐ I have a different perspective on this from you.
- ☐ You and I got our wires crossed.
- ☐ We seem to misunderstand each other.

比較・対照を示す

❶ Speech 25 ………… 219

- ☐ I believe the benefits outweigh the costs.
- ☐ The cons outweigh the pros.
- ☐ The advantages outweigh the disadvantages.
- ☐ The negative effects outweigh the benefits.
- ☐ The plusses far outweigh the minuses.
- ☐ A fund-raising dinner has more advantages than disadvantages.
- ☐ The benefits of surveillance cameras outweigh the drawbacks.
- ☐ The overall problems outweigh the benefits.

❷ Speech 28 ………… 243

- ☐ Some regulations are loosening in some schools in Japan. Conversely, some Australian regulations are stricter than those in Japan.
- ☐ Many countries still depend on limited energy sources like oil and gas. In contrast, some have started to use renewable solar energy.
- ☐ In my country, business conditions have been going smoothly recently. On the other hand, in France, the unemployment rate is high.
- ☐ Now, about 40% of people support the ruling party. On the other hand, 50% of them support the opposition parties.
- ☐ You think you're right, whereas I assume that you are wrong.

必要性を示す

Speech 07 ………… 075

- ☐ It's necessary for us to know that there is a fair outcome for all customers.

□ It's absolutely necessary to achieve our sales target.
□ It's essential to protect our online reputation.
□ It's a must to maintain strict quality control to improve the bottom line.
□ It's imperative to consider your opinion from different perspectives.
□ It's indispensable to satisfy all customers through exceptional customer service.

部分否定を示す

Speech 19 171

□ Not all students believe such a story.
□ Not all people behave the same way.
□ Winning the lottery doesn't necessarily bring happiness.
□ I don't necessarily agree with you, but I support your decision.
□ Even the richest people can't always get what they want in life.

問題を示す

❶ Speech 12 115

□ The drop in oil prices is a big problem for OPEC.
□ Many companies face a problem in their approach to big data analysis.
□ Bad company management may cause big problems.
□ Another issue is that stolen USB has confidential information.
□ We have to work together to tackle this perplexing problem.

❷ Speech 20 179

□ Air pollution used to be a big concern in China.
□ Another concern is that tipping at restaurants is not a common practice for Japanese.
□ Food safety is another big concern.
□ I worry about the tax payment on the assets after I inherit from my father.
□ I'm deeply concerned about the result of medical checkup.
□ I'm concerned that no effective method is available to control black hackers.

❸ Speech 21 187

□ Such chemicals are harmful to the environment.
□ The contents are legal but harmful to youth. They must be controlled by laws.
□ Food additives could be hazardous to human health.
□ Lack of sleep has a negative impact on work performance.
□ Sexual content on the Web has a negative impact on teenagers.

❹ Speech 24 211

□ Most smokers have big risks of getting cancer.
□ Investing in the market carries some risk.
□ The only way to gain something is to take a risk at something.
□ Some people take illegal drugs to improve their athletic performance. Such behavior is dangerous to their health.
□ Using a smartphone while walking on the street is very dangerous.

要約・結論・結果を示す

❶ Speech 26 227

□ To sum up today's lecture, I'd like to point out two things.
□ As a result, I completely agree with your suggestion.
□ In sum, the agenda is as follows. First, we'll discuss our monthly sales quota. Then, we'll review our budget.
□ In conclusion, there are some reasons why it doesn't work.
□ To conclude, it's essential for business people to get to know each other.

❷ Speech 27 235

□ The unemployment rate is high, prices are high; in a nutshell, the economy is in trouble.
□ First, make a to-do list. Then, prioritize what you need to do. In a nutshell, a to-do list makes you become a good time manager.
□ She is neither organized nor diligent. In short, she is hopeless.
□ Riding a bicycle is good for your health. Bicycles are environmentally friendly. In summary, it's obvious that commuting by bicycle has plenty of advantages.
□ To wrap up, we provide the best service with strict management.

理由を示す

❶ Speech 01 027

□ I have two reasons for this opinion.
□ I have two points to make.
□ I have two reasons to support my belief.
□ I have three reasons for believing so.
□ I have two reasons to give.

☐ I have five supporting reasons.
☐ I have three reasons for my disagreement.
☐ I have two reasons why I think so.
☐ I have three reasons for agreeing.

❷ Speech 16 147

☐ This is because I am against capital punishment.
☐ This is because I'm totally indifferent to this matter.
☐ There are several reasons why I'm optimistic about the future.
☐ I have several reasons for taking this stance.
☐ That's the reason why I don't agree with this statement.
☐ That's the reason why I can't back you up on this matter.

❸ Dialogue 10 301

☐ Are there any special reasons why we have so much food waste?
☐ Are there any special reasons why you overlooked such a mistake?
☐ Are there any good reasons to smoke?
☐ Are there any good reasons to work overtime for such a long time?
☐ Do you know why I'm satisfied with the result?
☐ Do you know why I took a detour today?
☐ Do you have a valid reason to convince us?

類似を示す

Speech 29 251

☐ These dishes are cooked in a similar way, but they taste very different.
☐ In the same way, we have to be more careful dealing with confidential client information.
☐ By the same token, you are required to submit your regular report this month.
☐ I don't love her, but by the same token, I don't want to hurt her.
☐ Likewise, we must develop good eating habits from childhood.

例を示す

❶ Speech 13 123

☐ I've heard about some terrible accidents. For instance, some parents left their kids in the car in the hot summer.
☐ Take watches, for example. If they are both high-quality and low-priced, many people would want to buy them.
☐ Their skill is often used in ballet, figure skating and gymnastics, just to name a few examples.
☐ This prepaid electronic money would be convenient for multiple purposes. For example, commuting, shopping, and the like.
☐ Your salary depends on your skills, such as computers, communication skills and so forth.

❷ Dialogue 18 333

☐ There are plenty of similar examples in other languages.
☐ There are numerous examples that support the theory.
☐ There is no other example in any scientific field.
☐ There are exceptions to every rule.
☐ Let me offer another example of joint collaboration.
☐ This project is a shining example of international cooperation.
☐ This is a prime example of why you should not judge a book by its cover.

連結語

❶ Speech 06 067

☐ Here is some drug abuse-related data.
☐ Car accident-related injuries happen a lot every day.
☐ How can we prevent alcohol-related accidents?
☐ A large number of people die from smoke-related diseases.
☐ Can you think of any allergy-related chemicals?
☐ I learned more about cancer-related pain.
☐ What is the most crucial diet-related issue?
☐ We should not underestimate drug-related side effects.
☐ Here are some computer-related business ideas.

❷ Speech 22 195

☐ Zero emission cars are eco-friendly.
☐ Is our website customer-friendly?
☐ This restaurant is kid-friendly.
☐ I'm satisfied with this hotel because of its budget-friendly service.
☐ You are requested to make user-friendly proposals.

あ

い

う

え

お

か

し

す

せ

そ

た

ち

つ

て

と

な

ふ

へ

ほ

ま

み

む

め

も

や

ゆ

よ

り

れ

ろ

わ

MEMO

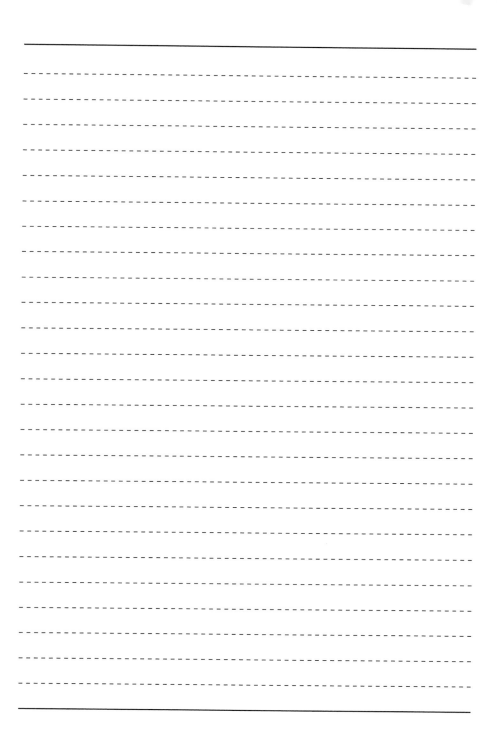

著者紹介

森 秀夫（もり ひでお）

麗澤大学外国語学部教授。上智大学大学院修士課程修了。英語教育・英語教員養成が専門。 25年以上、旺文社の『全国大学入試問題正解 英語』の解答者として、大学入試問題を分析している。その中で、なぜ多くの日本人が難解な大学入試の英文を理解できるのにもかかわらず、いつまでも話せるようにならないのかと疑問に思い、中学校や高校で学習する英文法と英単語の知識をいかに定着させるか、またそれらを実際の運用にどのようにつなげていくかに関心を持って研究を行っている。主な著書に、『英単語・熟語ダイアローグ 1800』（旺文社・共）、『50トピックでトレーニング 英語で意見を言ってみる』（ベレ出版）、『英語で論理的に賛成・反対が言えるトレーニング』（ベレ出版）、『中学英語だけで面白いほど話せる！ 見たまま秒で言う英会話』（ダイヤモンド社）などがある。

[PRODUCTION STAFF]

装丁デザイン　清水裕久（BOOK PLANT）
DTP　Pesco Paint
イラスト　飯山和哉
編集協力　恩田明香（BOOK PLANT）
英文校閲　CPI Japan
校正　鷗来堂
録音・編集　AtoZ English
ナレーション　Trish Takeda / Alex Fraioli

①